www.wadsworth.com

www.wadsworth.com is the World Wide Web site for Wadsworth and is your direct source to dozens of online resources.

At *www.wadsworth.com* you can find out about supplements, demonstration software, and student resources. You can also send email to many of our authors and preview new publications and exciting new technologies.

www.wadsworth.com
Changing the way the world learns®

Political Development in Emerging Nations

Is There Still a Third World?

HOWARD J. WIARDA
University of Georgia, Athens
The Woodrow Wilson International Center for Scholars
The Center for Strategic and International Studies (CSIS)
Georgetown University

THOMSON

WADSWORTH

Australia • Canada • Mexico • Singapore • Spain
United Kingdom • United States

THOMSON

WADSWORTH

Publisher: *Clark Baxter*
Executive Editor: *David Tatom*
Assistant Editor: *Heather Hogan*
Editorial Assistant: *Reena Thomas*
Technology Project Manager: *Melinda Newfarmer*
Executive Marketing Manager: *Caroline Croley*
Marketing Assistant: *Mary Ho*
Advertising Project Manager: *Nathaniel Bergson*
Project Manager, Editorial Production: *Kimberly Adams*

Print/Media Buyer: *Karen Hunt*
Permissions Editor: *Sarah Harkrader*
Production Service and Compositor: *Carlisle Communications*
Copy Editor: *Chris Feldman*
Cover Designer: *Sue Hart*
Cover Image: *Getty Images/Tim Bieber*
Printer: *Webcom*

For more information about our products, contact us at:
Thomson Learning Academic Resource Center
1-800-423-0563

For permission to use material from this text, contact us by:
Phone: 1-800-730-2214
Fax: 1-800-730-2215
Web: http://www.thomsonrights.com

Library of Congress Control Number:
ISBN 0-15-505104-0

Wadsworth/Thomson Learning
10 Davis Drive
Belmont, CA 94002-3098
USA

Asia
Thomson Learning
5 Shenton Way #01-01
UIC Building
Singapore 068808

Australia/New Zealand
Thomson Learning
102 Dodds Street
Southbank, Victoria 3006
Australia

Canada
Nelson
1120 Birchmount Road
Toronto, Ontario M1K 5G4
Canada

Europe/Middle East/Africa
Thomson Learning
High Holborn House
50/51 Bedford Row
London WC1R 4LR
United Kingdom

Latin America
Thomson Learning
Seneca, 53
Colonia Polanco
11560 Mexico D.F.
Mexico

Spain/Portugal
Paraninfo
Calle/Magallanes, 25
28015 Madrid, Spain

Contents

Preface

I f you've never been to the Third World before, you're likely to be shocked by what you see: the poverty, the squalor, the disease, the dirt, the grime, the inefficiency, the noise, the smells, the thick pollution, the chaos, the repression and frequent human rights violations, the low levels of literacy and health care, the malformed bodies of so many adults (usually from childhood diseases or broken bones that never received proper medical attention), and the malnourished, bloated stomachs (not from eating too much but from eating too little) of the children. The poverty and backwardness are so overwhelming that it often seems too much, even hopeless. Meanwhile, the rich in these countries often enjoy an extravagant lifestyle and appear to disdain and have no interest whatsoever in the plight of the poor. The sights and sounds of these poor nations are so overwhelming that, upon first encountering them, the visiting American or European, from wealthy, democratic, and more egalitarian societies, is likely to experience what the Peace Corps calls "culture shock": revulsion at what one sees, disbelief that people actually live this way, and a strong desire to get back home where, by comparison, everything is comfortable and familiar. After the shock wears off, however, most of us want to do something to help and to lend a hand. The first place to start is by reading about the developing nations and what can be done to assist them.

It has now been forty years since the concept—and reality—of the "developing nations" or the "Third World" burst upon the world scene and into its consciousness. In the early 1960s, a large number of former colonial territories in Africa, Asia, and the Middle East had just become new nations, independent of colonialism; in Latin America the Cuban revolution had just occurred, giving rise to the fear in Washington, D.C., that all of Latin America might explode in Castro-like revolution; and in the United States idealism toward the developing nations was in the air with the inauguration of John F. Kennedy and the launching of the Peace Corps and the Alliance for Progress. It seemed as if the developing or emerging nations (what we once called "backward," "primitive," or "uncivilized") were not only going to play an important role but were also going to receive major attention.

Up to this point the Political Science field of Comparative Politics had almost exclusively concentrated on the "developed," industrialized, and "advanced" nations of Western Europe and North America. And in International Relations the main theaters had long been Europe, then Japan and Asia-Pacific, and finally the Cold War conflict between the United States and the Soviet Union. Almost no one in the West paid serious attention to the non-West; the Northern Hemisphere was the main focus of power, wealth, and world events, while the South was all but completely ignored. Either the areas of the South, or Third World, were still under colonial rule or, if independent, the nations of the southern hemisphere were considered too poor, too underdeveloped, too weak, or too unstable to count for very much in the world's counsels of nations.

It is now four decades since these developing, emerging, or Third World nations exploded onto the world's stage and roughly half a century since serious scholars and policymakers began to grapple with the manifold problems and vicious circles of underdevelopment, the dilemmas posed by new nationhood, as well as the foreign policy implications of so many, often unstable, new states. It is time for an assessment and summation. Have the new or developing nations actually developed? Why has East Asia forged ahead while other developing areas, with a few exceptions, have lagged behind? Is there a formula for developmental success? What role have these nations played on the world stage? Now that the Soviet Union (the "Second World") has disintegrated, does it make sense anymore to talk about the "Third World," especially since within that category we have huge states (China) and tiny ones (Dominica), relatively wealthy countries (South Korea, Taiwan) and miserably poor (Ethiopia, Mozambique) ones. At this stage we urgently need an up-to-date appraisal of where the developing nations have been, where they are now, and where they are going.

It is therefore time for a new book on political development in emerging nations. A course on development is offered in virtually every anthropology, economics, sociology, and political science department in the country, yet the literature on the subject still dates mainly from the 1960s; there are few books that can be used as a text, and, meanwhile a series of truly epochal and earthshaking changes has occurred in the Third World that has not as yet been incorporated in the literature.

Among these major changes are the collapse of the Soviet Union and, hence, of the Marxist-Leninist model, the withering away of authoritarianism in many countries and the seemingly global triumph of democracy, the need in some form for all nations to accommodate to neoliberalism, the rapid development of the Newly Industrialized Countries (NICs) of East Asia (a number of which have left the Third World), the rising importance of such giants as China, Brazil, and India and their emergence onto the world scene, the plague of AIDS and its debilitating effects, and globalization in all its cultural, social, behavioral, technological, economic, and political dimensions. These monumental transformations have shaken and fundamentally altered the Third World, and yet we lack a clear, comprehensive, up-to-date volume that assesses these changes and puts them in perspective.

This volume helps fill that gap. It is well organized and well written. The book is written from a political science perspective and has major textbook possibilities in that field, but the author comes out of a multidisciplinary, cross-disciplinary background; as a result, the book will be useful for sociology, anthropology, and economics courses on development as well as those in political science.

The book is brief and readable, but it covers a wide range of issues and is designed for a variety of courses. It avoids jargon and instead tells the story of political development and the developing nations in a straightforward, clear manner. The book can be used in the introductory course in Comparative Politics, in upper-level courses on developing areas or the Third World, and in graduate-level seminars in Comparative Politics. It can be used in multidisciplinary courses in development, the Third World, and non-Western areas. The book is thematically organized; it is thus meant to serve as an introduction to the developing nations (rather than providing great detail or proceeding country-by-country); and it represents a summing up of much that we have learned about development in the last forty years. For that reason it can be used as a text in courses in economics, anthropology, and sociology of development as well as political science.

All the main themes and current hot-button issues are covered here: how and why we became interested in the Third World; the contributions of economics, sociology, anthropology, and political science to the field of development studies; the main literature in the field and the criticisms of it; and the disillusionment with developmentalism and the rise of alternative explanatory paradigms such as dependency theory, bureaucratic-authoritarianism, organic-statism, and corporatism. These background chapters are followed by chapters on the Asian success stories (the Newly Industrialized Countries, or NICs) and their implications; the "third wave" of democratization in the developing areas; neoliberalism, its critics, and the "end of history" thesis; and globalization and its multifaceted impact: cultural, social, economic, technological, behavioral, and political. A conclusion pulls all these diverse themes together and explains why some countries are making it in the twenty-first century modern world and others are not, and what strategies work in promoting development and which do not.

The author of this book has spent a large part of his life in the developing world. From 1960 to the present day, thus corresponding to virtually the entire life span of many of the new nations, he has lived, traveled, and studied in Latin America, Africa, the Middle East, Asia, Russia, and Eastern Europe. When not studying or living there, he has been working at various think tanks in

Washington, D.C., to increase U.S. attention spans and improve policy for the Third World. In other words, the developing nations have been for the author a lifetime commitment; moreover, his goal in all these efforts over four decades has been not only to study development but also to help *bring* development to less-favored nations. This book sums up what he has learned from this lifelong commitment.

The author wishes to thank those institutions in the United States who have assisted his research over this span: the Department of Political Science at the University of Massachusetts, the Center for International Affairs at Harvard University, the American Enterprise Institute for Public Policy Research (AEI), the Woodrow Wilson International Center for Scholars, and the Center for Strategic and International Studies (CSIS)—the latter three all in Washington. In the Third World, in Latin America, Africa, Asia, Russia, the Middle East, and East/Central Europe, I have had so many adventures, and the debts to the people encountered so many, that I cannot begin to list them all here; this book is in part my repayment for their generous hospitality. As always and in all ways, Dr. Iêda Siqueira Wiarda was a bulwark of support and good sense. Mrs. Doris Holden, as usual, worked her magic as editor, word processor, and good friend; and Ms. Barbara Ciesluk assisted greatly with the design and layout of the cover. All these persons and institutions contributed mightily to the final product, but the ultimate responsibility for what follows rests with the author alone.

Howard J. Wiarda
Athens, GA
August, 2003

1

Introduction:
The Wide World of the
Developing Nations

Whe know what an underdeveloped country is without having to define it very precisely. As described in the Preface, we can often tell we are in the developing world by the sounds, the smells, and the sights. The sheer poverty and disorganization that we see all about is likely to be the first and most lasting impression that we have. We are used to seeing *pockets* of poverty—poor people or the homeless—in our own country, but not the *extremes* of poverty—poverty that is society-wide; an entire culture of poverty affecting virtually the entire nation—as we see in the developing nations. The cacophony of misery, noise, unfamiliarity, and chaos (or at least seemingly so; there is often an order and system, although not *our* idea of an order and system, amidst the chaos) is often overwhelming. Some people never adjust to the differences and go home in frustration; others begin after a time to appreciate that, though very different from our own, the developing nations often have a dynamic, an energy, a lifestyle, a beauty, and even a system—including of politics—that is worth studying and understanding.

While impressions such as these are useful and worthwhile, we also have more precise measures to gauge underdevelopment. When I first started studying the developing nations in the early 1960s, the gauge of underdevelopment was usually a per-capita income of under $300 per person per year. Per-capita income is a figure arrived at by taking the gross national product (GNP) of a country and dividing it by the number of people in that country to arrive at the yearly per-person or average income. Earning under $300 per person per year classified that nation as poor and underdeveloped. In the early 1960s most of the Latin American nations fell under that amount. In Africa, however, the figures were even lower, with most countries under $100 per capita. Parts of Asia and the Middle East faced the same condition. Even today we frequently hear that sizable percentages of people in the developing world live on less than $1.00 per day.

Since this earlier time the numbers have changed somewhat, due both to inflation and to real improvement in some countries' standard of living. The World Bank, for example, has a fourfold classification of countries based on their per-capita income:

1. Low-income countries (LIC)—a per-capita income of $755 or less.

2. Lower-middle-income countries (LMC)—a per-capita income between $755 and $2,995.

3. Upper-middle-income countries (UMC)—a per-capita income between $2,996 and $9,265.

4. High-income countries—a per-capita income of $9,266 or higher.

These categories are, of course, somewhat arbitrary: a country does not wake up some fine morning and have a national celebration because it has moved from low income to lower-middle income—although such a step may occur and is certainly well worth celebrating. Informally, quite a number of us involved in development studies like to say that, when a country passes the $1,000 per person per year threshold, it is on its way, no longer caught in the vicious circles of underdevelopment but instead is in transition to greater development or a middle-income status. Another threshold comes when a country hits a per-capita income of $2,000 per year: at that stage it is often cut off from foreign aid, the assumption being that it has "graduated" into a period of *self-sustaining* growth and no longer needs outside aid to prime the pumps.

These numbers and the categories indicated are not magical, God-given, or derived from some metaphysical formula. Rather, they provide a useful, pragmatic way to describe and categorize the world's nations as well as to measure change over time. Note that these numbers measure *average* per-capita income; they do not tell us how evenly or unevenly income is distributed (we deal with that issue later in the book). For example, in some countries, especially in Latin America, a wealthy elite may monopolize most of the wealth, leaving the poor with virtually no income whatsoever, but still making the average come out looking fairly decent. Another flaw in the World Bank's methodology was pointed out with regard to the (former) socialist countries of the Soviet Union and East Central Europe where, it was argued, although individual per person income was low, the state provided extensive social services that made actual living standards somewhat higher. The World Bank adjusted for this flaw and introduced a new index called Purchasing

Power Parity (PPP) that, as shown in Tables 1.1 and 1.2, made a number of countries look better—although it must be noted that I have traveled in a large number of these formerly socialist countries where, by my own "eyeball index," the poverty is extreme and not what the PPP index indicates. I am skeptical of such adjustments in the index, consider it comparable to "dumbing down" or artificially raising up SAT (and other) scores, and prefer to use the simpler, unadjusted per-capita index. See the accompanying Table 1.1, the fifth column of which measures per-capita income for all the countries of the world.

Tables 1.1 and 1.2 also begin to get at some other points crucial to the analysis in this book. First, underdevelopment is *not* just a matter of low per-capita income, although that is the first and most obvious thing we think of. Underdevelopment is, therefore, not just an economic issue but also a social and political one. In Tables 1.1 and 1.2 it is clear that countries that are economically underdeveloped are also the ones that have low literacy levels, have low life expectancy and correspondingly high child mortality rates, and also tend to be more rural than urban. These social and economic indicators tend to reinforce each other—countries that are poor also have low levels of social modernization—but they also give rise to an interesting chicken-egg problem in the analysis of development that we deal with later in the book. In order to move out of underdevelopment, what is your initial step? Should you try to improve the economy so you can spend more on education and reduce illiteracy? Should you increase literacy and wealth standards first on the assumption that will improve the economy? Or should you try to do all of these at once? If so, remember that developing countries have scarce resources, so there are *never* enough funds available to do all you want to do in all areas. Development, therefore, is often a matter of choices, and the choices are not often pretty or easy.

When we get into the area of political development, the issues are even more problematic. At least with economic and social development we have some hard numbers (per-capita income, literacy, life expectancy, urbanization) to deal with. But what do we mean by *political development?* Scholars differ in their definition. Some mean greater freedom; some emphasize greater social and political pluralism; others mean greater complexity and differentiation (separation of church and state or strict segregation between military and civilian power); some emphasize government's ability to *deliver* real social and economic programs; and still others summarize all these other factors under the normative term of *democratization.* My own sense is that *all* of these factors are involved in a working definition of political development and that we don't need to worry too much if we differ slightly over the definition or the *relative* emphasis we give to the several parts of the definition. My own definition of a developed political system, thus, is one that is democratic; respects civil and political rights and liberties; reflects the pluralism of society; has differentiated (or "separated") religious, military, and political functions; and is effective in delivering real goods, services, and public programs.

Table 1.1 Key Indicators of Development

	Population			Gross National Income (GNI)[a]	
	Billions 2000	Avg. annual % growth 1999–2000	Density people per sq. km 2000	Billions of dollars 2000	per capita dollars 2000
Albania	3	0.4	124	. .	. .[c]
Algeria	30	1.9	13	48.3	1,590
Angola	13	3.2	10	3.1	240
Argentina	37	1.3	14	275.5	7,440
Armenia	4	0.8	136	2.0	520
Australia	19	1.2	2	394.1	20,530
Austria	8	0.5	98	204.2	25,220
Azerbaijan	8	1.2	93	4.9	610
Bangladesh	130	1.6	997	49.9	380
Belarus	10	−0.2	48	30.0	2,990
Belgium	10	0.3	312	252.5	24,630
Benin	6	2.8	57	2.4	.380
Bolivia	8	2.4	8	8.3	1,000
Botswana	2	2.3	3	5.3	3,300
Brazil	170	1.4	20	606.8	3,570
Bulgaria	8	−0.7	74	12.4	1,510
Burkina Faso	11	2.4	41	2.6	230
Burundi	7	2.2	265	0.7	110
Cambodia	12	2.7	68	3.1	260
Cameroon	15	2.7	32	8.6	570
Canada	31	1.0	3	647.1	21,050
Central African Republic	4	2.0	6	1.1	290
Chad	8	2.9	6	1.5	200
Chile	15	1.5	20	69.9	4,600
China	1,261	1.1	135	1,064.5	840
Hong Kong, China	7	1.8	..	176.4	25,950
Colombia	42	1.9	41	88.0	2,080
Congo, Dem. Rep.	51	3.2	23	5.0	100
Congo, Rep.	3	2.8	9	1.8	630
Costa Rica	4	2.0	71	14.4	3,960
Côte d'Ivoire	16	3.0	50	10.5	660
Croactia	4	−0.7	80	20.1	4,510
Czech Republic	10	−0.1	133	50.6	4,920
Denmark	5	0.4	126	171.0	32,020
Dominican Republic	9	1.9	177	18.0	2,100
Ecuador	13	2.1	46	15.3	1,210
Egypt, Arab Rep.	64	2.0	64	95.2	1,490
El Salvador	6	2.1	303	12.5	1,990
Eritrea	4	2.7	41	0.7	170
Estonia	1	−0.9	34	4.9	3,410
Ethiopia	64	2.3	64	6.7	100
Finland	5	0.4	17	129.0	24,900
France	59	0.4	107	1,429.4[e]	23,670[c]
Georgia	5	0.0	78	3.2	590
Germany	82	0.3	235	2,057.6	25,050
Ghana	19	2.6	84	6.8	350
Greece	11	0.4	82	126.2	11,960
Guatemals	11	2.6	105	19.2	1,690
Guinea	7	2.5	30	3.3	450
Haiti	8	2.1	289	4.0	510

PPP Gross National Income (GNI)[b]		Gross domestic product per capita % growth 1999–2000	Life expectancy at birth Years 1999	Under-5 mortality rate Per 1,000 1999	Adult illiteracy rate % of people 15 and above 1999	Carbon dioxide emissions Millions of tons 1997
Billions of dollars 2000	per capita dollars 2000					
12	3,550	5.9	72	..	16	1.7
153[d]	5,040[d]	1.1	71	39	33	98.7
16[d]	1,230[d]	−0.8	47	208	..	5.3
448	12,090	−1.7	74	22	3	140.6
10	2,570	5.5	74	18	2	2.9
487	25,370	3.0	79	5	..	319.6
213	26,310	3.5	78	5	..	62.6
22	2,760	10.4	71	21	..	32.0
213	1,650	3.8	61	89	59	24.6
76	7,550	6.3	68	14	1	62.3
282	27,500	3.5	78	6	..	106.5
6	970	2.2	53	145	61	1.0
20	2,380	0.2	62	83	15	11.3
12	7,190	2.5	39	95	24	3.4
1,245	7,320	3.2	67	40	15	307.2
45	5,530	5.5	71	17	2	50.3
12[d]	1,020[d]	3.1	45	210	77	1.0
4[d]	580[d]	−1.6	42	176	53	0.2
17	1,410	1.7	54	143	61	0.5
24	1,570	1.5	51	154	25	2.7
840	27,330	4.0	79	6	..	496.6
4[d]	1,210[d]	2.4	44	151	55	0.2
7[d]	860[d]	−2.1	49	189	59	0.1
139	9,110	4.0	76	12	4	60.1
4,966	3,940	7.3	70	37	17	3,593.5
174	25,660	9.3	80	5	7	23.8
249	5,890	1.0	70	28	9	71.9
33	*682*	..	46	161	40	2.3
2	590	4.8	48	144	21	0.3
30	8,250	0.0	77	14	5	5.4
24	1,520	−4.5	46	180	54	13.3
35	7,780	3.8	73	9	2	20.1
140	13,610	3.2	75	5	..	125.2
145	27,120	2.5	76	6	..	57.7
49	5,720	6.5	71	47	17	14.0
37	2,920	0.4	69	35	9	21.7
235	3,690	3.2	67	54	45	118.3
28	4,390	0.0	70	36	22	5.9
4	950	−11.4	50	105	47	..
13	9,050	7.0	71	12	..	19.1
42	660	2.2	42	166	63	3.8
127	24,610	5.4	77	5	..	56.6
1,440	24,470	2.9	79	5	..	349.8
13	2,470	1.8	73	20	..	4.5
2,054	25,010	2.9	77	5	..	851.5
37[d]	1,940[d]	1.8	58	109	30	4.8
179	16,940	3.8	78	7	3	87.2
43	3,770	0.6	65	52	32	8.3
14	1,930	−0.5	46	167	..	1.1
12[d]	1,500[d]	−0.8	53	118	51	1.4

(continued)

Table 1.1 Key Indicators of Development (continued)

	Population			Gross National Income (GNI)[a]	
	Billions	Avg. annual % growth	Density people per sq. km	Billions of dollars	per capita dollars
	2000	1999–2000	2000	2000	2000
Honduras	6	2.8	58	5.5	850
Hungary	10	−0.3	109	47.5	4,740
India	1,016	1.8	342	471.2	460
Indonesia	210	1.7	116	119.9	570
Iran, Islamic Rep.	64	1.6	39	104.6	1,630
Ireland	4	0.8	55	87.1	22,960
Israel	6	2.9	302	*99.6*	*16,310*
Italy	58	0.2	196	1,154.3	20,010
Jamaica	3	0.9	242	6.4	2,440
Japan	127	0.3	337	4,337.3	34,210
Jordan	5	4.3	55	8.2	1,680
Kazaklustan	15	−0.9	6	17.6	1,190
Kenya	30	2.4	53	10.7	360
Korea, Rep.	47	1.0	479	421.1	8,910
Kuwait	2	−0.7	111	. .	. .[f]
Kyrgyz Republic	5	1.2	26	1.3	270
Lao PDR	5	2.6	23	1.5	290
Larvis	2	−1.0	39	6.9	2,860
Lebanon	4	1.7	423	16.2	3,750
Lesotho	2	2.2	71	1.2	540
Lithuania	4	−0.1	57	10.7	2,900
Macedonia, FYR	2	0.7	80	3.5	1,710
Madagascar	16	2.9	27	4.0	260
Malawi	11	2.6	117	1.9	170
Malaysia	23	2.5	71	78.5	3,380
Mali	11	2.5	9	2.6	240
Mauritania	3	2.8	3	1.0	370
Mexico	98	1.6	51	498.0	5,080
Moldova	4	−0.2	129	1.4	400
Mongolia	2	1.3	2	0.9	390
Morocco	29	1.8	64	33.8	1,180
Mozambique	18	2.2	22	3.7	210
Myanmar	46	1.2	69	. .	. .[h]
Namibia	2	2.5	2	3.6	2,050
Nepal	24	2.4	167	5.3	220
Netherlands	16	0.6	469	400.3	25,140
New Zealand	4	1.1	14	50.1	13,080
Nicaragua	5	2.8	42	2.1	420
Niger	11	3.4	9	2.0	180
Nigeria	127	2.8	139	32.8	260
Norway	4	0.6	15	151.2	33,650
Pakistan	138	2.5	179	64.6	470
Panama	3	1.7	38	9.3	3,260
Papua New Guinea	5	2.2	11	3.7	760
Paraguay	5	2.6	14	8.0	1,450

PPP Gross National Income (GNI)[b]		Gross domestic product per capita % growth 1999-2000	Life expectancy at birth Years 1999	Under-5 mortality rate Per 1,000 1999	Adult illiteracy rate % of people 15 and above 1999	Carbon dioxide emissions Millions of tons 1997
Billions of dollars 2000	per capita dollars 2000					
16	2,390	2.1	70	46	26	4.6
121	12,060	5.7	71	10	1	59.6
2,432	2,390	3.9	63	90	44	1,065.4
598	2,840	3.1	66	52	14	251.5
378	5,900	3.5	71	33	24	296.9
97	25,470	9.8	76	7	..	37.3
120	19,320	3.5	78	8	4	60.4
1,348	23,370	2.8	78	6	2	424.7
9	3,500	0.0	75	24	14	11.0
3,354	26,460	1.7	81	4	..	1,204.2
20	4,040	0.8	71	31	11	15.7
82	5,490	10.1	65	28	..	123.0
30	1,010	-2.4	48	118	19	7.2
820	17,340	7.8	73	9	2	457.4
..	..	..	77	13	18	51.0
13	2,590	3.6	67	38	..	6.8
8[d]	1,530[d]	3.3	54	143	53	0.4
17	6,960	7.2	70	18	0[g]	8.3
20	4,530	-0.8	70	32	14	17.7
5[d]	2,490[d]	-0.1	45	141	17	..
26	6,960	3.3	72	12	1	15.1
10	4,960	4.6	73	17	..	10.9
13	830	1.6	54	149	34	1.2
7	600	-0.7	39	227	41	0.8
195	8,360	6.0	72	10	13	137.2
9	790	2.1	43	223	60	0.5
4	1,650	2.4	54	142	58	3.0
864	8,810	5.4	72	36	9	379.7
10	2,240	2.3	67	22	1	10.4
4	1,660	-0.3	67	73	38	7.8
98	3,410	-0.8	67	62	52	35.9
14[d]	820[d]	2.0	43	203	57	1.2[h]
..	..	..	60	120	16	8.8
11[d]	6,440[d]	1.6	50	108	19	..
33	1,360	3.1	58	109	60	2.2
417	26,170	3.8	78	5	..	163.6
72	18,780	3.1	77	6	..	31.6
11[d]	2,100[d]	1.7	69	43	32	3.2
8[d]	760[d]	-0.3	46	252	85	1.1
101	790	0.4	47	151	37	83.7
134	29,760	2.4	78	4	..	68.5
270	1,960	3.4	63	126	55	98.2
16[d]	5,700[d]	1.0	74	25	8	8.0
11[d]	2,280[d]	-1.8	58	77	36	2.5
24[d]	4,460[d]	-1.5	70	27	7	4.1

(continued)

Table 1.1 Key Indicators of Development (continued)

	Population			Gross National Income (GNI)[a]	
	Billions 2000	Avg. annual % growth 1999–2000	Density people per sq. km 2000	Billions of dollars 2000	per capita dollars 2000
Peru	26	1.7	20	53.9	2,100
Philippines	76	2.2	253	78.7	1,040
Poland	39	0.1	127	162.2	4,200
Portugal	10	0.1	109	110.7	11,060
Romania	22	−0.3	97	37.4	1,670
Russian Federation	146	−0.2	9	241.1	1,660
Rwanda	9	2.0	345	2.0	230
Saudi Arabia	21	2.7	10	*139.4*	*6,900*
Senegal	10	2.6	49	4.7	500
Sierra Leone	5	2.3	70	0.6	130
Singapore	4	2.8	6,587	99.4	24,740
Slovak Republic	5	0.2	112	20.0	3,700
Slovenia	2	−0.1	99	20.0	10,070
South Africa	43	2.0	35	129.2	3,020
Spain	39	0.2	79	590.1	14,960
Sri Lanka	19	1.3	300	16.6	870
Sweden	9	0.4	22	237.5	26,780
Switzerland	7	0.7	182	273.7	38,120
Syrian Arab Republic	16	2.8	88	16.0	990
Tajikistan	6	1.8	45	1.1	170
Tanzania	34	2.8	38	9.3[i]	280[i]
Thailand	61	0.9	119	121.8	2,010
Togo	5	2.8	86	1.4	300
Tunisia	10	1.6	62	20.1	2,090
Turkey	65	1.5	85	201.5	3,090
Turkmenistan	5	2.8	10	4.0	840
Uganda	22	3.0	111	6.8	310
Ukraine	50	−0.5	86	34.7	700
United Kingdom	60	0.4	247	1,463.5	24,500
United States	282	1.2	31	9,645.6	34,260
Uruguay	3	0.7	19	20.3	6,090
Uzbekistan	25	1.8	60	15.2	610
Venezuela, RB	24	2.1	27	104.1	4,310
Vietnam	79	1.7	241	30.7	390
Yemen, Rep.	18	3.9	33	6.7	380
Yugoslavia, Fed. Rep.	11	0.1	..	..	..[c]
Zambia	10	2.6	14	3.0	300
Zimbabwe	12	2.2	31	5.8	480
World	6,054 g	1.4 w	47 w	31,171.0 t	5,150 w
Low Income	2,459	2.0	76	1,029.6	420
Middle Income	2,693	1.2	40	5,307.7	1,970
Lower middle income	2,046	1.1	47	2,327.0	1,140
Upper middle income	647	1.4	28	2,986.0	4,620

PPP Gross National Income (GNI)[b]		Gross domestic product per capita % growth	Life expectancy at birth	Under-5 mortality rate	Adult illiteracy rate	Carbon dioxide emissions
Billions of dollars 2000	per capita dollars 2000	% growth 1999–2000	Years 1999	Per 1,000 1999	% of people 15 and above 1999	Millions of tons 1997
121	4,720	1.9	69	48	10	30.1
319	4,220	2.1	69	41	5	81.7
349	9,030	4.1	73	10	0[a]	357.0
169	16,880	3.0	75	6	8	53.8
143	6,380	1.7	69	24	2	111.3
1,168	8,030	8.8	66	20	1	1,444.5
8	930	2.8	40	203	34	0.5
223	11,050	. .	72	25	24	273.7
14	1,480	2.3	52	124	64	3.5
2	460	1.3	37	283	. .	0.5
100	24,970	8.1	78	4	8	81.9
59	11,000	2.1	73	10	. .	38.1
35	17,390	4.7	75	6	0[g]	15.5
393[d]	9,180[d]	1.4	48	76	15	321.5
757	19,180	4.0	78	6	2	257.7
67	3,470	4.2	73	19	9	8.1
211	23,770	3.9	79	4	. .	48.6
218	30,350	2.7	80	5	. .	42.6
52	3,230	−1.1	69	30	26	49.9
7	1,060	6.6	69	34	1	5.6
18[i]	530[i]	2.7	45	152	25	2.9
385	6,330	3.5	69	33	5	226.8
7	1,450	1.6	49	143	44	1.0
58	6,090	3.4	73	30	30	18.8
459	7,030	5.7	69	45	15	216.0
20	4,040	16.1	66	45	. .	31.0
27[d]	1,230[d]	2.2	42	162	34	1.2
184	3,710	6.7	67	17	0[g]	370.5
1,407	23,550	2.6	77	6	. .	527.1
9,646	34,260	4.0	77	8	. .	5,467.1
30	8,880	−1.8	74	17	2	5.7
59	2,380	2.9	70	29	12	104.8
139	5,750	1.2	73	23	8	191.2
159	2,030	5.4	69	42	7	45.5
14	780	3.7	56	97	55	16.7
. .	. .	. .	72	16	. .	50.2
8	750	1.3	38	187	23	2.6
31	2,590	−6.7	40	118	12	18.8
44,506 t	7,350 w	2.9 w	66 w	78 w	. . w	23,868.2 g
4,892	1,990	3.1	59	116	39	2,496.5
15,229	5,650	4.8	69	38	15	10,034.3
9,374	4,580	5.5	69	40	16	6,767.5
5,930	9,170	3.9	69	35	11	3,266.7

(continued)

Table 1.1 Key Indicators of Development (continued)

	Population			Gross National Income (GNI)[a]	
	Billions 2000	Avg. annual % growth 1999–2000	Density people per sq. km 2000	Billions of dollars 2000	per capita dollars 2000
Low & middle income	5,152	1.6	52	6,335.6	1,230
East Asia & Pacific	1,853	1.2	116	1,963.9	1,060
Europe & Central Asia	475	0.2	20	955.9	2,010
Latin America & Carib.	516	1.6	26	1,895.3	3,680
Middle East & N. Africa	296	2.2	27	602.0	2,040
South Asia	1,355	1.9	283	616.9	460
Sub-Saharan Africa	659	2.6	28	313.0	480
High Income	903	0.7	29	24,828.8	27,510

Note: For data comparability and coverage, see the technical notes. Figures in italics are for years other than those specified.

[a] Preliminary World Bank estimates calculated using the World Bank Atlas method. [b] Purchasing power parity; see the technical notes. [c] Estimated to be lower middle income ($756 to $2,995). [d] The estimate is based on regression; others are extrapolated from the latest International Comparison Programme benchmark estimates. [e] GNI and GNI per-capita estimates include the French Overseas departments of French Guiana, Guadeloupe, Martinique, and Reunion. [f] Estimated to be high income ($9,266 or more). [g] Less then 0.5. [h] Estimated to be low income ($755 or less). [i] Data refer to mainland Tanzania only.

Source: World Development Report, 2002, p. 232-233. Used by permission of the World Bank.

Table 1.2 Key Indicators for Other Economies

	Population			Gross National Income (GNI)[a]	
	Thousands 2000	Avg. annual % growth 1999–2000	Density people per sq. km 2000	Millions of dollars 2000	per capita dollars 2000
Afghanistan	26,550	4.1	41	. .	. .[c]
American Samoa	65	. .	325	. .	. .[d]
Andorra	67	. .	149	. .	. .[e]
Antigua and Barbuda	68	0.6	155	625	9,190
Aruba	101	. .	532	1,657[f]	16,900[f]
Bahamas, The	302	1.7	30	4,533	15,010
Bahrain	690	3.2	1,000	4,909	7,640
Barbados	268	0.4	623	2,487	9,280
Belize	255	3.0	11	751	2,940
Bermuda	63	. .	1,260	. .	. .[e]
Bhutan	805	2.9	17	441	550
Bosnia and Herzegovina	3,923	−1.3	77	4,930	1,260
Brunei	328	2.4	62	7,754	24,630
Cape Verde	441	2.6	109	587	1,330
Cayman Islands	35	. .	135	. .	. .[g]

PPP Gross National Income (GNI)[b]		Gross domestic product per capita % growth 1999–2000	Life expectancy at birth Years 1999	Under-5 mortality rate Per 1,000 1999	Adult illiteracy rate % of people 15 and above 1999	Carbon dioxide emissions Millions of tons 1997
Billions of dollars 2000	per capita dollars 2000					
20,056	3,890	4.2	64	85	25	12,530.8
7,631	4,120	6.5	69	44	15	5,075.6
3,145	6,620	6.3	69	26	3	3,285.6
3,627	7,030	2.3	70	38	12	1,355.4
1,527	5,170	. .	68	54	36	1,111.8
3,060	2,260	3.8	63	99	46	1,200.5
1,030	1,560	0.5	47	159	39	501.8
24,781	27,450	3.2	78	6	. .	11,337.4

PPP Gross National Income (GNI)[b]		Gross domestic product per capita % growth 1999–2000	Life expectancy at birth Years 1999	Under-5 mortality rate Per 1,000 1999	Adult illiteracy rate % of people 15 and above 1999	Carbon dioxide emissions Thousands of tons 1997
Millions of dollars 2000	per capita dollars 2000					
. .	. .	. .	46	220	64	1,153
. .	. .	. .	. .	. .	. .	282
. .	. .	. .	. .	. .	. .	. .
653	9,610	0.8	75	20	. .	337
. .	. .	. .	. .	. .	. .	1,872
4,981	16,490	3.1	73	21	4	1,740
7,798	12,130	. .	73	12	13	14,932
3,958	14,770	2.0	76	18	. .	984
1,313	5,140	4.6	72	37	7	388
. .	. .	. .	. .	. .	. .	462
1,088[g]	1,350[g]	3.9	61	. .	. .	472
. .	. .	8.4	73	18	. .	4,537
7,974[g]	25,320[g]	. .	76	11	9	5,454
2,063[g]	4,680[g]	1.9	69	50	26	121
. .	. .	. .	. .	. .	. .	282

(continued)

Table 1.2 Key Indicators for Other Economies (continued)

	Population			Gross National Income (GNI)[a]	
	Thousands 2000	Avg. annual % growth 1999–2000	Density people per sq. km 2000	Millions of dollars 2000	per capita dollars 2000
Channel Islands	149	0.4	481	..	..[e]
Comoros	558	2.6	250	213	380
Cuba	11,234	0.6	102	..	..[h]
Cyprus	766	1.2	83	9,086	11,950
Djibouti	660	2.4	28	556	840
Dominica	73	0.1	97	238	3,260
Equatorial Guinea	454	2.5	16	516	1,170
Faeroe Islands	45	..	32	..	..[g]
Fiji	810	1.0	44	1,480	1,830
French Polynesia	234	1.7	64	4,064	17,370
Gabon	1,237	2.5	5	3,928	3,180
Gambia, The	1,286	3.3	129	422	330
Greenland	56	..	0	..	..[e]
Grenada	98	0.5	288	345	3,520
Guam	155	1.4	281	..	..[e]
Guinea-Bissau	1,207	2.2	43	221	180
Guyana	863	0.8	4	667	770
Iceland	281	1.0	3	8,736	31,090
Iraq	23,264	2.5	53	..	..[b]
Isle of Man	75	..	131	..	..[d]
Kiribati	91	2.3	124	86	950
Korea, Dem. Rep.	23,620	1.4	196	..	..[e]
Liberia	3,130	2.5	32	..	..[c]
Libya	5,540	2.3	3	..	..[d]
Liechtenstein	32	..	200	..	..[g]
Luxembourg	438	1.4	169	19,420	44,340
Macao, China	442	1.8	..	6,161	14,200
Maldives	276	2.6	920	403	1,460
Malta	382	0.8	1,194	3,566	9,410
Marshall Islands	52	..	287	102	1,970
Mauritius	1,186	1.2	584	4,512	3,800
Mayotte	145	..	388	..	..[d]
Micronesia, Fed. Sts.	118	2.1	168	250	2,110
Monaco	32	..	16,410	..	..[g]
Netherlands Antilles	217	1.4	271	..	..[e]
New Caledonia	213	2.4	12	3,203	15,060
Northern Mariana Islands	72	..	151	..	..[e]
Oman	2,395	3.9	11	15,607[f]	6,720[f]
Palau	19	..	41	..	..[d]
Puerto Rico	3,920	1.0	442	..	..[d]
Qatar	585	1.9	53	..	..[e]
Samoa	169	0.6	60	246	1,460
San Marina	27	..	450	..	..[g]
São Tomé and Principe	149	2.6	155	43	290
Seychelles	81	1.5	181	593	7,310

PPP Gross National Income (GNI)[b]		Gross domestic product per capita % growth 1999–2000	Life expectancy at birth Years 1999	Under-5 mortality rate Per 1,000 1999	Adult illiteracy rate % of people 15 and above 1999	Carbon dioxide emissions Thousands of tons 1997
Millions of dollars 2000	per capita dollars 2000					
..	..	..	79	..	..	..
834[g]	1,490[g]	−3.6	61	86	41	66
..	..	..	76	8	3	25,967
14,511[g]	19,080[g]	..	78	9	3	5,954
..	..	0.4	47	177	37	366
381	5,210	1.0	76	18	..	81
2,166	4,770	18.3	51	170	18	612
..	..	..	..	..	..	634
3,645	4,500	−9.0	73	22	7	797
5,501[g]	23,510[g]	2.6	73	13	..	561
6,719	5,430	−0.4	53	133	..	3,430
2,109[g]	1,640[g]	2.4	53	110	64	216
..	..	..	..	..	..	520
640	6,540	4.1	72	18	..	183
..	..	..	78	10	..	4,078
843[g]	700[g]	6.7	44	214	62	231
3,016[g]	3,490[g]	1.7	64	76	2	1,022
8,084	28,770	2.3	79	5	..	2,140
..	..	..	59	128	45	92,339
..	..	..	..	..	..	..
..	..	−4.2	61	72	..	22
..	..	..	60	93	..	260,532
..	..	..	47	188	47	339
..	..	..	71	28	21	43,462
..	..	..	..	..	..	..
19,892	45,410	6.6	77	5	..	8,241
7,350[g]	16,940[g]	..	78	..	..	1,473
1,348[g]	4,880[c]	5.0	68	35	4	304
5,963[g]	15,730[g]	..	77	7	8	1,759
..	..	−1.4	..	..	..	..
11,795	9,940	7.5	71	23	16	1,704
..	..	..	..	..	..	..
..	..	1.2	68	33	..	..
..	..	..	..	..	..	..
..	..	..	76	16	4	6,760
4,654	21,880	0.3	73	12	..	1,801
..	..	..	..	..	..	..
..	..	..	73	24	30	18,418
..	..	..	..	..	..	238
..	..	..	76	..	7	17,054
..	..	..	75	22	19	38,264
861[g]	5,090[g]	6.6	69	..	20	132
..	..	..	..	..	..	..
..	..	0.8	65	66	..	77
..	..	−0.3	72	15	..	198

(continued)

Table 1.2 Key Indicators for Other Economies (continued)

	Population			Gross National Income (GNI)[a]	
	Thousands 2000	Avg. annual % growth 1999–2000	Density people per sq. km 2000	Millions of dollars 2000	per capita dollars 2000
Solomon Islands	442	3.2	16	278	630
Somalia	9,711	2.2	15	. .	. .[c]
St. Kitts and Nevis	41	−0.2	114	273	6,660
St. Lucia	156	1.5	256	634	4,070
St. Vincent and the Grenadines	115	0.7	295	309	2,690
Sudan	29,677	2.1	12	9,596	320
Suriname	415	0.3	3	558	1,350
Swaziland	1,045	3.1	61	1,350	1,290
Tonga	100	0.4	139	166	1,660
Trinidad and Tobago	1,301	0.7	254	6,477	4,980
United Arab Emirates	2,905	4.5	35	49,205	18,060
Vanuaru	200	3.0	16	228	1,140
Virgin Islands (U.S.)	121	1.5	356	. .	. .[e]
West Bank and Gaza	2,945	3.9	. .	4,745	1,610

[a] Preliminary World Bank estimates calculated using the World Bank Atlas method. [b] Purchasing power parity; see the technical notes. [c] Estimated to be low income ($755 or less). [d] Estimated to be upper middle income ($2,996 to $9,265). [e] Estimated to be high income ($9,266 or more). [f] Refers to GDP and GDP per capita.

Source: World Development Report, 2002, p. 240. Used by permission of the World Bank.

A quick glance again at Tables 1.1 and 1.2 reveals that there is a close correlation between economic, social, and political development. This is an important theme that the book will keep coming back to. That is, those countries that have high per-capita incomes and score high on the indices of social modernization also tend to be the most democratic. In contrast, those countries that have low per-capita income and low indices of literacy, life expectancy, urbanization, and so on, also tend to be *nondemocratic.* The correlations are not exact or 1:1 (which is why we say "tend to be"): Saudi Arabia, Bahrain, Qatar, Kuwait, the United Arab Emirates, and Brunei are rich but not democratic, whereas Costa Rica, Jamaica, Uruguay, Bangladesh, India, and Sri Lanka are democratic but not wealthy. Eventually we will want to explain these anomalies.

Most of us are strongly in favor of democracy so the correlation between economic and political development, or democracy, offers cause for optimism. But the reverse side of that equation is also true: countries that are economically underdeveloped also tend *not* to be democracies. In fact, many of them are unstable or authoritarian, human rights abusers, frequently breaking down into chaos, ungovernability, and failed states. Here is where the connection of comparative politics and the study of developing nations to policy comes in, for it is precisely these failed states—Somalia, Haiti, Bosnia, Ethiopia, Kosovo, Uganda, Afghanistan, and Liberia—that cause enormous problems for foreign policy and often call forth

PPP Gross National Income (GNI)[b]		Gross domestic product per capita % growth 1999–2000	Life expectancy at birth Years 1999	Under-5 mortality rate Per 1,000 1999	Adult illiteracy rate % of people 15 and above 1999	Carbon dioxide emissions Thousands of tons 1997
Millions of dollars 2000	per capita dollars 2000					
765[9]	1,730	−16.5	71	26	..	161
..	..	..	48	203	..	30
456	11,120	3.5	71	..	..	103
853	5,470	−1.2	72	19	..	198
584[9]	5,080[9]	−0.1	73	19	..	132
..	..	..	56	109	43	3,809
1,467[9]	3,550[9]	..	70	34	..	2,135
4,882[9]	4,670[9]	0.6	46	113	21	399
..	..	5.5	71	24	..	121
10,844	8,340	4.9	73	20	6	22,291
52,924[9]	19,430[9]	..	75	9	25	82,488
587	2,940	−1.3	65	44	..	62
..	..	..	77	12	..	11,553
..	..	−9.6	72	26	..	..

military interventions and occupations. So, on the one hand, we cheer the successful modernizers—Japan, South Korea, Chile, Taiwan, and others—who have not only developed economically but have also, in the process, become democracies, while at the same time we need to be politically prepared to act (or possibly be dragged) in those states and situations that have failed both economically and politically. The study of political development enables us to explain, understand, and maybe even predict the fate and behavior of countries at both ends of this spectrum: the successes as well as the failures.

THE GEOGRAPHY AND REGIONAL BASES OF UNDERDEVELOPMENT

In this section we begin to examine the patterns of underdevelopment. What countries are underdeveloped and where are they? We are interested in the geography and the regional bases of underdevelopment. Are there patterns and what are they? While this chapter is concerned with delineating the *where* of underdevelopment, the controversial issue of the *whys* of underdevelopment is reserved for later chapters.

As you read these pages, keep your fingers slotted for quick reference to the pages where Tables 1.1 and 1.2 and Figure 1.1 (pages 4, 14, and 22) are located. The discussion will generally proceed from the most developed nations to the least developed.

The first and most obvious fact to note concerns Western Europe: *all* of the countries of Western Europe are in the high-income category. Almost all of them have per-capita incomes between $20,000 and $30,000 per year, which makes them among the wealthiest, most prosperous nations on earth. Portugal is at the lowest end of the scale ($11,060) of the Western European countries even though it is still in the high-income category, while Switzerland ($38,120) is at the high end. There are still *pockets* of poverty in Western Europe, but not a *society-wide culture* of poverty.

North America (the United States, Canada) is just as wealthy, and maybe more so. The United States has a per-capita income of $34,260 per year, while that of Canada is $21,050.

Asia has a number of high-income countries led by Japan, whose GNP is second in the world behind only the United States, and whose per-capita income of $26,460 places it among the wealthier West European countries. Singapore and Hong Kong, both wealthy trading centers, are also in that range. South Korea, Taiwan, and Macao are also high-income countries but, by European standards, they are closer to the level of poorer Portugal than to richer Switzerland. Malaysia, Palau, and American Samoa have also made it to upper-middle-income status.

Once we move out of these core areas, the number of wealthier or high-income countries thins out, and it becomes more difficult to discern a pattern of development. One pattern includes former British colonies, whether in the Pacific (Australia, New Zealand) or the Caribbean (the Bahamas, Barbados, Bermuda, Cayman Islands), which are all relatively wealthy countries. Another pattern includes former French (French Polynesia) or Dutch (Aruba, Netherlands Antilles) colonies, which are also quite wealthy. Still a third pattern includes countries that are located in generally less-developed areas but are oil-rich—Brunei, Kuwait, Qatar, Saudi Arabia, United Arab Emirates. However, in these areas social modernization and political development lag behind.

While Western Europe is wealthy, Central and Eastern Europe, the countries that were formerly socialist countries and satellites of the Soviet Union, is not. But they are not poor and underdeveloped by Third World standards either, although the poverty in Central and Eastern Europe is clearly more visible and widespread than in Western Europe and is sometimes comparable to Third World conditions elsewhere. In contrast, the Baltic countries of Estonia, Latvia, and Lithuania, Poland, the Czech Republic, Slovakia, Hungary, and parts of the former Yugoslavia (Slovenia and Croatia) are all making it to upper-middle-income levels. Because they have recently made significant economic progress, these are also slated to join the wealthy "club" of the European Union (EU).

As we go farther into the Balkans (Albania, Bosnia, Kosovo, Montenegro, Macedonia, Bulgaria, and Romania), note that the countries are all poorer, in the lower-middle-income group. Then, moving farther east into those areas that were formerly part of the Soviet Union (Belarus, Ukraine, Georgia, Moldova, Russia itself), we start to see real poverty approaching the level of many Third World nations. Finally, as we move into Central Asia (Armenia, Azerbaijan, Kazakstan, Kyrgyz Republic, Tajikistan, Turkmenistan, Uzbekistan), we actually reach Third World levels.

We have already mentioned the wealthier countries of Asia; now we need to focus on the poorer ones. Note that in South Asia only the small Maldives and Sri Lanka have made it even to lower-middle-income ranks; in East Asia and the Pacific, Fiji, Kiribati, Marshall Islands, Micronesia, Papua New Guinea, the Philippines, Samoa, Thailand, Tonga, and Vanuatu (mostly small, foreign-dominated islands) have made it to the lower-middle-income category. China is also listed there but the author's research experience and travel in China leads him to conclude it belongs in the lower ranks. All the rest of South Asia (Afghanistan, Bangladesh, Bhutan, populous India, Nepal, populous Pakistan) and East and Southeast Asia (Cambodia, populous Indonesia, North Korea, Laos, Mongolia, Myanmar, Solomon Islands, and Vietnam) are in the low-income category.

Moving to Latin America we again see a mix of some countries that are making it and others that lag behind. Latin America is a transitional area: although *none* of the Latin American countries are in the upper-income brackets, only Haiti and Nicaragua are still stuck in the low-income category. In contrast, Antigua and Barbuda, Argentina, Brazil, Chile, Costa Rica, Dominica, Grenada, Mexico, Panama, Puerto Rico, St. Kitts and Nevis, St. Lucia, Trinidad and Tobago, Uruguay, and Venezuela are all in the upper-middle-income range. Belize, Bolivia, Colombia, Cuba, the Dominican Republic, Ecuador, El Salvador, Guatemala, Guyana, Honduras, Jamaica, Paraguay, Peru, St. Vincent and the Grenadines, and Suriname are in the lower-middle-income group but, of these, several are developing rapidly.

In the Middle East and North Africa we find some similar patterns: most of the countries are in the middle ranges. Bahrain, Lebanon, Libya, Oman, and Saudi Arabia are in the upper-middle-income category; Algeria, Egypt, Iran, Iraq, Jordan, Morocco, Syria, Tunisia, and the West Bank and Gaza are in the lower-middle-income group. Only Yemen Republic is listed as lower-income. Note, however, how many of these, plus the high-income countries mentioned earlier, rely on a single product for their wealth: oil. And that, simultaneously, makes them prosperous but also potentially vulnerable to changing world market prices for that one product.

It is in Sub-Saharan Africa where the real poverty is to be found. However, before we jump to too hasty conclusions about that, look at the (surprising?) number of upper-middle-income countries (Botswana, Gabon, Mauritius, Mayotte, Seychelles, and South Africa) in Africa as well as the lower-middle-income countries (Cape Verde, Equatorial Guinea, Namibia, Swaziland). These are hopeful signs and examples, but we must also recognize realistically that *most* of the countries of Sub-Saharan Africa are extremely poor and in the low-income column.

FIGURE 1.1 Classification of Economies by Income and Region, 1999

Income group	Subgroup	Sub-Saharan Africa		Asia	
		East and Southern Africa	West Africa	East Asia and Pacific	South Asia
Low income		Angola	Benin	Cambodia	Afghanistan
		Burundi	Burkina Faso	China	Bangladesh
		Comoros	Cameroon	Indonesia	Bhutan
		Congo, Dem. Rep.	Central African Republic	Korea, Dem. Rep.	India
		Eritrea	Chad	Lao PDR	Nepal
		Ethiopia	Congo. Rep.	Mongolia	Pakistan
		Kenya	Côte d'Ivoire	Myanmar	
		Lesotho	Gambia. The	Solomon Islands	
		Madagascar	Ghana	Vietnam	
		Malawi	Guinea		
		Mozambique	Guinea-Bissan		
		Rwanda	Liberia		
		Somalia	Mali		
		Sudan	Mauritania		
		Tanzania	Niger		
		Uganda	Nigeria		
		Zambia	Sáo Tomé and Principe		
		Zimbabwe	Senegal		
			Sierra Leone		
			Togo		
Middle-income	Lower	Djibouti	Cape Verde	Fiji	Maldives
		Namibia	Equatorial Guinea	Kiribati	Sri lanka
		South Africa		Marshall Islands	
		Swaziland		Micronesia. Fed. Sts.	
				Papua New Guinea	
				Philippines	
				Samoa	
				Thailand	
				Tonga	
				Vanuatu	

Europe and Central Asia		Middle East and North Africa		
Eastern Europe and Central Asia	Rest of Europe	Middle East	North Africa	Americas
Armenia		Yemen, Rep.		Haiti
Azerbaijan				Honduras
Kyrgyz Republic				Nicaragua
Moldova				
Tajikistan				
Turkmenistan				

Eastern Europe and Central Asia	Rest of Europe	Middle East	North Africa	Americas
Albania		Iran, Islamic Rep.	Algeria	Belize
Belarus		Iraq	Egypt. Arab Rep.	Bolivia
Bosnia and Herzegovina		Jordan	Morocco	Colombia
Bulgaria		Syrian Arab Republic	Tunisia	Costa Rica
Georgia		West Bank and Gaza		Cuba
Kazakhstan				Dominica
Latvia				Dominican Republic
Lithuania				Ecuador
Macedonia. FYR[a]				El Salvador
Romania				Guatemala
Russian Federation				Guyana
Ukraine				Jamaica
Urbekistan				Paraguay
Yugoslavia. Fed. Rep.[b]				Peru
				St. Vincent and the Grenadines
				Suriname

(continued)

FIGURE 1.1 Classification of Economies by Income and Region, 1999 (continued)

| Income group | Subgroup | Sub-Saharan Africa | | Asia | |
		East and Southern Africa	West Africa	East Asia and Pacific	South Asia
Middle-income	Upper	Botswana Mauritius Mayotte Seychelles	Gabon	American Samoa Korea, Rep. Malaysia Palau	
Subtotal	157	26	23	23	8
High-income	OECD			Australia Japan New Zealand	

Europe and Central Asia		Middle East and North Africa		
Eastern Europe and Central Asia	*Rest of Europe*	*Middle East*	*North Africa*	*Americas*
Croatia	Isle of Man	Bahrain	Libya	Antigua and Barbuda
Czech Republic	Turkey	Lebanon		Argentina
Estonia		Oman		Barbados
Hungary		Saudi Arabia		Brazil
Poland				Chile
Slovak Republic				Grenada
				Guadeloupe
				Mexico
				Panama
				Puerto Rico
				St. Kitts and Nevis
				St. Lucia
				Trinidad and Tobago
				Uruguay
				Venezuela
26	2		10	5 34
	Austria			Canada
	Belgium			United States
	Denmark			
	Finland			
	France			
	Germany			
	Greece			
	Iceland			
	Ireland			
	Italy			
	Luxembourg			
	Netherlands			
	Norway			
	Portugal			
	Spain			
	Sweden			
	Switzerland			
	United Kingdom			

(continued)

FIGURE 1.1 Classification of Economies by Income and Region, 1999 (continued)

Income group	Subgroup	Sub-Saharan Africa East and Southern Africa	West Africa	Asia East Asia and Pacific	South Asia
High-income	Non OECD	Reunion		Brunei	
				French Polynesia	
				Guam	
				Hong Kong, China[c]	
				Macao	
				New Caledonia	
				N. Mariana Islands	
				Singapore	
				Taiwan, China	
Total	**211**	**27**	**23**	**35**	**8**

[a] Former Yugoslav Republic of Macedonia. [b] Federal Republic of Yugoslavia (Serbia/Montenegro). [c] On July 1, 1997, China resumed its sovereignty over Hong Kong.

Source: World Development Report, 1999/2000, p. 290-291. Used by permission of the World Bank.

A close examination of these tables reveals some interesting conclusions:

1. Poverty and underdevelopment occur in diverse regions with diverse histories, religions, cultures, sociologies, and racial backgrounds. No one area or region has a monopoly on underdevelopment.

2. Underdevelopment is *mainly* found in parts of Africa, Asia, Latin America, and the Middle East.

3. Of all these areas, the worst and most widespread poverty is to be found in Sub-Saharan Africa.

4. There is a discernible arc of poverty[1] that begins in Sub-Saharan Africa, swings up to include the poorer Middle Eastern countries, then moves to parts of the Balkans and Southeast Europe, parts of the former Soviet Union, and Central Asia, followed by Mongolia, Afghanistan, Pakistan, India, probably China and much of the rest of South and Southeast Asia, and ends in the Pacific islands of Indonesia, the Philippines, and East Timor. Within this arc of poverty lies much potential instability and trouble.

UNGOVERNABILITY, FAILED STATES, AND FOREIGN POLICY

Poor nations tend to be unstable nations. They are not only underdeveloped economically but their social bases, in terms of levels of literacy, education, health and life expectancy, and organizational or associational infrastructure,

| Europe and Central Asia | | Middle East and North Africa | | |
Eastern Europe and Central Asia	Rest of Europe	Middle East	North Africa	Americas
Slovenia	Andorra	Israel	Malta	Aruba
	Channel	Kuwait		Bahamas,
	Islands	Qatar		The
	Cyprus	United Arab		Bermuda
	Faeroe	Emirates		Cayman
	Islands			Islands
	Greenland			French
	Liechtenstein			Guiana
	Monaco			Martinique
				Netherlands,
				Antilles
				Virgin
				Islands
				(U.S.)
27	27	14	6	44

tend to be weak. And if both the social and the economic base is weak and underdeveloped, the political system tends to be wobbly and uncertain as well. Underdevelopment is, therefore, *multifaceted,* with economic, social, and political underdevelopment all closely interrelated.

Not only is underdevelopment multifaceted, affecting all areas of society, but it is also characterized by a series of vicious circles that are very hard to escape. For example, to break out of economic underdevelopment, a country needs capital for investment that can only come from three possible sources: domestic investment, foreign investment, or foreign aid. But if the country is politically unstable, and if property and investments are not protected by the rule of law and a functioning judicial system, little foreign investment will want to come in and potential domestic investors will want to quickly transfer their money out of the country and into safer havens in Switzerland, the tax-free Caymen Islands, or the United States. At the same time, foreign aid, which is always scarce and never enough to solve the manifold problems involved, will have a hard time justifying assistance to unstable, often corrupt governments. Underdeveloped countries need capital to grow economically, but without social and political modernization they cannot attract it; ironically, they cannot modernize society and the political system unless they grow economically. Determining how to break out of these vicious cycles and what resources to use where is a terrible dilemma for almost all developing nations.

Underdeveloped nations that lack infrastructure and viable institutions tend to be not just unstable but also *chronically unstable.* Instability often lasts over a long period of time; fragmentation and collapse are frequent. When nations reach that point, we often call them "ungovernable" or "failed" states. Haiti, Somalia, Sierra Leone, Zaire, Liberia, Uganda, Afghanistan, East Timor, and the former Yugoslavia are cases in point. Pakistan, India, the Philippines, Colombia, and Indonesia are also teetering dangerously close to falling into the ungovernable category. Poverty and underdevelopment are the chief causes of state failure but, more than that, social and political unraveling and then disintegration into warring factions are also involved.

When a state fails, it often attracts the attention of its neighbors as well as the great powers and the international community, or it may get sucked into the vortex of great power politics and rivalries. Look again at the previous list of failed states: every one of them has recently been the subject of high-level international attention and diplomatic or military intervention. Poverty and underdevelopment, therefore, are not just problems of internal interest to the countries affected; for good or ill, they attract international attention and often intervention as well. Sometimes they are better off as a result of such interventions, and sometimes they are worse off.

The writer-journalist Robert Kaplan (*Balkan Ghosts, The Coming Anarchy*) sees a pattern in all this poverty, misery, and failed-state phenomenon. Go back to our discussion in the previous section. Recall that much of Latin America (Haiti is the main exception), Central and Eastern Europe, and East Asia are now doing fairly well, having made it out of low-income ranks to middle-income ranks. These countries, for the most part, are now also stable democracies. But that leaves most of Africa, parts of the Middle East, Southeast Europe, Central Asia, and South and Southeast Asia in the poor or low-income category. This list includes almost all the countries that are in the actual or potential failed-state category.

If one were to predict where United States and international attention and possibly military intervention would occur in the next twenty years, it would be in this "arc" of poor countries whose political systems are often failing and collapsing. Underdevelopment thus becomes not just an economic and a humanitarian issue; it is a political and an international one as well.

FIRST, SECOND, THIRD, AND OTHER WORLDS OF DEVELOPMENT

When the new or emerging nations first burst onto the world's stage and consciousness nearly half a century ago, social scientists invented a new nomenclature and set of categories to help describe them. The French term *Tiers Monde* or *Third World* was used to describe these countries that were not part of the *First World* of modern, democratic, capitalistic countries (North America, Western Europe, eventually Japan, and a few others), nor a part of the *Second World* of (presumably) developed communist nations (the Soviet Union, Eastern Europe). The developing nations not only deserved a category of their own but their politics and sociology, to say nothing of their economics, immediately marked them as different from the other categories; hence, the term *Third World*. This categorization[2] also had foreign policy implications as many Third World nations sought to navigate a "middle way" between the two main representatives of the First and Second Worlds, the United States and the Soviet Union, respectively.

Nearly everyone recognized right from the beginning that this three-part division of the world was inadequate in various ways. First, there were enormous differences between the nations (Japan, Europe, United States) of the First World; second, the Second World (Soviet Union and Eastern Europe) proved to be far less developed than had been thought. Latin America, with almost two hundred years of independent history behind it, was never sure if it belonged in the New Nation or Third World categories. Questions arose about whether Marxist-Leninist China belonged to the Second or the Third World. In the rest of the Third World there were immediately recognizable differences between those countries that were "making it" into the ranks of middle-income countries and those that were falling farther behind. Additionally, the social and cultural differences between Latin America, Sub-Saharan Africa, Asia, and the Middle East made it hard to lump all of them into one catch-all category.

Now that the Cold War has ended, these categories make even less sense than they did before. First, the political and ideological differences among the First World nations, principally the United States and Europe, have grown wider than before. Second, with the collapse of the Soviet Union and of communism in Eastern Europe, the Second World has disappeared; there are no longer any developed Marxist-Leninist states, although there are a handful of underdeveloped ones (Cambodia, Cuba, North Korea, Vietnam). Third, without a Second World, the Third World category, which was always problematic, makes no sense at all anymore—even though it is still often used in popular discourse, including this book.

Since this book is about the developing nations, we concentrate on that issue here. New categories are needed that are both easy to use *and* help us understand the widening differences among Third World nations. The World Bank, whose figures for economic development are the best available, has also moved helpfully in this direction by its distinction between low, lower-middle, upper-middle, and upper-income countries. Those useful categories are utilized here, but they are tied exclusively to economic indices that, by themselves, tell us nothing about the countries' political institutions, stability, and whether or not they are democratic. Similarly, the U.S. government has been talking in the post-Cold War era about the Big Emerging Markets or BEMs (Argentina, Brazil, Chile, China, Egypt, India, Indonesia, Mexico, Nigeria, Pakistan, South Africa, South Korea, and Taiwan) as real or potential large markets for U.S. trade. But again, the emphasis is on economics, not politics.

What is required is a set of categories that enables us to combine measures of economic and social development with a measure of political development (i.e., democracy, stability, strong pluralist and representative institutions). Here, and throughout our analysis, we suggest three categories to help us distinguish among the developing nations. The first category includes those countries who are "making it" both economically and politically, in the sense of having developed more or less stable, effective, democratic governments. Examples include Chile, Costa Rica, virtually all the countries of Central, Eastern, and Northeast (the Baltics) Europe, Mexico, South Korea, Taiwan, Singapore, and *perhaps* India, a marginal case.

The second category includes a large number of in-between countries. These are countries that have made *some* progress toward democracy, but their economies are often still fragile and their political institutions remain weak and are not yet consolidated democratically. Most of the other countries of Latin America fall into this category as does Russia, a number of members of the Commonwealth of Independent States (CIS—formerly a part of the USSR), Egypt, Jordan, Lebanon, India (again), Indonesia, and the Philippines.

A third category is that of failed states: those that are stagnating, showing little progress, or are on the path to disintegration. We have already described the geography of this category: Haiti and perhaps Nicaragua in Latin America, much of Sub-Saharan Africa, Southeast Europe (the Balkans), parts of the Middle East, Central Asia, and parts of South and Southeast Asia. Not only are these nations economically and politically unsuccessful, but they are also, in a foreign policy sense, the most likely countries where the United States and the international community will have to intervene to rescue them from misery and chaos.

It is important to emphasize, first, that these are not fixed but fluid categories: countries can move from one category to another, up or down. Second, the categories themselves are not always precise: witness our difficulty in deciding whether India and Indonesia are "making it" or are failed states; there are trends pointing in both directions. Third, while we all can recognize what a successful country (democratic, developing) looks like, or a failed one for that matter (chaotic, crumbling), the middle category tends to be more ambiguous and imprecise. It consists of countries that show some hopeful signs and some negative ones, may move ahead for a time and then slip back, and may be democratic at some times and less than democratic at others. These are countries that show all the ambiguities, uncertainties, and mixed features of *transitional* regimes and societies.

Finally, we need to say that these categories, while useful for categorizing nations, are not strictly neutral. The author's bias, and that of most readers, to say nothing of persons in the developing nations themselves, is in favor of development and democracy. We all know that modernization brings some unwanted changes (uprooting of peoples, breakup of the family, etc.) as well as desired ones; but most people prefer development over underdevelopment and freedom over tyranny. *On balance* it is surely far better to be literate, wealthy, live longer, have better housing, and live under a democratic regime—the features of a developed country—than to live with the misery of underdevelopment.

These categories carry policy implications as well. The bias, if it can be called that, is toward helping people and countries "make it" to more developed, democratic status and to assist them in staying there once they arrive.

Our wish is to help those countries in the middle or transitional category consolidate their economic and political gains and to grow further. The goal is to prevent countries from slipping into the ungovernable or failed-state categories, with all their attendant misery and potential for disaster. Our categories, therefore, not only help us differentiate better among the many developing nations but also suggest policy guidelines as well. We will return to these themes later in the discussion.

NOTES

1. The phrase comes from Robert Kaplan, whose books (*Balkan Ghosts, The Coming Anarchy*) focus on the poorest, most miserable countries.

2. Irving Louis Horowitz, *Three Worlds of Development* (New York: Oxford University Press, 1966).

2

The Concept
of Development: Origins
and Main Themes

The concept of individual and national *development* goes back to the Enlightenment and the eighteenth-century idea of progress, both for countries and for individuals. Prior to that, society, nations, and individual persons were assumed to be fixed in their stations in life. There was no sense of development or progress, or the possibility of modernization; life simply went on as it always had before, or perhaps in cycles. One was born into a certain station in life, one died there, and one's children continued in the same station through time immemorial. One had to have a sense of fatalism about it all: birth, life, death, and stagnation. As the Christian Bible, then accepted almost universally in Europe, put it rather starkly: "Dust thou art and to dust thou wilt return."

History and its writing were conceived in the same terms. There was no idea of progress or development. Societies and nations as well as individuals were fixed in place; they were born, lived, and died. The dominant conception was that history was cyclical, as in the *rise and fall* of Rome, or the *rise and fall* of civilizations in Arnold Toynbee's multi-volume study of the subject.

Only in the eighteenth-century Enlightenment did the idea of progress or development, both for individual persons and for nations, become fashionable and widespread. Knowledge, study, hard work, industry, rationality, and education were the keys to improving one's individual lot, and by similar diligence and effort societies and nations could also show progress, develop economically, and industrialize. It is no accident that at the end of the eighteenth and the beginning of the nineteenth centuries the first great economists to study the conditions for the wealth and *progress* of nations emerged: Adam Smith, Thomas Malthus, and David Ricardo.

It was similarly out of this background that the great, alternative, nineteenth-century, developmentalist theories—economic, social, and political, many of whose ideas and debates are still with us today—emerged. For example, in economics, Karl Marx, in his analysis of how societies move through the stages of feudalism, capitalism, and socialism, presented a clear developmentalist perspective. In the field of sociology, the positivist thinker Auguste Comte, whose writings are well-known in Europe and much of the developing world but never achieved popularity in the United States, posited a developmentalist sequence in which societies move from "supernatural" or traditional forms based on religious or transcendental beliefs, to what he called the metaphysical stage, and finally to the positivist stage where rational or "scientific" laws of behavior take charge.

Similarly, the sociologist Emile Durkheim showed that, as societies industrialize, develop, and become more modern, tasks become more specialized, a division of labor takes place, and society becomes more differentiated in terms of roles and functions. Finally, in the areas of law and governance, the great German scholar Max Weber showed how societies evolve from traditional authority (chiefs, clan heads, men on horseback) in their traditional stages, to charismatic or colorful and personalistic authority in transitional phases, to regularized, merit-based, bureaucratic, or rational authority at a fully developed stage.

These writers and theorists of the nineteenth century provided many of the ideas and concepts by which later, twentieth-century scholars and activists would try to analyze and/or promote development in the new or emerging nations.

THE FOCUS ON THE DEVELOPING NATIONS

A number of reasons can be offered to explain the growing focus beginning in the 1950s and continuing into the 1960s and beyond, on the part of both scholars and policymakers, on the developing nations. These reasons are related to intellectual trends, to international events and policy issues, to political and economic opportunities, and to transportation and logistical changes.

The first and foremost reason was the sudden emergence in the late 1940s, 1950s, and early 1960s of a host of newly independent nations onto the world stage. After World War II, colonialism proved to be too expensive and difficult for most of the earlier colonizers to maintain; hence, over a two-decade period the British, French, Dutch, Belgians, and eventually the Portuguese began pulling out of the possessions they had colonized in centuries past. The result was a large number of newly independent countries in Africa, Asia, the Middle East, and the Caribbean, most of which had little or no experience in nationhood or self-government, whose borders were often unclear, who were poor and underdeveloped, and who lacked basic social and political institutions—schools, universities, health care, civil society and interest groups, political parties, and bureaucracies. All these new nations quickly doubled the number of countries in the world, and then doubled it again.

The literature during this early period largely focused not only on issues of underdevelopment but also on the problems previously mentioned of "new nationhood." Many of the new countries faced similar problems: writing new constitutions, settling border disputes, developing political parties and government institutions, and so on. In many of these former colonialist areas the problems were compounded by the fact that the borders drawn by the colonial powers which the new nations then inherited had little to do with the realities of culture or ethnicity, often cutting tribal or ethnic units in pieces and putting them, irrationally, in separate countries. Hence, the common "new nations" focus made sense. But in the case of Latin America that designation made no sense since most of the nations there had already been independent for almost a century and a half, since the 1820s. So already we have a problem of analysis and interpretation: while Latin America shared some common problems of underdevelopment with the nations of Africa, Asia, and the Middle East, it did not share the other problems associated with new nationhood. Right from the beginning, therefore, rather like apples and oranges, it was hard to find an analytic framework or set of common concepts that all of the developing nations shared.

A second reason for the rising interest in the developing nations during this period was strategic. The 1940s through 1970s—precisely the time when these new nations were emerging—were the high point of the Cold War, and the developing nations often became the pawns in the Cold War conflict between the U.S. and the Soviet Union. Earlier in the 1950s, the main focus of the Cold War had been the Iron Curtain divide between Western and Eastern Europe; but with the Castro revolution in Cuba and the sudden emergence of so many new and often unstable nations, frequently with internal communist movements, onto the world stage, much of the emphasis shifted to the developing countries. That was particularly true after Cuba not only broke relations with the U.S. and allied itself with the U.S.S.R., but then also imported Soviet missiles which it aimed at the U.S. and also began assisting revolutionary guerrilla movements in Africa, Asia, Latin America, and the Middle East. Fearing that other nations might go the way of Castro's Cuba and that the balance in the Cold War might tip toward the Soviet side if other countries became Marxist-Leninist, the U.S. began to pay far more attention to the developing nations than it had previously. Both the U.S. and Soviet Union, through their assistance and other programs, competed for power and influence there.

The third reason for greater attention being given to the developing nations was economic. Here were areas of vast natural resources as well as immense actual or future markets for U.S., European, and eventually Japanese manufactured goods. Just the thought of a *billion* consumers of Coca-Cola and washing machines in China and another billion in India made the mouths of multinational corporations drool with anticipation. Similarly, in Latin

America, Africa, and Asia, the emerging, consumer-oriented middle class was seen as a major potential buyer of U.S.-produced goods.

While expansion into the developing nations was an end in itself for U.S. companies, it was a means to an end for U.S. policymakers, who were less interested in economic investment per se than in what it brought. Investment and economic growth tended to mean stabler political systems in the developing nations, a growing middle class that would be the bastion of stability, and, therefore, the greater ability of these countries to resist communism, which was *the* main (and often virtually only) U.S. foreign policy preoccupation during these decades. In this way investment by private U.S. companies in the developing nations *and* U.S. foreign-policy interests went hand-in-hand. U.S. private companies saw these new areas as future sources of profit, while the U.S. government tended to see private investment as assisting in the larger foreign-policy goal of promoting stability and anti-communism.

A fourth reason for the new attention to the developing world was the sheer intellectual excitement of it. Here were *dozens* of new nations, with greatly diverse histories, cultures, and sociologies, which no one had ever studied before. The challenge was not just to understand these new nations but to fashion new models or frameworks to comprehend the processes of development and the developing world as a whole. Here were new and exciting "living laboratories" to not only try out new policy prescriptions but also areas where the new, hybrid, innovative, interdisciplinary fields of political anthropology, political sociology, and political economy could be utilized, as well as the new and more scientific approaches in the fields of political science and comparative politics.[1] There was a palpable intellectual excitement in the air in the early 1960s as the first generation of scholars and students set off for the green fields of the developing areas. Part of that excitement was reflected in the new government agencies created during this period to focus on the developing nations: the Peace Corps, the Agency for International Development (AID), and the Alliance for Progress.

Fifth, one cannot discount as a factor in explaining the new interest in the developing nations the new technologies as well as the funding then available. Technologically, the late-1950s to early 1960s was the period when widespread jet travel became available on a large-scale basis for the first time. In the early 1950s, using propeller planes, it took travelers three to four days to go to far-flung places abroad; by the early 1960s, virtually every corner of the globe was within one-day's travel time by jet. Scholars who had once thought themselves lucky to go abroad three or four times in a lifetime now often found themselves making that many foreign trips or more per year to the developing nations. Accommodations abroad, in the form of hotels, rental cars, computers, and travel facilities, also greatly improved. In addition, there was more grant and research money to do these things.

That takes us to the final factor in explaining the new shift in attention to the developing areas. With the Cold War in full bloom in the developing world, the U.S. government initiated a variety of new scholarship programs, language and area studies training programs, and fellowships to lure faculty and students into studying the developing nations. Most of the big foundations—Rockefeller,

Ford, and McArthur—followed suit, both on the humanitarian grounds of wanting to assist poor nations but also as a way of supporting U.S. government programs. The present author was himself a product of this largesse, going all through graduate school and living abroad for long periods on the basis of new U.S. government and foundation grants aimed at training a new generation of specialists in the developing world. Such grants and fellowships were meant to shift the focus of scholarly attention and inquiry away from Western Europe, where it had traditionally been concentrated, and toward the developing nations.

The program succeeded magnificently. By means of these inducements it attracted many of the best young minds to the new field of development studies. By the end of the 1960s, such academic professional associations as the African Studies Association, Asian Studies Association, and Latin American Studies Association were as big as or bigger than the more established European Studies Association. From this point on, the study of the developing nations would emerge as one of, if not *the,* major focuses of the social sciences.

THE EARLY DEVELOPMENT LITERATURE

The Economists

Development was initially seen as mainly, in fact almost exclusively, an economic issue, and the earliest major books on the subject were written by economists. Writers in the classic tradition of Adam Smith, David Ricardo, Thomas Malthus, Karl Marx, and Thomas Marshall were all concerned with how nations grow, become affluent, and prosper or share the wealth more equitably. But their focus, given the time period in which they wrote (the eighteenth and nineteenth centuries), was on the nations that we would today call industrialized or already developed. It was not until World War II and its aftermath, corresponding with the emergence of India, Pakistan, the Philippines, Egypt, Indonesia, and eventually many other new nations, in the 1940s, 1950s, and 1960s, that the emphasis on development in the emerging nations came.

A classic in the literature is Karl Polanyi's *The Great Transformation: The Political and Economic Origins of Our Time* (1944), which focused on European industrialization and economic development but which set the tone for at least two more generations of economists by its problematic suggestion that what worked in Europe to stimulate and achieve growth would, despite very different cultures, sociologies, histories, and backgrounds, work also in the developing nations. In the 1950s and 1960s, quite similar arguments were set forth by such developmentalist economists as Everett von Hagen, Bruce Morris, Robert Heilbrouer, and W. W. Rostow. A number of economists from the Third World, such as Raúal Prebisch, also began writing during this period on developmentalist themes but, with some acknowledgment of locally different conditions, it is striking how many of them echoed the argument of the Western economists that Europe or the United States provided the model for their countries to emulate.

The economists shared a number of related assumptions and understandings that proved in long-range terms to be biased, mistaken, or incomplete. First, they shared the belief—naturally enough; these are economists writing—that economic growth was *the* driving motor force in development, not culture, history, sociology, or politics. Second, they believed that social change and political development/democratization flowed from economic development and not the other way around. However, an equally plausible argument is the one that suggests that *first* you get your political house in order in the form of honest, efficient government, and *only then* can economic growth occur that benefits the whole nation rather than going into the private pockets of some dictator, elite, or clique.

Third, the economists believed that the European model of development, which was generally the only one they knew or had experienced, was *universal,* applying to all countries everywhere at all times, rather than particular and based on a unique European history and culture unlikely to be replicated elsewhere. Finally, the economists believed their formula was automatic and *inevitable:* that all you needed to do was pump-prime the economy, achieve self-sustained growth, and that, once started, economic growth would go forward inevitably, producing not only ongoing development but also, inevitably, the positive social and political changes of greater affluence, a large middle class, and democracy. Little thought was given to reversals, stagnation, or the consequences if social and political mobilization of the people outstripped the government's ability to provide much-needed social reform or jobs.

During this period the single most influential book, because of its impact not just intellectually but also on American foreign policy, was W. W. Rostow's *The Stages of Economic Growth,* subtitled *A Non-Communist Manifesto* (1960). As the title implies, Rostow presented the process of economic growth as proceeding through five stages: traditional society (backward, undeveloped), establishment of the preconditions for take-off (political stability and national unity), the take-off (rapid economic growth but in limited areas), the drive to maturity, and the age of high mass consumption. *All societies,* he said, had to go through these stages. Rostow's stages-based model was derived exclusively from the pattern of U.S. and Western European development which the developing nations were presumably fated to exactly follow. Progression from one stage to the next was both inevitable and universal. The driving force in change was always economic. Moreover, at each stage certain social and political consequences of economic growth followed: the growth of a larger middle class, democracy, and greater social justice. Thus, all the flaws previously noted in the approach of the major economists to development were present in Rostow's analysis. His model was parochial, ethnocentric, and, based on the experience of the already-developed nations, had little to do with the real situation in most developing countries.

Of course, you need economic growth to create jobs, provide investment for future growth, build infrastructure, dynamize the economy, and pay for social services. Economic growth is the *sine qua non* for development. But it is mistaken to assume there is a universal model, derived from the in-many-ways unique and special experiences of the United States and Western Europe, that can be applied to all countries at all times, without taking account of local cultures, histories, sociologies, and ways of doing things. Nor are these processes inevitable and universal; rather, they occur by fits and starts, through sideways steps as much as forward ones, with each society and culture providing its own unique path. Nor are democracy and social justice the inevitable outcomes; in much of the developing world, by contrast, it was authoritarianism, conflict, and civil war that resulted. In terms of sequences, moreover, a good case can be made that it is first necessary to put in place a decent political system that wants genuinely to stimulate democracy and development so that the economic growth occurs for the benefit of society as a whole and is not channeled off to benefit only the ruling elites.

In short, the earliest models of economic growth were fatally flawed in conception and gave rise to many of the problems of development that are still with us today.

The Anthropologists

Cultural anthropologists had in the past taken a position very different from that of the developmental economists. Whereas economists tended to see their categories as universal, pertaining to all countries at all times, anthropologists inclined toward the view of the uniqueness and particularity of all cultures. In the research and writings of such pioneering anthropologists as Franz Boas, Margaret Mead, Ruth Benedict, George Foster, and others, every culture has its own internal dynamic, logic, and rationality. One has to study each culture *on its own terms, in its own language,* and *in its own context.* Seen in this light, each culture has special features of its own; it may be affected by outside forces but, contrary to the economists, there is no one, single, inevitable, and universal model of development. Cultural distinctiveness and relativity are the norms, not some global pattern to which all nations must conform.

Most scholars in the development field accept the notion, contrary to the economists' idea of the universality of their model, that all societies have unique and distinctive characteristics. But while siding with the cultural anthropologists on that issue, they also tend to believe that there are *patterns* in the development process. Each society and culture is different and responds to stimuli in often distinctive ways, but there are general trends in the development process that are also discernible. We often call these "tendency statements." That is, while each society does things in its own way, there are common trends or tendencies that can also be analyzed. Contrary to the economists, each country is unique; but contrary to the anthropologists, there are certain common patterns. Understanding development is a matter both of comprehending the unique characteristics of each society and of identifying the common tendencies at work.

Developmental anthropology, as distinct from the earlier individual case study approach of Mead and others, builds upon this understanding while also going in some quite new and innovative directions. One of the most influential papers written in this regard is by Francis X. Sutton, then of the Ford Foundation.[2] His paper, while not well-known at the popular level, was enormously influential in the early (1950) studies and literature of development. Sutton's paper was important not so much in its own right but through the influence of his writing on other, better-known scholars of development (discussed later) such as political scientist Gabriel Almond. Sutton suggested that *distinct cultures* go through certain *common processes* en route to development and modernization. In particular, Sutton analyzed and mapped out the processes and a set of indicators to measure societal transitions from traditionalism to modernity. In his formulation, modern, industrial societies were characterized by broadly accepted legal standards, increasing social mobility, and increased differentiation of specialized structures and function. By contrast, traditional or agricultural countries were characterized by time-honored custom and fatalism, rigidly hierarchical status considerations, and absence of specialization. Development, in his view, consisted of countries moving from the second set of conditions to the first.

Presumably all societies could be categorized in the "traditional" or "modern" categories, or found to be "strung out," so to speak, somewhere on a continuum between these two polar points. Such dichotomous thinking— traditional versus modern, as compared with the reality that most societies are complex, overlapping mixtures of both—would dominate much of the subsequent thinking and writing about developing nations. Moreover, the march from traditional to modern was presumably universal, inevitable, and one-way; it also followed the example of the already-developed and modern nations, the United States and Western Europe. In this way, some of the best-known anthropological writings on development came to closely parallel the writings of developmentalist economists such as Rostow.

The Sociologists

The field of sociology also offered its contributions to the new thinking about developing nations. We have already mentioned the great German sociologist Max Weber and his idea that societies go through three successive stages on the route to development: traditional authority, charismatic authority, and then rational-legal authority. Weber's translator (from German to English) and major disciple in the United States was Talcott Parsons of Harvard University; other major figures in sociology who wrote about developmental themes included Daniel Lerner, Seymour Martin Lipset, and (although a political scientist, he often used sociological approaches) Karl Deutsch.

Parsons, so far as we know, never spent any time in the developing nations; his contribution was at the level of "grand theory." He presented a set of categories for comparing modern and traditional societies that in his view would have universal validity. He called these categories "pattern variables," of which there are three. Parsons suggested that traditional societies are based on *ascription* (birth, family name, clan or tribe; *who* you know or are related to rather than *what* you know) whereas modern societies are based on *merit*. Second, traditional societies are narrow, parochial, and *particularistic* in their viewpoints, whereas modern societies are based on broader, *universal* values. Third, traditional societies are *functionally diffuse* (religious, economic, military, and political authority may overlap and get mixed up) whereas modern societies are *functionally specific* (i.e., religious or military authorities should not interfere in the political process). In each pattern variable, the direction of change would be from traditional behavior to modern traits; moreover, the *cluster* of traits previously indicated constituted the differences between traditional society and modern society, as shown in Table 2.1.

Table 2.1 Parsons' Pattern Variables

Traditional Society	Modern Society
Ascription	Merit
Particularism	Universalism
Functionally diffuse	Functionally specific

These are useful distinctions in some ways and, as we will see shortly, they further provide political scientists with a method and model to distinguish between developing and developed nations. However, to anticipate the criticisms that were later made, in reality most societies (even the United States) are complex mixtures and overlaps of ascription and merit, of particularism and universalism, of functional diffuseness and functional specificity. Nor in the Parsons formulation is there any indication of how societies move from one form or stage to another. Is it culture and changing values that drive the change; is it economic development and industrialization; or something else? Do we learn why these three pattern variables are singled out and not others (Parsons actually changed his mind on the issue a couple of times, sometimes including other pattern variables)? In addition, the dichotomous, either-or categories of traditional and modern are too absolute; they tell us little about the mixed or hybrid cases (most countries in the world) that lie in-between these two polarized ideal types; and, therefore, they probably present a false picture of both traditional and modern societies. Plus, if a modern society is defined by the three traits Parsons ascribes to it, it is likely that *no* developing country can ever achieve that position, a disappointment that is likely to lead to frustration and mass discontent. The pattern variables seem almost antiseptic: is there any room in them for clash and conflict, coups d'etat, revolutions, exploitation, civil war, genocide, AIDS, and other realities of the poorer nations? One will not find an answer in Parsons' pattern variables.

In contrast to Parsons' "grand theory," Lerner was more down-to-earth and factual, with real countries and facts involved.[3] He studied the effects of increased means of communications on modernization and development in the

Middle East, arguing that greater access to the media would produce greater awareness, greater egalitarianism, and ultimately greater democracy. But Lerner's study rested on many of the same assumptions as did those of the other economists, anthropologists, and sociologists surveyed here: that the process of going from traditional to modern was one way, that all societies regardless of distinct cultures went through essentially the same processes, and that the final outcome would be democracy and pluralism. But the Islamic revolution of the Ayatollah Khomeini in Iran and his use of tapes ("modern communications") to get his hateful, anti-Western, anti-democratic message across, or the use of the Internet (again "modern communications") by Osama bin Laden and his terrorist cells, should be sufficient to give us pause as to just how one-way, inevitable, universal, and pro-democratic the changes produced by modern communications really are.

Two other seminal articles, published about the same time as these others, and just as the flood of new nations was washing across the globe in the late 1950s and early 1960s, attracted widespread attention and were highly influential in shaping thinking about the developing areas. Karl Deutsch[4] and Seymour Martin Lipset[5] focused, respectively, on "social mobilization" and the "social requisites of democracy." Although derived from distinct research projects, the two articles were remarkably parallel in their arguments and conclusions. Both argued forcefully that certain social requirements (high literacy, mobilization of peasants and workers, education, modern communications, basic agreement or consensus on political institutions and procedures) must be met before a society could become developed and democratic.

The analyses offered were similar to those discussed earlier of Rostow, Sutton, Parsons, and Lerner: that all countries go through similar processes of modernization, that economic development and social change give rise to democracy, and that these processes are inevitable and universal. Actually these scholars were careful to point out that greater education did not necessarily *cause* democracy (many authoritarian and totalitarian regimes at the time had used education not to enhance democracy but to teach the cult of the leader or of the party and thus to inhibit democracy), only that there was a close *correlation* between high levels of education and democracy. But some of their followers and disciples, especially in U.S. policymaking circles, were not as careful as Deutsch and Lipset were; and hence the belief grew that by just pumping in money (Rostow), mobilizing the lower classes (Deutsch), and educating the masses (Lipset), democracy and development would automatically flower.

For a long time, and often continuing to today in the programs of the World Bank, USAID, and others, these ideas of the causative relationship between economic growth, social change, and political development (viewed by most in the United States as "democratization") constituted the ideological and theoretical bases of the U.S. foreign aid program directed at the developing countries. That program had been in large part designed by Rostow according to his "Stages of Economic Growth" analysis. In his analysis, recall, the motor force in moving from one developmental stage to the next was always economic development; social and political changes followed *automatically* from economic growth.

In turn, in the analyses of Sutton, Parsons, Lerner, Deutsch, and Lipset, political change followed from social change. The arguments were highly deterministic; to use social science jargon for a minute, economic development and social change were always the driving forces in development while politics and governance seemed to be the dependent variables, never independently important but rather an offshoot of other factors. All the United States and the international foreign aid community needed to do, the argument ran, was to pump in economic aid, build dams and highways, expand communications, finance education, and assist with social mobilization, and *somehow* democracy would inevitably, automatically, and universally follow out of this. It does not take a huge amount of logic and understanding to see that there are immense holes in this argument. Democracy did not inevitably, automatically, and universally follow upon economic growth and social change; indeed, a strong argument can be made (and was, forcefully, by Samuel P. Huntington) that such changes, instead of aiding democracy, in fact undermined it and helped lead to the huge wave of authoritarianism and repression throughout the developing world that followed in the later 1960s and 1970s.[6]

There was, in addition, a foreign policy goal and underpinning attached to the early literature on development. Rostow had subtitled his famous book *A Non-Communist Manifesto,* and there is no doubt many of the scholars writing in this early period saw a relationship between achieving development and serving U.S. foreign policy or Cold War goals. By achieving economic growth, a sizable and literate middle class, and so on, a society could carry itself through the dangerous earlier stages of development when it might be subject to communist takeovers. A carefully formulated U.S. foreign aid program to assist development, therefore, was not only ethically and morally good (aiding poor nations) but it would also serve then high-priority U.S. foreign policy goals by preventing developing countries from "going communist." However, the plan did not work as anticipated either as a development strategy or as a Cold War policy.[7]

Political Scientists

As early as the 1950s political scientist Roy Macridis had been urging his fellow comparative politics scholars to move away from the almost exclusively European focus of the field and to study other areas.[8] He had also urged that Comparative Politics be more truly comparative and analytic, and should concentrate on the *informal* processes of politics (public opinion, interest groups, political parties) rather than the *formal structures* or institutions of government. These injunctions seemed to apply particularly to the emerging areas where, it was already assumed, the formal institutions of government would not work very well and, therefore, informal processes of politics merited greater attention.

In his path-breaking edited book *The Politics of the Developing Areas* (1960), Gabriel Almond followed precisely the Macridis suggestions. Note also that the date *exactly* corresponds with the Rostow, Lipset, and Deutsch studies and is right at the point when so many of the developing nations were achieving independence. The Almond volume was not only influential but its approach was closely in keeping with that of the other studies here surveyed.

In his Introduction, which was accompanied by chapters on all the world's major developing areas, Almond set forth a framework for studying development that was to have enormous influence in the field. First, Almond accepted the emphasis on process, informal actors, non-Western countries, and genuine comparison as argued by Macridis and others. Second, Almond adapted the *systems approach* (input → government decision making → policy outputs) advanced earlier in political science by David Easton for the study of developing nations. Third, Almond took Parsons' pattern variables (ascription → merit, particularism → universalism, functionally diffuse → functionally specific) and made them the core of his understanding of the differences between developing and developed political systems.

Almond further reasoned, fourth, that the same basic functions (choice of lenders, mobilization of support, delivery of services, etc.) had to be performed in all political systems, developed or developing. He therefore set forth a *functionalist* model of the political system which was presumably valid for all countries. On the "input" side (influences going "into" the political system) Almond had four functions:

1. Political socialization—how people learn about or are inculcated with political values through their families, schools, religious background, and so on.

2. Interest articulation—how interests are articulated and conveyed, which sounds similar to American-style interest group activity or lobbying.

3. Interest aggregation—how interests are combined or aggregated, which sounds like political party activity.

4. Political communication—how influence and interests are transmitted to decision makers, á la Lerner.

On the output or policy delivery side there were three more functions:

5. Rule-making—who makes the rules or laws, which sounds like a U.S.-style legislative activity.

6. Rule-execution—carrying out or administering the laws, which sounds like the U.S.-style executive branch.

7. Rule-adjudication—deciding conflicts over rules or laws, rather like the U.S.-style judicial branch.

Note how close all of these functions are to the American political system, or at least an idealized version of it. Where in this scheme is the patronage function, partisan politics, political log-rolling, and "I'll scratch your back if you scratch mine?" In other words, the supposedly "universal" model that Almond presented was really a disguised picture of the American political system, and a cleaned-up, idealized, sanitized version if that. But is the romanticized, antiseptic American model, albeit hidden by Almond's functional categories, really applicable to all the world's political systems? Therein lies one of the great problems of understanding the developing countries, both in the past and today. Can they be properly comprehended only by whether they live up to the U.S.

model, or must they be understood only in *their own* cultural, historical, and developmental context? Most scholars believe the latter.

Right from the beginning skepticism arose about the Almond approach. Specialists in Europe did not find his categories very helpful in studying advanced, industrial societies. Similarly, senior Asian and Latin American specialists felt the Almond design was an effort to stuff their areas or countries into a preconceived set of categories that had only limited applicability. Even within the prestigious Committee on Comparative Politics of the Social Science Research Council (CCP/SSRC), which Almond chaired and which played a dominant role in the study of the developing nations over the next decade, many doubts existed about Almond's approach, the pattern variables, the use of the traditional-modern dichotomy, and the functional perspective.

Nevertheless, and especially for younger scholars and students, the approach of *The Politics of the Developing Areas* proved to be very attractive. First, it provided a logical, coherent outline of the political process which was presumably applicable to all the world's political systems. Second, it told young scholars what to look for in the developing world: interest articulation, interest aggregation, and so on. Third, the approach seemed neutral and unbiased; unlike other approaches in the past, it was not condescending or racist toward the developing nations. Fourth, not only was it scientifically sound (or so it appeared), but it was also morally correct: one could not only study development but, additionally, also work to advance it. And fifth, since it reflected U.S. government and foundation thinking at the time, it came with the promise of fellowships, grants, and the opportunity to study abroad.

So, armed with the Rostow-Lipset-Sutton-Parsons-Almond categories, a whole generation of young scholars went off to Africa, Asia, Latin America, and the Middle East to study "development." But what they found often bore little resemblance to what the Almond framework had led them to expect. Later in the chapter we will explore what they *did* find and how that led to entirely new and quite different approaches to studying and/or assisting the developing nations. But first we continue the story of the immense proliferation of developmentalist writings.

THE PROLIFERATION
OF DEVELOPMENT STUDIES

During the decade of the 1960s, studies of development proliferated, and the developmentalist approach became the dominant one in the field. In addition to the path-breaking *The Politics of the Developing Areas,* a series of other trailblazing books was issued by the leading scholars in the field and published by the prestigious Princeton University Press on such topics as communications and political development, political culture and political development, political parties and political development, education and political development, bureaucracy and political development, religion and political development, armed forces and political development, trade unions and political development, peasants and political development, and so on. A bibliography published in the mid-1960s contained over two thousand entries dealing with development themes; by this point, the developmentalist approach had established itself as the dominant one, not only in economics, sociology, and anthropology, but also in the fields of political science, comparative politics, and Third World studies.

Developmentalism was not only the dominant academic approach but it had also become *the* approach underlying U.S. assistance programs and policy toward the emerging nations. Here the key person had been W. W. Rostow, author of the earlier summarized *The Stages of Economic Growth,* who had gone from his academic position at MIT in the late 1950s, where he had written his main works on development; to head of the Policy Planning Staff at the State Department, where he had also been the chief architect of John F. Kennedy's foreign aid program through the newly created Agency for International Development (AID), and specifically for Latin America in the form of the Alliance for Progress; to National Security Adviser under President Lyndon Johnson, where he had been one of the leading planners of the war in Vietnam. Rostow is one of those rare individuals who has had the opportunity to convert his academic ideas and writings into policy practice.

Indeed, the fingerprints of Rostow, Almond, Lipset, and the entire developmentalist approach can be seen all over the U.S. foreign aid program during this and subsequent periods, and in U.S. foreign policy toward the Third World. With regard to foreign aid and development assistance, the assumption á la Rostow and Lipset was to build infrastructure (dams, roads, etc.), pour in foreign aid, and stimulate investment; that, in turn, will create stability, a middle class, and societal pluralism; and all of this combined will cause political pluralism and, hence, democracy to flower. Recall that this sequence, according to Rostow, was automatic, inevitable, and universal. All countries went through the same processes, which was, of course, a model based on the U.S. and West European experiences.

To accomplish these goals, a number of regional development banks for Africa, Asia, and Latin America were created to go along with the older World Bank and International Monetary Fund (IMF) to channel money into the developing areas. In addition, a host of new development-related programs—the Peace Corps, agrarian reform agencies, economic planning agencies, institutes for dam projects and hydraulic resources, electrification programs, and a large variety of others—were put in place to help the emerging countries achieve "take-off." And in all of this the familiar assumptions applied: if only we can stimulate economic development, then we can create middle class, democratic societies that will also be socially just and that, therefore, will resist the appeals of communism. Development assistance, therefore, was not just a way of raising up Third World countries; it was also designed to serve U.S. security policy and Cold War goals. In the early, optimistic (pre-Vietnam) years of the early-to-mid-1960s, no contradiction was seen between these two goals.

Almost no one disagrees with the goals sought: to achieve development, farm-to-market roads need to be built, dams constructed and power capacity increased, loans and investments secured, productivity increased, and so on. The questions are not over the goals but how best to achieve them, whether the U.S./European model is appropriate for today's developing nations, and what the sequence of development ought to be. For example, the model of agrarian reform pushed by developmental economists often has a striking resemblance to rural Wisconsin (where, in fact, the principal advising agency on Third World agrarian reform, the Land Tenure Center at the University of Wisconsin, was located); the model of citizen participation came out looking like a romanticized version of a participatory New England town meeting; and Parsons' "pattern variables" as well as Almond's "functional categories" produced a political system that too closely reflected an idealized version of the United States. Now, most of us are admirers of the American political system but *no one* in their right mind believes it can be replanted and imitated, lock, stock, and barrel, in such impoverished places as Haiti, Somalia, East Timor, Afghanistan, or Iraq.

A key issue revolved around the sequencing of development. Rostow, himself an economist, had, of course, argued that economic development is the great motor force of development and, therefore, comes first, followed by social change, then democratization. So the implication is: pour in the money, stimulate economic growth, and democratization will automatically follow. But in many countries it did not work that way. There, corrupt rulers, oligarchies, and militaries in the 1960s and 1970s (think of Marcos in the Philippines, Suharto in Indonesia, the Shah of Iran, the Somoza family in Nicaragua, and *numerous* African, Latin American, and Middle Eastern dictators and strong-arm regimes), instead of using aid and investment for development, *stole* the money, diverted it for their personal use, or funneled it patronage-like to favored friends and supporters.

Rather than economic development, much of the money went into private pockets. Instead of economic development producing and leading automatically to democracy, it only produced greater corruption and the enforcement and perpetuation of authoritarianism. The case began to be made that Rostow and early development theory got it all wrong and backward: rather than economic development leading to democracy, what was required *first* was a decent democratic regime that was committed to using the funds honestly, and only then would genuine economic development occur. (An exception to this rule was East Asia where, in the big and little "tigers"—Japan, South Korea, Taiwan, Hong Kong, and Singapore—real, noncorrupt, *massive* economic development *did* occur that led to social change that eventually produced democratization. Later in the analysis, in Chapter 4, we seek to explain this Asian "exceptionalism.")

A similar fatal flaw appeared as regards to the sociological literature (Lipset, Deutsch) and the argument that social mobilization needed to accompany and perhaps precede democratization. But instead what happened was the following: in the face of the rapid social mobilization of peasants and workers in the early 1960s that occurred in considerable part as a result of the developmentalist argument and numerous U.S. foreign aid programs (Peace Corps, Alliance for Progress, agrarian reform, etc.), the elites, oligarchies, and armed forces in many developing countries became frightened that they would be overwhelmed from below, either violently through Marxian revolution or electorally by being out-voted. They therefore organized to prevent that from happening by banding to-gether and staging a wave of right-wing military takeovers in the 1960s and 1970s that overthrew fledgling democracies, suppressed and often repressed the work-ing and peasant classes, restored the old oligarchic and authoritarian regimes, and led to a decades-long period of human rights violations, a turning back of the clock, and an end to democratic life. Instead of social change and mobilization leading to democracy as the development literature suggested, they had the op-posite effect, producing oppression, counter-change, and authoritarianism.

The strongest and most powerfully argued book making this case was Samuel P. Huntington's 1968 study, *Political Order in Changing Societies.* There, Huntington argued that, rather than economic development, social change, and political development or democratization all going forward harmoniously to-gether, in fact economic and social modernization, if they proceeded too fast and threatened traditional groups, often had the reverse effect of undermining democracy and paving the way for a reassertion of authoritarianism. With the strong Huntington critique, the developmentalist model of the 1960s, which had once seemed both so positive and so benign, lost its luster. On top of that came a *flood* of case studies of the developing areas that failed to find the kind of "development" that Rostow, Lipset, and Almond had hypothesized, and whose cumulative critical weight soon challenged the basic theory and logic of developmentalism. Meanwhile, the Vietnam War, Watergate, the assassinations of Robert F. Kennedy and Martin Luther King, and other demoralizing cur-rents in American society undermined the presumption that the United States provided an attractive model for the developing nations to emulate.

There were other biases in the developmentalist approach that soon became obvious as more and more actual studies (as distinct from the earlier theoretical formulations—often by scholars who later confessed they had never been in a developing country) of developing nations appeared. First, in all the literature on development, no one seriously studied the relations of business, entrepre-neurship, and the private sector to development—possibly because in those days the widespread assumption was that a centrally planned, socialist, or perhaps mixed economy was the best way to achieve development, and few scholars or developmentalists thought seriously about the contribution of business to de-velopment. Another glaring omission was the lack of studies of oligarchies and ruling classes and development—again, presumably, because this element was seen as inevitably fading away or being destroyed as modernization went for-ward, and because those who studied and promoted development tended to fa-vor democracy and pluralism over elite rule. But in the short run at least these elite groups did not disappear; moreover, a strong case can be made that, if we are in favor of development, we had better be well informed about those elite groups with the capacity to control, advance, coopt, or frustrate it.

A third, major omission was the inability to see that there were more than two paths to development. Early writers like Rostow, caught up in the Cold War calculations of the time, envisioned only two routes to development, a commu-nist one and its obviously preferable democratic alternative. But, in fact, there are many diverse paths to development besides these two: an authoritarian path, a statist path, a corporatist path, and—most likely of all in most developing countries—a confused, often chaotic, hodge-podge alternation between, or mixed combination of, *all* of these. The proper image to use is not that of "the two paths" but rather of a trellis of the kind one uses in a garden for roses or other climbing vines, with *multiple* routes to development, numerous crossing patterns, and a great variety of mixed, overlapping, crisscrossing sprouts—which also sometimes get reversed, blocked from growing, or stymied.[9]

Confusion also continued about what, precisely, development meant. In the less-divisive, more-consensual atmosphere of the early-to-mid-1960s when writing about and attention to development themes began, people simply assumed they knew what it meant and that others of goodwill (Westerners and people in the developing areas who thought like Westerners) would arrive at the same understanding. But, in fact, the term continued to involve different understandings and to mean different things to different groups and people, which then was reflected in what they wrote about it or the policies they advocated. Perhaps the dominant orientation at least initially was to conceive of development in purely economic terms, as *economic development,* but which would then have the social and political consciences already analyzed. Sociologists, in contrast, tended to see *development* as the growing division of labor and differentiation of functions in society or, following Parsons and Lipset, to focus on such indicators of *modernization* (a term they often preferred over development) as urbanization, rising literacy, or longer life expectancy. Political scientists had still a third definition, equating development with the growth and effectiveness of such institutions as political parties, interest groups, and state bureaucracies and public programs. In the policy arena still a fourth definition prevailed, which equated development with stability, democracy, and anti-communism. Political scientist Lucian Pye once counted over twenty distinct uses and definitions of *development.*[10]

Although the definitions of development were often vague, unclear, and potentially contradictory, in the consensual, pre-Vietnam 1960s that was not seen as a major problem. Most scholars incorporated several or all of the definitions just mentioned—economic development, specialization and differentiation of functions, institutionalization, democracy, stability, even anti-communism—into their understanding, and assumed that all of these features went pretty closely together. Such vagueness was not so bad so long as there was a solid general understanding of what was meant, but the very looseness and imprecision of the concept provided an open opportunity for critics to attack it, particularly as the earlier consensus (see the following chapter) on both the concept and American foreign policy started falling apart.

Moreover, unlike economic development which can be measured quite precisely in terms of rising per-capita income, or social development which can also be measured fairly precisely as rising literacy, rising urbanization, and rising life expectancy, political development is far more difficult to measure. How do we know when a country is politically developed? Especially when, as previously noted, there are so many definitions of development? What criteria would we use, and what measures? Is it when a country is democratic, and how precisely do we measure that; when it has developed political parties, interest groups, and government agencies? If we look back at Tables 1.1 and 1.2, we see that economic and social development can be measured with the use of several criteria but there is not a single gauge for political development. These definitional and measurement problems would continue to plague the political development approach.

Despite the problems and omissions, the developmentalist approach became *the* dominant approach in the 1960s to studying and recommending policies for the emerging nations. Thousands of articles and hundreds of books were written about development in the Third World during this period; at the same time, almost the entire U.S. and international aid program and foreign policy toward the developing nations were based on developmentalism. Pour in economic aid, build infrastructure, and stimulate social modernization, the argument was, and political development and democratization would automatically and universally follow. But soon the criticisms of the developmentalist approach began to mount, and in the Third World, development was not working out as the theory of development had posited. By the end of the 1960s and on into the 1970s the developmentalist approach was under strong attack at the academic level, but little of the academic criticism had much effect on the U.S. foreign aid program which continued (and continues today) much as it had before: outdated, not very effective, and often irrelevant.

NOTES

1. For an overview, see Howard J. Wiarda, *Introduction to Comparative Politics* (Fort Worth: Harcourt Brace, 2000).

2. Francis X. Sutton, "Social Theory and Comparative Politics." Paper prepared for the Committee on Comparative Politics, Social Science Research Council, Princeton University, June 1954.

3. David Lerner, *The Passing of Traditional Society: Modernizing the Middle East* (Glencoe, IL: The Free Press, 1958).

4. Karl Deutsch, "Social Mobilization and Political Development," *American Political Science Review,* 53 (March 1959), 493–514.

5. Seymour Martin Lipset, "Some Social Requisites of Democracy: Economic Development and Political Legitimacy," *American Political Science Review,* 53 (March 1959), 69–105.

6. Samuel P. Huntington, *Political Order in Changing Societies* (New Haven: Yale University Press, 1968).

7. For the early history of developmentalism including U.S. government involvement, see Donald L. M. Blackmer, *The MIT Center for International Studies: The Founding Years, 1951–1969* (Cambridge, MA: MIT Center for International Studies, 2002).

8. Roy Macridis, *The Study of Comparative Government* (New York: Random House, 1955).

9. The "trellis" or "lattice" image derives from Philippe C, Schmitter, "Paths to Political Development in Latin America," in Douglas Chamers (ed.), *Changing Latin America* (New York: Academy of Political Science, Columbia University Press, 1972).

10. Lucian Pye, *Aspects of Political Development* (Boston: Little Brown, 1965).

3

Disillusionment with Development: Military Coups and the Emergence of Bureaucratic Authoritarianism

The shift in the 1960s, in both the Comparative Politics and the Foreign Policy/International Relations fields, away from Europe and toward a focus on the developing nations, represented what scholars call a *paradigm shift*. That meant a change not just in the geographic areas and countries studied but also a shift in the assumptions, theory, preconceptions, student interest, and emphases—indeed, in a whole way of thinking—of scholars and policymakers alike about how nations change, develop, and modernize. The Europe-NATO focus represented one paradigm, dominant from World War II through the 1950s; the developing areas or Third World was a new paradigm that emerged and gradually supplanted the older one during the course of the 1960s.

But developmentalism, as this new paradigm was labeled, seemingly fell and went into eclipse just as rapidly as it had arisen. Two major causes for this decline were involved, one intellectual and the other quite practical, having to do with events on the ground in the Third World itself. The first, beginning in the late 1960s and suggested in the previous chapter, was a withering critique of developmentalism's assumptions, theory, and main models, a critique that was so powerful that it all but undermined the developmentalist approach. The second involved a *wave* of military coups, authoritarianism, and accompanying statism and corporatism in Africa, Asia, Latin America, and the Middle East that seemed to undermine all of developmentalism's assumptions about the relations between socioeconomic development and democracy. Both of these subject matters—the critiques of developmentalism and the rise of military authoritarianism (now referred to as "bureaucratic-authoritarianism," to distinguish the new, more complex, *institutionalized* armed forces' or civil-military regimes from the old-fashioned one-man dictatorships of the past)—receive major attention in this chapter.

But while the strong critiques served to undermine the developmentalist approach and while the rise of bureaucratic-authoritarianism severed the hoped-for connection between modernization and democracy, we must also remember that in quite a number of countries actual development continued to go forward. Economies continued to grow, often at miracle rates in some countries, regardless of the kind of regime in power; literacy increased; life expectancy increased; and social change—the rise of new business groups, the emergence of a larger middle class, and the mobilization and urbanization of much of the peasant population—continued to go forward. So here we have a curious phenomenon: the main theories of developmentalism had been discredited and military-authoritarianism had dimmed the lights of democracy, yet *on the ground,* in the lives of real people, change, modernization, and actual, real development continued to advance.

One of the interesting questions, therefore, becomes: were the military regimes as effective, or perhaps more so, at achieving development as the civilian democracies they replaced? Or, alternatively, did real development continue to go forward *regardless* of the theory scholars had devised to try to understand it and *regardless* of the type of regime, democratic or authoritarian, in power? A Brazilian proverb captures this last alternative nicely: "Development occurs at night while the government, of whatever kind, sleeps."

CRITICISMS OF THE DEVELOPMENTALIST APPROACH

The criticisms of the developmentalist approach were many and telling. We have already hinted at some of them. First, the developmentalist approach was based on abstract, theoretical formulations of persons (Rostow, Parsons, Lipset, Almond) who later admitted they had not, to that point, ever visited, let alone lived or had field experience in, a developing nation. The theoretical models they used were derived either from abstract deductive reasoning (if this, then that) or from the experience of the already developed nations of Western

Europe and the United States, but not on empirical research in the Third World. To the legion of young graduate students, Peace Corps volunteers, and foreign aid workers now fanning out to the developing areas for the first time, neither Rostow's "stages," Parsons' "pattern variables," nor Almond's "functional" categories had anything to do with what they saw in actual practice. The reality was usually not "interest aggregation" or "rule adjudication" but instead vast misery, power grabs by military and civilian elites, violence, corruption, vast patronage networks, special favoritism, repression of change-oriented groups, revolution, civil war, and political breakdown. Eventually several of these young scholars came to the conclusion that the developmentalist approach was guiding them to ask the wrong questions and look for the wrong things. Over time they came to believe that the entire developmentalist model and paradigm were wrong and eventually advanced other, alternative approaches.

A second negative influence of developmentalism was the war in Vietnam, from the mid-1960s to the mid-1970s. Vietnam was a severe test case for U.S.-conceived developmentalism, as well as for U.S. foreign policy. In South Vietnam the United States had tried virtually every program that the developmentalist school suggested: agrarian reform, community development, infrastructure growth, aid to labor and peasant organizations, political party creation, military reform, government reform, massive assistance and pump-priming through the transitional stages, and so on. But nothing the United States did seemed to do the trick of achieving development and democracy. Not only was South Vietnam defeated and overrun by the communist North but, in the process of trying to "develop" Vietnam, the United States seemed wrongheadedly to be destroying it as well. The fact that many of those who had been leading architects of developmentalism (Rostow, Lipset, Almond) had also been involved in designing programs for the failed Vietnam effort seemed to discredit the entire developmentalist approach. Out of Vietnam came the strong conclusion that neither the United States nor developmentalism had the right answers for the Third World; indeed, they were the wrong and very destructive answers.

A third blow to developmentalism came with the previously noted publication of Samuel P. Huntington's devastating critique of modernization theory.[1] Coming at the end (1968) of a decade of extensive theoretical writings about development by Almond and many others, and after many failed developmentalist experiments at the policy level, Huntington's critique was particularly damaging because it attacked the basic assumption on which all the developmentalist literature was based. The development literature had been grounded on the assumption that economic development, social change, and democratization all went forward in harmony, but Huntington showed convincingly that rapid economic growth and social mobilization, rather than leading to stability and democracy, could be so upsetting of traditional ways that they produced chaos and breakdown. Social modernization leads people to have increased expectations for a better life before their political institutions are capable of providing it, producing disappointment and frustration on a national scale leading to societal unraveling or even revolution. Or else social mobilization of peasants, workers, and other lower-class elements may so frighten traditional elites and militaries that they abandon democracy, seize power, and rule through authoritarianism—precisely what was happening in a *wave* of coups in Africa, Asia, Latin America, and the Middle East at the very time that Huntington's book came out. Huntington suggested that, instead of focusing on mobilization and social change, scholars and development practitioners should concentrate on building strong institutions capable of handling the immense changes underway, such as political parties, bureaucracies, and armed forces.

A fourth criticism of developmentalism, mainly growing out of the experience of many young scholars doing extensive field work in the emerging areas in the 1960s, was that it was biased and ethnocentric. The development categories, the stages of growth, and the institutions and processes involved all seemed to derive from the Western (European, U.S.) experiences, not from the developing areas themselves. There was little attempt to take the developing nations on their own terms, in *their own* cultural, social, historical, or political settings, or to consider that they themselves might know best concerning their own development needs. The experience of many young scholars in non-Western developing nations during this period often led them to conclude that the Western experience was of doubtful applicability when imported into Third World areas whose background and culture were entirely different.

A fifth criticism was that the international context of development for today's Third World nations was very different from that of the earlier developers (Great Britain, Germany, France, the United States) in the eighteenth and nineteenth centuries. Then, nations could develop autonomously and largely on their own, but today's emerging nations are much more strongly affected by international market forces, modern communications, globalization, war and conflict, international trade, and complex patterns of dependency and interdependency with the outside world. They cannot develop independently but are constantly caught up in powerful global currents over which they have only limited control.

Sixth, the timing, sequences, and stages of development that the West experienced cannot be repeated in today's developing world. As regards timing, while the West took a long time—hundreds of years—to develop, in today's developing nations peoples and societies are aroused (social mobilization), impatient, and unwilling to wait the centuries that it took the West to develop. Concerning sequences: whereas in the West industrialization drew people out of the countryside and into urban areas, thus creating jobs and the basis for an organized working class, in today's developing nations rapid urbanization is occurring *before* industrialization, thus creating high unemployment and gigantic urban shantytowns with immense social and political problems. In terms of stages, the West went sequentially from feudalism to capitalism to various forms of social welfare states, but in the developing nations feudalism, capitalism, and varying kinds of socialism or statism often exist simultaneously, side by side, in a confused, overlapping form.

A seventh criticism was that the developmentalist approach misrepresented the role of such "traditional" institutions as the family, the tribe, the caste, the clan, the patronage network, or the ethnic group. Most of the development literature suggested that these traditional institutions would either die of natural causes or be overthrown and destroyed as modernization went forward. But many of these institutions are sources of pride in the Third World and quite functional *within their own settings* (as noted in the fourth criterion). They often provide the "glue" that holds these countries together as they go through the wrenching process of transition. Moreover, in many developing countries, rather than being swept aside as development proceeds, such institutions as a "tribe" and "caste" often themselves undergo modernization, convert themselves into interest groups or political parties, and deliver about the only public policy programs (education, welfare, justice, protection) that local communities in poor countries have. The terms *traditional* and *modern* thus represent false or misplaced bipolarities; instead, what we have is a mix and fusion of the two, with many so-called traditional institutions adapting themselves and taking on new, transitional, even modernizing roles.

There were a variety of other criticisms leveled at the developmentalist approach. It underestimated the difficulties and length of time needed to achieve development (three to four *generations* rather than three to four years) and portrayed it in too peaceful, almost antiseptic terms—instead of the realities of disease, malnutrition, and violence. There were also difficulties in lumping Africa, Asia, Latin America, and the Middle East all together in the "underdeveloped" category—rather like the difficulties of adding up apples, oranges, and grapefruit. Radical critics, in addition, argued developmentalism was just another way for the United States to dominate the Third World; less radical critics suggested that, even with the best of intentions, the United States and the international lending agencies, primarily the World Bank and the International Monetary Fund (IMF), did not emphasize democracy and human rights enough, or got its priorities wrong, or undermined older and often still viable institutions before the newer and presumably more modern ones had been created, thus producing chaos and instability and adding to the Third World's already long list of woes.

These criticisms of the literature, approach, and program of developmentalism were powerful and quite devastating. By the end of the 1960s the criticisms were so widespread and so many case studies had been written finding the developmentalist approach wanting that its entire theory and body of assumptions were questioned. A good part of this also had to do with the fact that a new generation had grown up with vast experience in the field whose research work in the developing areas led to the questioning and eventual rejection of the work of their elders.

ALTERNATIVES
TO DEVELOPMENTALISM

Concurrent with the attacks on and gradual fading of the developmentalist approach, a number of new approaches began to appear in the late 1960s that then reached maturity as alternative explanatory models in the 1970s. Three main alternatives emerged: cultural explanations, the dependency approach, and institutional explanations. To these we add, later in the chapter, a focus on authoritarianism and corporatism as alternatives to the earlier emphasis on democracy. These alternative approaches and models gradually shunted developmentalism to the sidelines and into the ashcans of discarded academic theories—although the concept continued to dominate most U.S. foreign aid programs.

The cultural approach, of course, favored development but argued that scholars and policymakers needed to pay far more attention to the distinct cultures and histories of the non-Western countries and areas involved. Development, they said, was not automatic and universal; rather, different societies and cultures responded differently to global stimuli. Each country or culture filtered development through its own culturally derived values, institutions, and ways of doing things, accepting *some* practices and institutions from the West but always doing things their own way. Or else they worked out fusions and blends of imported and local or indigenous ways and institutions.

For example, new development institutions (planning agencies, agrarian reform institutes, technical offices) might be created, but they would often be dominated by the clan, caste, tribe, or patronage loyalties and practices of the past. Elections might be held and "democracy" instigated, but the state, president, or armed forces usually kept large controlling or limiting powers in its own hands. Similarly, liberalism might be introduced in the economic sphere but the government usually maintained a strong role in the economy. In other words, the culturalist approach also accepted development but insisted foreign aid and other programs had to be sensitive to cultural differences and that there was no one single model that would fit all countries. This approach further stated it could explain the differences between Asian (successful) and African, Latin American, and Middle Eastern development (less so) by focusing on cultural factors—for example, Asian emphasis on education, discipline, hard work, loyalty, and order. The cultural approach, therefore, introduced a useful and constructive corrective to development theory by forcing it to pay greater attention to cultural differences (1) between the West and the non-West, and (2) between distinct developing areas.

A second and more radical alternative to developmentalism was dependency theory. At its most basic level, dependency theory suggested that the developing nations were *dependent* on, and *dependencies* of, the already developed nations. More than that, it argued that the earlier development of the West had come at the *cost* of the underdevelopment of the non-West, that the Western countries had achieved their development on the backs of and by exploiting the non-West. Dependency theory brought to our attention that countries do not develop in isolation as so much of the development literature suggested, but are caught up in international market forces over which they have no control, are victimized by multinational corporations and other international agencies, and are falling even farther behind—as part of a conscious strategy by their exploiters, according to the dependency argument—the wealthier countries. From the dependency perspective, therefore, *development* is a fraud and a sham, a means for the rich countries to continue to exploit the poorer ones and keep them underdeveloped. Assessing dependency theory, one can say that it was correct to emphasize the international and economic forces in development, but that its sometimes heavy-handed ideological Marxist approach detracted from its usefulness.

A third alternative to developmentalism was what came to be called institutionalism or "the new institutionalism." As the name suggests, this approach sought to focus mainly on political and governmental institutions, not on the cultural, anthropological, or sociological bases of politics. The institutional approach was used to study such issues as parliamentarism versus presidentialism, federalism versus unitarism, and then, as many developing countries in the late 1970s and 1980s moved away from authoritarianism, issues of the transition to democracy. The latter included the writing of new constitutions; the legalization and organization of political parties; stability "pacts" agreed to between labor, business, and government; and the creation of other new, democratic institutions. All these are important matters and, for societies in transition, it is, of course, essential to get your institutions correct; however, most scholars remained convinced that cultural, historical, religious, and sociological factors are similarly important in shaping the political arena and that these should be studied *along with* the institutional factors.

The emergence of these alternative approaches to thinking about development had several important implications. First, it further undermined the earlier (Rostow, Lipset, Almond) 1960s consensus on how development occurs. Second, it gave rise to a greater diversity of approaches and insights from different perspectives, which most scholars thought was healthy for the study of development. But third, while the academic study of development was exploring new directions and approaches, much of the foreign aid and official U.S. government policy toward the developing nations continued to be based on the same tired, largely discredited Rostow categories, stages, and ways of thinking of the past.

A RECONSIDERATION OF THE DEVELOPMENTALIST APPROACH

Developmentalism was the dominant paradigm or approach to thinking about Third World nations in the 1960s, the first decade in which the United States and other Western nations paid serious attention to the developing countries. But then the developmentalist approach was subjected to some withering criticisms and largely went out of fashion during the 1970s and 1980s.

In recent years, however, the developmentalist approach has been reconsidered. First, quite a number of countries—Brazil, Hong Kong, Mexico, Singapore, South Korea, and Taiwan—did, in fact, develop, often quite impressively. Second, after many Third World countries made impressive transitions to democracy in the 1980s and 1990s, the correlations and patterns that the earlier developmentalists had posited began to look better and better. With a flood of military-authoritarian regimes in power in the 1970s, the supposed correlations between economic development, social modernization, and democracy were not correlating well at all; however, with the restoration of democracy in later decades, these interrelations between economic, social, and political development looked far better. Could it be that the Rostow-Lipset-Almond approach, while wrong in the short run and containing many errors, might turn out yet to be right in the longer run? And if so, could a reformulated, nonethnocentric, corrected developmentalist approach be resurrected and still provide us with valuable insights concerning the development process?

We return to that theme and question later in the book, but first we need to discuss that wave of military-authoritarian regimes that washed ashore in the 1960s and 1970s, and the relationship between authoritarianism and development.

ON THE GROUND: BUREAUCRATIC AUTHORITARIANISM

The second major change affecting development theory (in addition to its intellectual bankruptcy) in the mid-to-late 1960s and through much of the 1970s occurred on the ground, in the developing nations themselves: the rise of bureaucratic-authoritarianism. By this time, not only had developmentalism been subjected to a withering academic critique but *within* the developing countries the assumptions of development—the close correlation between economic growth, social change, and democratization—were not working out very well either.

The early 1960s, with John F. Kennedy as President, the founding of the Peace Corps and the Alliance for Progress, the fall of a number of bloody dictators in Latin America (Fulgencio Batista in Cuba—actually overthrown in 1958, Rafael Trujillo in the Dominican Republic), and the end of colonialism in much of Africa, Asia, and the Middle East, had been a heady, optimistic time for development and democracy. But then in 1962 a military coup overthrew democracy in Argentina; the following year there were military coups ousting democracy in the Dominican Republic and Honduras, and in 1964 big, important Brazil succumbed to military authoritarianism. Over the course of the next few years other countries succumbed, including such well-established democracies as Chile and Uruguay, until by the mid-1970s twelve of the twenty Latin American countries—Argentina, Bolivia, Brazil, Chile, Ecuador, El Salvador, Guatemala, Honduras, Panama, Paraguay, Peru, and Uruguay—were under military-authoritarian rule. In five others—the Dominican Republic, Mexico, Haiti, Cuba, and Nicaragua—civilians remained in office but the military was so close to the surface of power as to make the usual distinction between civilian and military regimes all but meaningless, and authoritarianism was clearly in sway. That left only three countries as democracies (Colombia, Costa Rica, and Venezuela), and even these three were generally referred to as elite-directed democracies, not genuine or participatory ones. Latin America had been the main test case of both the Alliance for Progress and the economic-growth-brings-democracy thesis, and with at least seventeen of the twenty countries now ruled by authoritarianism, that thesis looked pretty threadbare.

Much the same had occurred in Sub-Saharan Africa. There, too, the early 1960s was a period of optimism. In 1959, 1960, and 1961, throwing off colonialism, a *host* of new African nations had emerged with great hope onto the world stage. Almost all of them wrote new constitutions, organized political parties (often single-party systems), installed civilian leaders, and began their independence as hopeful democratic nations. But the new constitutions, political parties, and democracies proved to be superficial and ephemeral. Few of their institutions, largely imported from outside, sank deep roots in the African soil, culture, or consciousness.

For example, as a young graduate student during this period, I remember reading the hopeful, often wishful new-development literature on African single-party regimes by David Apter, Ruth Schachter Morgenthau, and others[2] which sought to make the case that they could be instruments of integration, unity, and of a particularly African form of "democracy." But I also had a professor, Henry Brennan, who was skeptical and openly derisive of these new parties, calling them facades, or "paper parties," that lacked substance, organization, and institutionalization. Sadly, when the military challenge to the new African democracies came in the mid-to-late 1960s, Brennan proved to be correct and the others wrong. The parties, constitutions, and formal institutions of democracy quickly collapsed and disintegrated, while the first generation of democratic leaders faced the unhappy choice of fleeing into exile, imprisonment, or death.

From the mid-1960s through the 1980s, the dominant form of political system in Sub-Saharan Africa was authoritarianism. During this quarter-century, authoritarian regimes were in power, sometimes off-and-on, in fully three-quarters of Africa's countries. Authoritarianism could take different forms: monarchy, Marxist regimes, military regimes, and single-party-dominant regimes, with the latter being most prevalent. Authoritarianism was often brutal, corrupt, and dominated by considerations of enrichment and special privilege for those in power. Authoritarianism was often employed in the service of the clan, tribal, and ethnic identity of those in power. Moreover, it took place in a context of generally poor preparation by the departing colonial powers of their former colonies for independence and democracy, of weak indigenous institutions within the new African nations, and of wholesale dependence of these nations on the outside world and international lending agencies for capital and investment.

The situation in Asia was more diverse and more complex, and fails to correspond closely or generally to the patterns observed in Latin America and Africa. The world's most populous nation, China, had had, under Mao Tse-tung, a communist revolution in the 1940s and in subsequent decades continued to champion its Marxist-Leninist model for the rest of the Third World. India, the world's second most populous nation, emerged from British colonialism in 1947 and was a functioning though often tumultuous democracy which also practiced socialism in the economic sphere. Japan emerged from defeat in World War II, was militarily occupied by the United States from 1945 to 1952 and obliged to adopt many U.S.-designed constitutional and political institutions, and then in subsequent decades developed as one of the world's most dynamic and powerful economies. Meanwhile, Southeast Asia (Vietnam, Laos, and Cambodia, and to a considerable extent Thailand and Burma, too) was torn by revolution, civil conflict, war, and U.S. intervention that disrupted, set back, and greatly skewed their processes of development.

None of these countries, including obviously big and important countries, conforms to the model of bureaucratic-authoritarianism set forth earlier.

The best examples of B-A regimes in Asia were the Philippines under Ferdinand Marcos (1965–1986), Indonesia under Radan Suharto (1966–1998), and Pakistan under Ayub Khan (1958–1969) and then later under Muhammed Zia-ul-Huq (1977–1989) and once again under Pervez Musharraf. In addition, it is possible to put Taiwan under the Kuomintang Party, Singapore under authoritarian leader Lee Kwan Yew, and South Korea under a succession of authoritarian civilian *and* military regimes from the 1950s through the 1980s in the bureaucratic-authoritarian category.

It is important to emphasize several general characteristics about these regimes. First, they emerged or were strongest in the 1960s and 1970s. Second, they were all authoritarian, albeit in varying degrees, as distinct from the earlier, often failed democracies. Third, they tended to be long-lived, enough to accomplish real development, rather than just short term change. Fourth, there were considerable differences among them in terms of longevity, level of development, harshness of rule, and so on. And fifth, their ranks included not just military regimes but also civilian or civil-military (combined) regimes, such as in Mexico, Singapore, or Taiwan. But whether civilian, military, or a combination of the two, they were all authoritarian, and that is the trait we wish to emphasize here.

A considerable controversy exists as to the causes of this shift from democratic development in the early 1960s to more authoritarian forms in the later 1960s and 1970s. In a famous formulation, the Argentine political sociologist Guillermo O'Donnell, thinking in Marxian terms, attributes the cause to what he calls the "crisis of import substitution industrialization."[3] Import Substitution Industrialization, or ISI, was the model of economic growth followed in many Latin American countries from the depression years of the 1930s through the 1960s. Under ISI, Latin America (and presumably the other developing areas as well) sought to change from being merely suppliers of primary products (coffee, bananas, sugar, copper, tin, etc.) to being producers of manufactured goods which they had previously imported. In other words (and, hence, the origin of the ISI term), they attempted to *industrialize* by *substituting* their own manufactured goods for the increasingly expensive *imported* ones. By the 1960s, according to O'Donnell, this ISI model had "run its course," and that explains the collapse of Latin American democracy.

The O'Donnell formulation has been roundly attacked as a not very accurate effort to impose an economic determinist explanation on a process that is actually political in origin. Here, in this alternative explanation, is what really happened. In the late 1950s and early 1960s a considerable number of elected, democratic governments had come to power in Latin America. But these democratic regimes, under the influence of developmentalist thinking, often mobilized peasant, worker, and lower-class support, in countries that had not experienced mass mobilization before, and these activities severely frightened and even threatened the traditional wielders of power in Latin America: the armed forces, the business and landed elites, and the Roman Catholic Church. These conservative groups then coalesced to overthrow democracy and bring the military into power, often for long stays. This *political* crisis and confrontation may have been in several countries *exacerbated* by an economic downturn, but it was not *caused* by economic breakdown.

If O'Donnell's explanation failed adequately to explain the rise and triumph of bureaucratic-authoritarianism in Latin America, it was even less useful in Africa and Asia. In Africa, the explanations for military takeovers were not a crisis of ISI but sheer disorder, chaos, civil war, or perhaps the desire for corruption or power that obliged or encouraged the armed forces to take over from often-incompetent civilians. In Asia the situation was quite different but even less supportive of the O'Donnell thesis. There, countries like South Korea, Taiwan, and Singapore continued very successfully to follow a model of export-led growth, even while perpetuating authoritarian rule. In addition, in all these areas, the arrival of the Cold War in the 1950s and 1960s, which as in the case of Korea often became quite hot, meant that the United States, while earlier supporting democracy, was not averse to military-authoritarian regimes that kept order (often with a vengeance), suppressed communist and left-wing groups, and thus protected U.S. strategic interests.

THE AUTHORITARIAN ROUTE TO DEVELOPMENT

With authoritarian regimes replacing democratic ones in so many areas of the world, the question now becomes: are authoritarian regimes better at achieving development than democracies?

The question is particularly difficult for Americans to deal with. The United States has been such a stable, successful, and democratic country for so long that we find it hard to conceive that there could be any other way to achieve modernization except through democracy. But in the developing world, the answer is not so clear.

Even though this may not be our own political preference, there *is* a compelling case to be made for authoritarianism. Authoritarian regimes tend to provide order, discipline, and stability, precisely what most Third World nations need to achieve development. Since most developing nations are (by definition— that is often why they are developing and not developed) weakly institutionalized, lacking well-organized, pluralist, interest associations, functioning political parties, and effective government agencies, they often require a strong hand at the helm if they are to develop. Authoritarian regimes, particularly during the Cold War, also made the argument that they kept the communists and leftists under control, prevented disruption by labor unions, and were successful at attracting foreign investment. Authoritarians further argue that elections, political campaigns, and democratic give-and-take are disruptive, divisive, and destabilizing, which most Third World nations—often operating without a wide margin for error—cannot afford. Authoritarian regimes, it is said, get results faster and better than democracies. Authoritarians, in addition, tend to be good at building things: highways, bridges, dams, port facilities, and factories—precisely the kind of large infrastructure projects that most Third World countries require if they hope to develop.

The literature is replete with arguments and justifications from authoritarian leaders, most of them self-serving but also with a considerable degree of accuracy. It was said famously of Italian dictator Benito Mussolini that "he made the trains run on time." Similarly, dictator Rafael Trujillo of the Dominican Republic used to say, "You can't speak of democracy in a country that has no roads, no highways, no bridges, no public buildings, no order, no discipline, no literacy." In that same country a prominent presidential candidate, waving a menacing cattle prod in the air, declared, "I need authority for my cattle, and I will need authority for my people"—while the gathered peasants cheered. Similarly, dictator Alfredo Stroessner of Paraguay used to argue, "My country is 75 percent illiterate. It has no roads and no institutions. The people require a strong guiding hand. Democracy is good for the United States but it doesn't work in Paraguay."

There was also a strong national security argument in support of authoritarianism. Especially during the Cold War it was argued that authoritarian regimes preserve stability, keep communism and subversion under control, and guarantee American interests. When faced with a choice in the Third World between an idealistic, well-meaning, but usually wobbly democracy, and the prospect of stable authoritarianism, the United States almost always opted for the authoritarian. The logic of this argument stood for several decades, but then came the overthrow of Cuba's dictator Fulgencio Batista, the triumph of communist Fidel Castro, and Cuba's subsequent alliance with the Soviet Union. From this experience the United States learned that, rather than protecting against communism, right-wing regimes might instead make the conditions ripe for communism to grow. This realization forced a revaluation of U.S. policy, leading to a greater emphasis on supporting democratic development as the best guarantee of *long-term* stability, but still holding in reserve the option of supporting authoritarianism if anti-communist Cold War considerations so demanded.

Of course, there are large negatives that go with authoritarian development as well. Authoritarian regimes, by definition, suppress democracy and tend to be repressive of human rights—although there are degrees and gradations of that. Authoritarian regimes, lacking checks and balances or political pluralism, often make mistakes or become corrupt and brutal; and then there is no institutionalized way of making corrections. Authoritarian regimes are usually not very good about dealing with change, or adapting to new social and political realities; and, therefore, while they may provide needed stability over a one-, two-, or, in the case of the most long-lived, three-decade period, in the long run most authoritarian regimes break down eventually into instability as they prove unable to solve the problem of succession from one dictator to the next. Still, if you're an emerging country and you can get two or three decades of stability, you can accomplish a lot of development in that time period.

There is no one single pattern for the authoritarian model; instead, there are many variations. Such notorious Latin American dictators as Rafael Trujillo, Anastasio Somoza, Fulgencio Batista, and Alfredo Stroessner were all bloody, corrupt tyrants, but they also accomplished major development during their long periods of rule, before leaving their countries in chaos at the end. It is said that Somoza, while corrupt, at least shared the corruption "democratically"; his son, who inherited power, was greedy and failed to continue his father's policy of "democratizing" the corruption, which helps explain his violent overthrow. The Brazilian generals came to power in 1964 delivering honesty, probity, and efficiency, and the economy expanded magnificently, producing miracle growth rates (8, 9, and 10 percent) for several years; however, over time the military proved as inefficient and eventually as corrupt as the civilians they replaced and was forced to relinquish office. The military regime of Augusto Pinochet in Chile similarly accomplished miracle economic growth, but it had an atrocious human rights record that went beyond the pale. The regimes of Ferdinand Marcos in the Philippines and Suharto in Indonesia were similar to those of Somoza or Stroessner: anti-communist, stable at least for a time, corrupt, but also achieving significant development.

These examples from Latin America and Southeast Asia illustrate the dilemma of the trade-off between economic development, on the one hand, and democracy and human rights, on the other, or between short-term stability and growth and long-term instability and slow-down. In contrast, many of the authoritarian dictatorships in Sub-Saharan Africa—such as Sese Seko Mobutu in the Congo, Jean-Bedel Bokassa in the Central African Republic—seemed to be motivated almost exclusively by kelptocracy—stealing from the national treasury or using political power for self-enrichment—rather than a desire to develop the country economically. In the Middle East there have been numerous military-authoritarian regimes in recent decades—Gamel Abdul Nasser in Egypt, Saddam Hussein in Iraq, Hafez al-Assad in Syria, Hosni Mubarak again in Egypt—who seem to be motivated mainly by nationalism, Arab socialism and statism, an often vaguely Islamic ideology, and pan-Arabism; but which have proved, by comparative standards, remarkably *unsuccessful* in achieving economic development. The lack of success in so many Islamic states in achieving either democracy or development helps explain their often simmering resentment, tinged with envy, toward the United States and Western Europe.

Several of these authoritarian regimes operated as *institutionalized* systems and not as just single-person or military dictatorships. They, thus, avoided five of the most egregious faults of the authoritarian model: (1) they were civilian or civil/military regimes and not just narrowly dominated by the armed forces; (2) their human rights records were usually better than those of the military dictatorships and they did not become internationally despised pariahs (like

Chile's Pinochet); (3) because these systems were institutionalized rather than resting on the shoulders of a single person, they were able to solve the succession problem better than the one-man dictatorships; (4) they were also able to adjust to social and political change better than did the more rigid dictatorships; and (5) because they were more open and inclusionary than the closed, exclusionary military regimes, they tended to be nascently democratic or at least had the capacity to move in that direction. Obviously these features make these regimes much more attractive than pure military authoritarianism or one-man dictatorships. And they may provide a model, between democracy and authoritarianism, that would be particularly attractive in the Third World where democratic institutions are still weak.

Mexico provides one of the best cases. There, a single-party regime, under the hegemony of the Revolutionary Institutional Party (PRI, to use its Spanish-language initials), dominated national politics and provided stability and continuity for seventy years—1930–2000. Stemming from the great social upheaval, or revolution in Mexico from 1910–1920, which largely destroyed the traditional wielders of power (the Church, the Army, and the landed oligarchy), the PRI was organized on a sectoral basis that included the rising new groups in society: organized labor, organized peasants, and a catch-all "popular" category that incorporated government bureaucrats and much of the emerging middle class. Under the umbrella of this monopolistic, dominant, and dominating political party, Mexico maintained stability for all these seventy years while also adapting, slowly but still much better than other authoritarian regimes, to change. At the same time, human rights violations were not overly atrocious and, by incorporating the main groups in society into the official party, Mexico managed to call its regime "democratic."

Not only was Mexico politically stable under one-party government but, because of this stability, it attracted major foreign investment and its economy, over a thirty- or forty-year period, grew steadily by 4, 5, or 6 percent or more per year. That is significantly better than almost any other developing country, particularly over the long term, enabling Mexico to double, and then double again, its per-capita income within a relatively short period. With this steady, impressive growth, Mexico was one of the great success stories in the Third World.

Many countries in Latin America and Africa have sought to emulate the Mexican example of a single-party, integrating, developmentalist regime, but few have succeeded, mainly because their social, economic, and political situations were different from those of Mexico. Nor should one idealize the Mexican case: it remained an authoritarian regime; it offered voters little or no choice; it was very corrupt; and its human rights record often left much to be desired. Nevertheless, its accomplishments—stability and long-term growth—were major. Moreover, once Mexico did begin to democratize, the inclusionary nature of the PRI made that process easier and more successful than other post-authoritarian transitions. A long process of liberalization in both the economic and political spheres culminated in 2000 with the democratic election of opposition candidate Vicente Fox.

A second example is Taiwan. It was on that small island off the coast of China that in 1949 the remnants of the "nationalist" or conservative forces, defeated in the civil war by the communists of Mao Tse-tung, took refuge. Their organization, which evolved into a single-party regime not unlike the Mexican PRI, was called the Kuomintang (KMT), the heir on the island of the organization founded in 1912 on the mainland as a nationalistic, reformist, unifying party to overthrow the Manchu dynasty. In 1925 the KMT had been taken over by General Chiang Kai-shek, who dominated Chinese politics for the next quarter century until forced to flee to Taiwan. There, General Chiang Kai-shek established an authoritarian regime, ruling under a system of martial law. Most Taiwanese eschewed politics and concentrated on making money and developing their small island, at which tasks they proved to be enormously successful: in the period from 1950 to today Taiwan emerged as an economic powerhouse, one of the most dynamic nations in the world, and another one of the Third World's great success stories.

Chiang Kai-shek died in 1975 and was succeeded by his son, Chiang Ching-kuo, who considerably relaxed his father's martial law regime and abolished it altogether in 1987. Thereafter, Taiwan moved gradually toward democracy and a freeing up of the society until in 1989 the opposition won power in a democratic election. The human rights situation also improved greatly; meantime, Taiwan continued its aggressive economic growth, although it was slowed somewhat by the general Asian downturn of the 1990s.

The model followed by Mexico and Taiwan is interesting for a number of reasons. First, one should have no illusions: these were frankly authoritarian regimes. But, second, instead of being one-man or narrowly based military dictatorships, these were regimes dominated by a single party which maintained remarkable stability over a long period (seventy years in Mexico, forty in Taiwan). Third, because of the stability, investors felt confident; investment funds poured in; and these two countries achieved steady, long-term, even miracle economic growth. And fourth, both these regimes, perhaps because they were more civilian than military, had the good sense eventually to evolve gradually and peacefully away from authoritarianism and toward democracy, thus not only avoiding the violent overthrow to which many authoritarian regimes succumbed but also maintaining all-important economic growth even during the transition period. We will have more to say on this model in the following chapter.

Other Third World regimes tried to emulate the Mexico/Taiwan model but none of them so successfully. South Vietnam in the 1960s, Greece under the colonels, Iran under the Shah, Nicaragua under the Somozas, the Dominican Republic under Trujillo, the Philippines under Marcos, Indonesia under Suharto, Paraguay under Stroessner, Chile under Pinochet, Zaire under Mobutu, Pakistan under Generals Ayub Khan and then Zia, and Brazil under the generals—all *tried* to maintain long-term authoritarianism while stimulating major economic growth, but none succeeded. The major problems appear to be (1) these regimes were either one-man tyrannies or narrowly based military dictatorships; (2) they failed to develop a genuine *party* that incorporated civilian leadership and thus broadened the regime; (3) they failed to adjust adequately to social and political change; and (4) because they were one-man regimes and/or politically insensitive, they failed to adequately arrange for their own succession.

In the case of South Africa, the (white) National Party was able to monopolize political life for several decades and achieve significant economic growth, but its rule was part of the overall apartheid regime that excluded 90 percent of the population from participation and thus was doomed to failure. Turkey also had a one-party authoritarian regime during 1923–1946, which helped stimulate development and Westernization, but since then it has been mainly a democracy, although with three military re-incursions into politics in the decades since then.

AUTHORITARIANISM
AND CORPORATISM

Almost all of the authoritarian regimes described here used one or another form of *corporatism* as an instrument of their rule. They ruled not just by blood, tyranny, and dictatorship alone but also employed a more *institutionalized* system of domination that usually took corporatist forms. Corporatism here means controls, limits, and regulation of social and interest-group life that often took one of two directions (or both simultaneously): cooptation into the regime of new and rising interest groups like organized labor and peasants, or else repression of them. The literature further distinguishes between state (authoritarian) and societal (more participatory and democratic) corporatism, and between closed (rigid, repressive, dictatorial) and open (inclusive) corporatism.[4]

Corporatism has a long history in Western political thought, going back to ancient Greece and Rome and to medieval Christianity. It also has a foundation in the "communalist" societies of many Third World nations. Corporatism suggests an organic and integral view of the state and society in which all of the parts are interconnected. Whereas liberalism suggests the separation of the state or government from society (interest groups), and totalitarianism means the *total* control and destruction of all interest groups by the state, corporatism *absorbs* the interest groups *into* the state. It does not destroy them as in totalitarianism, but they are not independent either as in liberalism. Under corporatism, such groups as organized business, labor, farmers, professionals, religious bodies, and so on, become a part of the state, as official government agencies. Thus, in a corporatist system there is usually just one official labor organization, one official farmer group, and so on. Usually in return for some benefits from the state (hence, cooptation), such as higher wages or better working conditions, these groups give up their autonomy and independence and become a part of the official state or government system.

While corporatism had a long history in Catholic political theory, which helps explain why it has been particularly strong in the predominantly Roman Catholic countries of Eastern and Southern Europe, Latin America, and the

Philippines, there are also secular versions. Dictator Benito Mussolini proclaimed Italy to be a corporatist state; particularly in the interval between World Wars I and II, corporatist regimes in one form or another sprang up all over Europe and in the major countries (Argentina, Brazil, Chile, and Mexico) of Latin America. In that period, both Soviet communism and German fascism were unacceptable to most people, while liberalism and capitalism seemed to be collapsing in the Great Depression; hence, corporatism's popularity as seemingly the only viable acceptable alternative, as a "third way."

It is easy to understand why corporatism would be so attractive to so many authoritarian regimes. It enables the regime to regulate, limit, control, and absorb the interest group life that goes on around it rather than giving it independence that might lead to democracy. Corporatism does not permit free associability or, as in the United States, the almost anarchic competition (so much so that it often paralyzes government activity and leads to gridlock) of thousands of interest groups. Rather, it *structures* interest group activity, coopts some interest groups that it can control while repressing others, and absorbs these interest groups into the state *not* as free actors but as integral parts of the authoritarian state itself.

As economic development proceeds and accompanying social change also occurs, a shrewd authoritarian regime can thus create, legitimize, and absorb into itself new corporatist groups—usually one each for the new social sectors that modernization spurs, such as official labor organizations, official peasants' groups, official women's associations, and so on. In this way, an authoritarian regime can continuously adapt to change, even while maintaining its control and absorbing these new and otherwise potentially threatening social groups into the official state system, which thus removes their threat of opting for revolution or overthrow.

Authoritarian regimes tend to be fearful of all the new social movements, demands for greater participation, and unfettered pluralism to which the very process of modernization gives rise. They do not like all those unregulated, competitive interest groups "out there," outside of the state's or regime's control. They fear democracy, pluralism, and uncontrolled interest-group activity as constituting a threat to their power. And, from their point of view, repression also has its limits, as too much abuse may turn the entire population against you. Hence, corporatism's popularity: it enables an authoritarian regime to adapt to change by absorbing the new social forces which modernization stimulates into its state-controlled ranks, even while enabling the authoritarian regime to stay in power indefinitely.

While corporatism as a theory was born in the Western tradition and had its heyday in Europe in the interwar period, in the 1960s and 1970s, during the period of widespread bureaucratic-authoritarianism, it spread widely throughout the Third World. Almost all the military regimes of Latin America (and some civilian ones as well), the Shah's Iran, Nasser's and then Mubarak's Egypt, Suharto's Indonesia, Taiwan of the Kuomintang, the South Korean military regime, Marcos's Philippines, and quite a number of the Sub-Saharan African military dictatorships *all* employed one or another form of corporatism to keep rising social groups in check and under state control. Corporatism seemed to be ubiquitous and omnipresent throughout the Third World, especially as earlier, hopeful democracies gave way to authoritarian regimes.

The connection between authoritarianism and corporatism was so close that many scholars began to see them as (1) inevitably linked, and (2) perhaps permanent. As to their linkage, corporatism was seen as one of the main props of authoritarian regimes, critical for controlling the emergence of new socioeconomic groups, especially during the early stages of modernization. That meant that, when quite a number of these authoritarian regimes transitioned to democracy in the 1970s and 1980s, presumably corporatism would disappear as well. But, in fact, that did not happen, as we see in Chapter 5; instead, corporatism proved to have amazing resilience and persistence, continuing on in many developing nations, albeit in modified form, into the period of democracy as well.

As for authoritarianism's and corporatism's permanence, we know now in hindsight that, in fact, authoritarianism did not live on indefinitely in most countries. Instead, almost all the authoritarian regimes previously mentioned eventually underwent a transition to democracy. But from the perspective of the early 1970s, when most of the literature on authoritarianism and corporatism was written, it *appeared* as if there might be permanent features of most Third World and developing regimes. After all, Francisco Franco in Spain, Antonio Salazar in Portugal, the Shah in Iran, Marcos in the Philippines, the Kuomintang in Taiwan, Suharto in Indonesia, the South Korean generals, the PRI in Mexico, and many military-authoritarian regimes in Latin America had all been in power going on twenty or thirty years or more, and they were still going strong. Moreover, it had begun to appear that these many authoritarian regimes had figured out a proven method both to achieve economic growth through the imposition of order and stability and to handle and control, through corporatist cooptation, the sociopolitical effects of modernization. We know now that was a mistaken interpretation, but in the 1970s it appeared that authoritarianism and corporatism might be permanent features of most Third World developing countries.

FRIENDLY TYRANTS: AN AMERICAN DILEMMA[5]

These authoritarian-bureaucratic or authoritarian-corporatist regimes of the 1960s, 1970s, and often continuing on into the 1980s presented American foreign policymakers with a terrible dilemma. On the one hand, most of these authoritarian regimes were staunchly anti-communist, friendly to the United States (hence, the term *friendly tyrants*), and supported what were then seen as all-important U.S. strategic interests in the Cold War. On the other hand, they were not democratic, were often gross abusers of human rights and the values most Americans hold dear, and often (like dictator Batista in Cuba), by their very actions, prepared the way for future problems, upheaval, or even revolution.

What to do? After all, most American foreign affairs officials were not sympathetic to these regimes' authoritarianism, absence of democracy, or human rights abuses. The authoritarian regimes violated American values and their sense of fair play, human and civil rights, and democracy. At the same time, they *did* protect our interests, were sympathetic allies, and could often make decisions faster and more efficiently than more deliberative democracies.

The debate over what to do about these friendly tyrants had a long history in American foreign policy. It reflected and was the latest incarnation of the old idealism versus realism arguments. Idealists would have the United States keep a firm distance from all these authoritarian regimes so as to keep our hands pure and clean from these nefarious characters, and often suggested that, in the name of our democratic and human rights values, we should try to overthrow them—even if they are "friendly." Realists, in contrast, argued that the United States has to deal with the realities of these regimes and not just wish them away, that the *internal affairs* of these countries are not our concern, and that, in any case, fundamental U.S. security interests should have precedence over idealistic human rights campaigns.

The issue has waxed and waned in U.S. foreign policy. Of the presidents in power during this period, Richard Nixon and Gerald Ford were in the realist camp, while Jimmy Carter was in the idealist one. The realist position, seemingly in conflict with America's democratic values, was often controversial in domestic politics, while Jimmy Carter's often quixotic quest for human rights produced few tangible results at first, often undermined American allies abroad (the Shah, Somoza), antagonized the countries the United States criticized, and in the Iranian and Nicaraguan cases led to regimes that, in terms of American interests, were worse than the authoritarians who had gone before.

We learned several things from this policy debate. Among other things, we learned that it is far harder for the United States to engineer a transition from authoritarianism to democracy than had earlier been thought. We learned something of the limits of U.S. policy to positively influence the process. We learned that U.S. foreign aid is a weak lever in influencing these events. We learned that in most cases, in the early days of the debate, the national security interests or realist position often take priority; but as the debate goes on, and especially as the issue gets television coverage, the human rights issues (murdered nuns in El Salvador, blacks being beaten in South Africa) or the idealist position gain ascendancy. That is because bodies bloodied by the police or dictatorship shown night after night in our family rooms makes "better," more dramatic TV (and thus supports the idealist position that *we* must do something to change these horrible conditions) than any picture images of oil tankers or strategic interests which, since they are not very dramatic, are only good for one night's television.

In the end, the issue largely resolved itself and, over the course of the 1980s and 1990s, faded away. That is because most of the authoritarian regimes described previously, which once looked so strong, impregnable, and permanent, declined or disappeared, eventually giving way to a new wave of democracy, as described in Chapter 5. Sometimes U.S. pressure and blandishments were instrumental in forcing these authoritarian regimes from power, but mainly they fell as a result of internal changes *within* their own countries. Many of these military and authoritarian regimes got old, ran out of gas, proved ineffective or excessively corrupt, became increasingly narrowly based, often antagonized their own supporters, were unable to adjust to changed circumstances, lost popular backing, and eventually retreated back to the barracks. Few of them were actually overthrown or driven from power; rather, in most cases they retired from power of their own volition.

The debate between idealists and realists over the "friendly tyrants" issue thus ended most often with a whisper rather than a bang. But that also meant that the era of bureaucratic-authoritarianism was also coming to an end. Both had run their course and become discredited. We will want to trace these processes in detail, particularly as they led to the nearly global triumph of democracy. But first we need to interrupt this narrative to analyze one of the truly phenomenal changes during this period: the rise of a number of exceedingly successful Third World nations to the rank of Newly Industrialized Countries or NICs.

NOTES

1. Samuel P. Huntington, *Political Order in Changing Societies* (New Haven, CT: Yale University Press, 1968).

2. David Apter, *Ghana in Transition* (New York: Athenium, 1963); Ruth Schachter Morgenthau, "Single Party Systems in West Africa," *American Political Science Review* (June 1961).

3. Guillermo O'Donnell, *Modernization and Bureaucratic-Authoritarianism* (Berkeley, CA: Institute of International Studies, University of California, 1973). For a critique, see David Collier (ed.), *The New Authoritarianism in Latin America* (Princeton, NJ: Princeton University Press, 1979).

4. Howard J. Wiarda, *Corporatism and Comparative Politics: The Other "Great Ism"* (New York: M. E. Sharpe, 1997).

5. After the title of a book of the same name edited by Daniel Pipes and Adam Garfinkle (New York: St. Martin's Press, 1991) to which the author contributed to the Mexico and a theoretical chapter.

4

Developmental Success Stories: The Rise of the NICs

L et us state the obvious: the trait that is most characteristic of developing nations is that they are poor. Poverty, malnutrition, disease, the bloated bellies of the children, illiteracy, low life expectancy, low standards of living, helplessness—all these and other traits seem to go together to form a composite picture of underdevelopment. A variety of measures is used: some define underdevelopment as having a per-capita income of under $500 per year, while others use the World Bank's now-popular measure of poverty of $1 per day per person, or $365 per year. Whatever index is used, we all know poverty when we see it and would like to do something to alleviate it. But *how* to do so, what is the best formula, how to raise oneself and one's country out of poverty—those are the questions.

There are actually only a very few Third World countries in the world that have succeeded in raising themselves out of poverty. Quite a number of others have made progress but not spectacularly so; we need to face the hard reality that development is a long, difficult, slogging process, and there is no magic formula that will quickly blaze the way to progress. Most developing countries, sad to say, show little progress in lifting themselves up from poverty; viewed from a global perspective, the gap between the wealthier and the poorer nations continues to widen rather than narrow. Nevertheless, there is a lot that a developing country can do to improve its prospects and raise itself up. In this chapter, we analyze the success stories, what the Newly Industrialized Countries, or NICs, have done to improve their chances, what formula they followed, and what *package* (since development has to be a multipronged effort) of policies and circumstances furthered their development. And, obviously, we will want to know if their successes are replicable in other countries.

Most of the NICs or success stories are located in Asia, although there are some from other areas as well. Japan was the first non-Western nation to achieve the status of being a developed, industrialized nation; today Japan, even with its current economic problems, is so dynamic and prosperous that it is hard to believe it was once a poor, underdeveloped country. Japan's development goes back over a hundred years, however; it was already industrialized before World War II; it was devastated by the war and then *re*-covered (like similarly defeated Germany) in the postwar period to achieve its status as the world's second most powerful economy (after the United States) with one of the world's highest standards of living. Following the Japanese model of growth in the postwar period were South Korea, Taiwan, Hong Kong, and Singapore. These are the nations that are usually thought of as the world's most successful developers.

Brazil, Mexico, and Chile have been among the most successful developers in the Latin American area, and several of the Arab states—Saudi Arabia, Kuwait, Qatar, Bahrain, United Arab Emirates, and Brunei—are fairly advanced on the list of countries with high per-capita income. But these last countries almost literally float on oil, which is the main factor accounting for their developmental success; however, social and political modernization in these countries is still retarded. Of course, it helps if a developing country has vast resources ready for extraction, but at the same time, if we are looking to fashion a model or road map to development, it seems a bit unfair and not very useful to attribute development to sheer "dumb luck," the mere "accident" as a country of having been born atop such rich natural resources that, no matter the country's social, economic, or political system, it is bound to make it anyway *purely* on the basis of vast mineral or oil wealth. It is worth noting that the countries mentioned in Latin America—Brazil, Chile, Mexico—as the most successful developers are also rich in natural resources, but that is not the *only* reason for their success. We must, therefore, explore the other factors involved.

THE TIGER AND THE FOUR LITTLE TIGERS: SEARCHING FOR THE REASONS FOR ASIA'S SUCCESS STORIES

The world's most impressive developmental success stories may be found in Asia: Japan, South Korea, Taiwan, Hong Kong, and Singapore. Probably it is no accident that the *most successful* of the developing nations are all found in Asia, and we will want to explore later on the reasons for that. Japan was devastated in World War II, but only two or three decades later it developed into a global powerhouse, second only to the United States in economic production (with a population only one-third that of the United States) and with a per-capita income that made it, even in the absence of many natural resources, one of the richest nations in the world, on a par with or ahead of the United States or the wealthiest European countries.

In some ways the accomplishments of South Korea and Taiwan are even more impressive because they started much later and at a lower base than Japan. South Korea and Taiwan were both poor, underdeveloped countries in the 1950s, but by the 1990s they had not only developed impressively but—and this is rare among nations—had *leapfrogged* over many other nations to achieve a rank of high income or upper-middle income in the World Bank's ratings—and even with aspirations to surpass Japan! Singapore is another Asian wonder, a small city-state with no natural resources, on the tip of the Malay Peninsula; and yet over thirty years Singapore became a commercial, manufacturing, and shipping center with a standard of living that rivals Japan and the other wealthiest countries. Hong Kong is similar, a small state on the edge of China (and now absorbed into China and no longer independent) that made it on the basis of shipping, banking, commerce, and trade.

While these are the great Asian success stories, in the last two decades such countries as Malaysia, Thailand, India, Indonesia, the Philippines, and now giant China have also begun to achieve impressive growth rates. But these are all still at the level of most of the Latin American countries and with many of the same problems of social dislocation and unstable (actual or potential) political institutions, so we cannot—yet—put them in the same category as the other Asian tigers. However, in the next decade or two these countries may also make a great leap forward out of the ranks of underdevelopment and into the modern world.

What then accounts for the tremendous success of Japan and the other Asian tigers? Obviously, if we can answer that question, we may have a formula that will also help other countries achieve the same miracle development. The problem is: there are several competing explanations for the Asian tigers' success, and scholars are in disagreement over which is the most important. At the same time, by sorting through and analyzing these various explanations, we can probably come very close to a consensus definition of the factors accounting for successful development over failure. Herewith is a list of possible explanations:

1. *A long history of development.*   Some countries have a long history of development and they are able to build upon past accomplishments. Great Britain, France, the United States, and Germany were among the early developers, beginning their drive to growth in the eighteenth and early nineteenth centuries. Similarly, among the Asian countries, Japan was the first to break out of isolation, undertake societal modernization, and begin economic and industrial development as early as the 1860s and 1870s. It, therefore, had a mammoth head start on its neighbors, most of whom did not begin development

until almost a century later. Japan's development, like Germany's, was interrupted and set back by World War II but not destroyed by it; and in the postwar period their development was enormously aided by the fact they had to *re*-build their economic and industrial base, not start from scratch which is much harder.

2. *Defeat in war and military occupation.*   Both Germany and Japan were defeated in World War II and subsequently occupied by U.S. and allied forces. Military defeat and occupation, it is argued, discredited and destroyed an older, failed, quasi-feudal system and enabled the United States and its allies to press for social reform, new constitutions, a new and democratic political system, and enlightened policies of economic growth. In addition, since they had been largely destroyed in the War, completely new factories and the industrial base had to be rebuilt, using only the most modern, efficient technological methods. Undoubtedly, among our cases, this factor of military defeat and rebuilding was important in Germany and Japan; but among the other success stories, only Taiwan's forces had suffered military defeat (but not occupation), while South Korea had fought a civil war with the North that ended in stalemate and a large U.S. military presence.

3. *U.S. aid and influence.*   These were undoubtedly high in Japan, South Korea, and Taiwan but not in Singapore or Hong Kong. U.S. aid and influence were important in the early stages of development of the first three countries, in terms of what economists call "priming the pumps" of development and also in opening its markets to Asian products; but within a decade or two these countries were basically on their own economically.

4. *The right economic model.*   *All five* of these countries basically "made it" by following an economic model of building up industry and *exporting* manufactured goods (plastics, automobiles, televisions, electronic equipment, clothing) to the already-developed countries. In contrast, most of Latin America followed the Import-Substitution-Industrialization (ISI) model which called for protection from outside competition, production for non-competitive local markets, and the discouragement of both imports and exports. By now, the Latin American countries have largely abandoned the ISI model in favor of Asia-style export-led growth, but they argue that, because of protectionism by the importing countries, U.S. and European markets are less open to them and their products now than was the case for the Asian countries at their earlier, critical stage of growth. Others dispute this claim, suggesting the United States is still mainly an open market and that the fault still lies with the Latin American countries themselves.

5. *Authoritarianism.*   In their early decades of development, South Korea, Taiwan, Hong Kong, and Singapore were all governed by authoritarian or top-down regimes. Japan was *formally* a democracy, thanks to the U.S.-style constitution imposed on it by the occupation, but it, too, functioned as a one-party, statist, top-down regime. The argument is that, in the early stages of development, a country needs the peace, order, stability, and discipline of an authoritarian regime to achieve growth. Only later, it is argued, once

a country achieves self-sustaining growth, can it afford the "luxury" of greater pluralism and democratization. We return to this theme later in the discussion.

6. *Institutional design.* It is, of course, important for development to get your institutions—laws, constitution, form of government, bureaucracy, and state structure—correct. In the Japanese case especially, and the other Asian tigers, too, what seemed to be especially important for development were the extremely close, even intimate ties between the government, the bureaucracy (especially the trade ministry), the banks, and the private sector. In the United States and other capitalist systems, trade and commerce are based more on a *laissez-faire* or free-market system, but in Asia it was the state in alliance with private-sector allies that organized a *coordinated, integrated,* growth model.

7. *Culture.* Is there something in Asian, or more specifically Confucian (thus encompassing *all five* of our Asian tigers plus China), that helps explain the success of Asian development? Most of us think, yes; but then the arguments get tricky. For a long time, Confucianism in Asia, with its emphasis on rank and hierarchy, respect for elders, and deference and conformity, was thought to hold back development. Only recently have these traits, plus the equally strong Confucian focus on education, honor, loyalty, striving, hard work, and consensus, been viewed positively for development. For example, in Japan and the other tigers, one frequently sees people *running* to work, *hurrying* to get the work done well and on time, and *bowing* to consumers or those served at the end of a successfully completed task. How long has it been since you've seen people *running* to work in the United States or Europe as if they're eager to get there, *hurrying* to do it well and efficiently, and then *bowing* to those served?

8. *Resources.* We began this analysis with a discussion, in the cases especially of the oil-rich states, of the advantages of having vast natural resources. Clearly that is one way to achieve development: witness the United States, France, Germany, and others—all resource-rich countries *and* among the most-developed countries in the world. But then look at Denmark, the Netherlands, Switzerland, and the Asian tigers already mentioned—all poor in natural resources but, nevertheless, among the richest countries on earth. The other side of this coin is represented by the cases of Argentina, Brazil, China, and Russia, which are fabulously rich in natural resources but historically unable to get their economic and political acts together and organized sufficiently to achieve sustained development. So at some level, in order to achieve development, it helps to have vast resources; but, as in the Argentina, Brazil, China, or Russia cases, that is not enough by itself, and in some other cases it is likely that the very absence of natural resources stimulates, to compensate for this lack, the hard work, ambition, and energy needed for development.

9. *The neighborhood.* Here the argument is that it helps to have rich neighbors. Especially in modern times when trade, commerce, investment, and growth are strongly tied to globalization and international factors, it is beneficial

to live near a wealthy neighbor whose wealth also rubs off on you. Thus, Mexico benefits from being close to the huge U.S. market; small, poor, and weak Paraguay profits from being close to big, dynamic Argentina and Brazil; the small European countries mentioned in explanation 7 benefit from being next to bigger, stronger economies (France, Italy, Germany); and some of its neighbors now (but earlier this was not the case) gain advantages from being close to Japan. In Eastern and Central Europe, in fact, there is a close correlation between levels of individual country development and proximity to the rich economies of Western Europe—for example, the Czech Republic, Hungary, the Baltics, Poland, and Slovenia benefit from being close to such wealthy countries as Germany, Austria, and Italy, and are all wealthier than their neighbors farther to the east who are, thus, also farther away from Western markets, capital, and affluence. Yet it is striking that, in the early decades of their development, the Western European countries, the United States, and the Asian countries that are our main focus here *all* developed in relative autonomy and did not really feel much rub-off effect from richer neighbors (there were no richer neighbors at that time).

There we have it: Nine possible (and plausible) explanations for why some countries develop and others do not. Already from our preliminary discussion, some conclusions are possible:

1. There is probably no one, single explanation, let alone a magic formula for growth.
2. In most countries a combination of several factors is involved.
3. These factors and their combinations may vary somewhat from country to country.
4. Nevertheless, there is an emerging pattern as to which factors are *most important* in *most cases.*

We return to these themes later in the discussion. Now let us take up some of the individual case studies.

Japan

Japan, which among the industrialized nations is relatively resource-poor, has had a long history of development (see explanation 1 on page 73), which was then interrupted by World War II. Militarily defeated and occupied by the United States in the aftermath of the war, Japan's economic and industrial base was crippled and destroyed. The American occupation forces helped write a new U.S.-style constitution for the country, rebuilt the shattered economy, instigated an agrarian reform that led to greater social equality, and poured in aid to the defeated country to help put it back on its feet. Japan was not too proud to accept the American influence even while continuing to run the country in time-honored Japanese ways. Thus, even though the constitution, parliament (Diet), and party system appeared to be liberal and democratic, in fact the system remained, in many respects, autocratic, top-down, illiberal, and closed to all except a small coterie of patronage politicians. Similarly, although the economy was supposed to be free enterprise, in fact it was closed, bureaucratic, statist, and run by an interlocking directorate of banks, party leaders, business groups, and government officials, especially in the crucially important Ministry of Trade or MITI.

The party system, elections, and democracy were not entirely a sham but nearly so, because one party, the Liberal Democrats, (almost) always won. That provided the political stability for several decades that enabled the Japanese economy to take off. Economic development was also aided by the interlocking directorate previously noted which made it virtually impossible to separate, as in America, the public and the private sectors. In Japan all the key groups—government, private, financial, bureaucratic—were tied together in a crash program of integral national development. It also helped that the United States provided its security blanket for Japan so it would not have to expend investment capital on defense, that the United States opened its markets wide to Japanese products, and that Japan is very well organized, disciplined, educated, and hard-working, so that it could take advantage of these opportunities.

For four decades, from the 1950s through the early 1990s, the Japanese model of export-led growth in the context of a remarkably efficient, unified, productive, stable, and authoritative, if not authoritarian, governmental-bureaucratic system worked remarkably well. During many of these years Japan achieved "miracle" economic growth rates of 7, 8, 9, or 10 percent per year, enabling per-capita income to double several times over and vaulting Japan to the very top ranks of the world's most prosperous nations. At one point Japan's prosperity made it the wealthiest nation in the world on a per-capita basis (over $40,000 per person per year) before falling back slightly; productivity was so great and rising so fast that there was talk of Japan as "The New Superpower" or "Japan as Number One," meaning that its gross national product might in the future surpass that of the United States.

But then in the 1990s Japan's economy began to slip somewhat. The precise reasons for this are still unclear and are subject to disagreement among economists as well as the Japanese themselves, but they have to do with bad bank loans to some inefficient and badly run enterprises, the closed nature of the Japanese system which makes it very difficult to root out corruption and inefficiency, the undemocratic nature of the political system which makes accountability and responsibility difficult to assign, and the system of honor and status which makes getting rid of old deadwood almost impossible. In addition, there is what the Japanese call "McDonald's kids," kids born of affluence who sit around all day eating high cholesterol, fast-food hamburgers and French fries, get fat in the process, and who over time lose the energy, ambition, and work ethic of their fathers and grandfathers. These habits have received much attention in the U.S. press, on the assumption that it must be gratifying to Americans to learn that the Japanese are becoming fat and lazy just like we sometimes seem to be!

But any recent visitor to Japan will see immediately that there are actually very few fat and lazy Japanese; that the economic and industrial base of Japan is still tremendously productive; that the population is well educated, disciplined, organized, and efficient; and that once the present spate of administrative/banking/economic troubles are resolved, Japan will be poised once again to resume its remarkable growth, perhaps even to achieve that number one position. The Japanese miracle of the preceding fifty years has to be one of the great success stories of the last half of the twentieth century, a story (and model) not lost on Japan's Asian neighbors.

South Korea

As compared with Japan, Korea was a very poor and traditional society up through World War II. Divided by the Cold War between a communist north and a non-communist south, the two Koreas fought an inconclusive civil war in the early 1950s with the United States and the United Nations intervening on behalf of the south and subsequently providing guidance (as in postwar Japan) and assistance, as well as large-scale military forces aimed both at deterring the north from further attacks and keeping a peaceful lid on the volatile, potentially unstable political situation in the south. Syngman Rhee emerged out of the turmoil of the 1950s and established an authoritarian regime that nevertheless, like Japan, had a democratic, constitutional facade. With stability reestablished under Rhee, the Republic of South Korea (ROK) began a process of crash economic development and industrialization in the late 1950s that was patterned after Japan's already-ongoing miracle.

As Japan's expanding economy progressively "graduated" into high-tech goods like televisions, VCRs, Walkmans, computers, and quality automobiles, South Korea (and Taiwan) filled the gaps of low-tech textiles, plastic toys, and kitchen utensils previously supplied by Japan. South Korea also stressed, like Japan, the organization of state-associated big-business combinations and monopolies similarly tied in with major banks and economics/trade ministries, but without the same egalitarianism and paternalism of the Japanese firms. On the other hand, Korea's labor unions were more militant than their Japanese counterparts and, in alliance with disgruntled students, considerably more disruptive.

President Syngman Rhee was toppled in 1960 by one of these student-labor protests with the military watching from the sidelines; a year later the army under strongman Park Chung Hee seized power with General Park ruling until his assassination in 1979. The regime remained authoritarian or bureaucratic-authoritarian, keeping a tight grip over all political movements and not allowing democracy to develop, even of the controlled kind as in Japan. The economic model of export-driven growth continued, now reaching quite spectacular, almost Japan-like development, dominated by those large public-private conglomerates—except in South Korea's case with military officers as well as civilians serving on their boards of directors and profiting from the growth.

Park's overthrow was followed by a brief democratic opening, which was quickly closed with another coup by Chun Doo Huan. Thus, authoritarianism continued in a virtually unbroken string from the 1950s to the 1980s. Meanwhile, South Korea's economic development continued unabated at "miracle" growth rates to match Japan's; South Korea also began to match Japan in automobiles and higher-tech products and even had visions, assuming eventually the reunification of North and South, of one day overtaking Japan in productivity. For Korea, also formed by the Confucian culture, is similarly dedicated to ambition, energy, hard work, and getting ahead—maybe even more so than Japan itself.

A democratic breakthrough occurred in 1987. Dictator Chun indicated a desire to extend his presidential term beyond what he had earlier promised, which split his own ruling coalition; at the same time, South Korea had become a better-educated, more-urban, and pluralist country; the opposition had grown; and it had taken heart from recent democratizing movements in the Philippines and Latin America. The Chun dictatorship gave way and South Korea, though still not fully consolidated as a democracy, has been governed by elected, not military, regimes ever since.

The South Korean model is interesting to us because, like Japan, it had more-or-less stable authoritarianism for over three decades which provided a climate in which the economy could really take off. Then, as social pluralism took hold in the 1980s, the opposition grew, and the threat from the North receded, South Korea ever so slowly evolved toward democracy. It had in its early years viewed democracy as a potentially unstable luxury which it could not afford; but as development proceeded and pluralism grew, it came to see democracy not as a luxury but as a necessity, alone capable of peacefully handling rising social pluralism. We will see this process elsewhere in Asia.

Taiwan

Taiwan, or the Republic of China (ROC), is another "wonder" or "miracle" of East Asian modernization, a tiny island that has taken its place as an economic giant and a prosperous, high-income society. It shares with Japan, South Korea, Hong Kong, and Singapore the Confucian and general East Asian work ethic and the values of education, discipline, hierarchy, and honor. The growth model that Taiwan has pursued, export-led growth, is very similar to that of Japan and South Korea. Its recent sociopolitical development is also remarkably similar to that of South Korea, although its historical background is quite different.

The island of Taiwan, once called Formosa, lies off the coast of China; although ethnically the native Taiwanese are different from the mainlanders, the island has long been considered a part of Greater China. From 1895 to 1945 it was occupied by Japan; then, briefly, it became a part of communist China when Mao's revolution triumphed in 1948. However, the following year the defeated Nationalist (anti-communist) forces of Chiang Kai-shek, expelled from the mainland, took refuge on Taiwan and established an authoritarian state whose main props were the army, the police, the government bureaucracy, a well-educated and skillful technocratic elite, and the Kuomintang or Nationalist Party (KMT).

Chiang Kai-shek ruled until the early 1970s when he was succeeded by his son Chiang Ching-kuo, who governed until 1988. Taiwan, therefore, like South Korea and to some extent Japan, had forty years of stability under authoritarian auspices, during which it modernized, industrialized, and became the economic wonder that we know today. During this four-decades period, its growth *averaged* 8 percent per year, better even than that of South Korea and comparable to that of Japan, albeit starting from a lower base. Taiwan's per-capita income catapulted it to the front rank of nations and eventually reached the level of the developed, West European countries.

In his last years Chiang Ching-kuo, as in South Korea in the same time period, feeling pressure from new, rising social groups, principally the middle class, opened up the regime, reactivated democratic constitutional functions, and turned power over to Vice President Lee Teng-hui. Lee continued on the path of democratization, strengthened democratic institutions, and paved the way for the opposition to win the election of 2000. Taiwan is now a democratic state with the main threat to it being not internal but external: the (communist or mainland) People's Republic of China (PRC), which has never recognized Taiwan's right to independence.

Taiwan, though geographically small, is still an economic giant. Significantly, it achieved its phenomenal growth record under authoritarianism, the KMT, not democracy. Authoritarianism provided the order, stability, discipline, and continuity that helped Taiwan to grow. Other factors—open U.S. markets, an ethic of hard work, U.S. security protection—were also important, but for the purposes of this analysis it is the *political* model that Taiwan employed to move ahead that commands our attention.

Both Taiwan and South Korea, and to a somewhat lesser extent Japan, tended to see democracy as a luxury they could not afford in the early stages of their development. Democracy tends to divide and fragment developing countries and, thus, slow their economic growth. South Korea and Taiwan, in contrast, argued that they *first* had to establish their economic base; only later could they permit democracy. Hence, they both had forty years of authoritarianism. Then, when the economic structure was sufficiently strong and secure, they felt they could move to democracy. Aiding this transition were (1) mounting pressure from the outside (United States, human rights groups, etc.) to democratize; (2) rising internal social pressures that threatened the authoritarian regime's stability if it failed to democratize; and (3) a lessening of the external security threat (from North Korea in the case of South Korea and from Communist China in the case of Taiwan) to the extent the regime felt it could now afford that "luxury" called democracy. Nevertheless, keep in mind the East Asian formula: economic development *first, then* democracy later on.

Hong Kong

Hong Kong is another of the miracle economies of Asia. But its future position is precarious.

Hong Kong was built up in the nineteenth century as a British trading post on the south coast of China. It occupies a very small amount of land at the entrance of China's Pearl River, which leads to major trading centers in the interior. Its strong points have always been shipping, banking, trade, commerce, insurance, and manufacturing. But, of course, it did well and prospered in all these areas because (1) it enjoyed the protection of the British crown as well as the profitable connections with British banks and commerce, and (2) it served as a privileged gateway to the vast China market and, indeed, to all of Asia.

Hong Kong has almost all the same attributes as Japan, South Korea, and Taiwan. It is tremendously energetic, well organized, educated, well disciplined, and hard-working. It also enjoyed the security blanket and aid of an outside power—in this case Great Britain. Its economic model is similar to that of export-driven growth. And as a colony, its political model was that of authoritarianism or autocracy.

Hong Kong's economic accomplishments have been phenomenal. It is ranked in the highest-income category by the World Bank and, like the other Asian tigers already mentioned, it has *leapfrogged* over other countries to reach that high ranking.

Without meaning to detract from Hong Kong's remarkable accomplishments, it must be said that this is a special case and perhaps not representative or repeatable in other countries. Its value as a British colonial outpost and as a gateway to the China trade not only made it unique but also made its position precarious. In 1997, sovereignty over Hong Kong was transferred from Great Britain to China. While China promised in the transfer agreement to respect Hong Kong's freedoms and independence, in fact China has been exerting greater control over the enclave and, as a still-Marxist-Leninist state, is not at all comfortable with the political freedoms Hong Kong enjoys. And in the economic sphere, China also has the power to undermine Hong Kong's prosperity through further restrictions or by making Shanghai its preferred center for banking and commerce rather than Hong Kong.

Singapore

Singapore is like Hong Kong: dynamic, busy, energetic, and entrepreneurial. And, like Hong Kong, it is a small city-state that has taken its place as one of the most prosperous places on earth. Singapore is 90 percent Chinese so it shares the Confucian ethic of education, discipline, and hard work found in our other cases.

Singapore was also a former British colony and trading post. It occupies a crucial strategic and commercial position at the tip of the Malay Peninsula, commanding all the shipping routes between the Indian and Pacific oceans and between Europe and Asia. It is either the top or second-ranked shipping center in the world. Like Hong Kong, it is also an important banking, commercial, trading, insurance, and manufacturing center. Many of these industries, as in Hong Kong, are among the biggest and busiest in the world. Hong Kong and Singapore, along with Tokyo and Osaka in Japan, are among the great trading-commercial hubs of Asia.

Singapore achieved its independence in 1965, separating from Malaysia. At that time it was quite poor and underdeveloped. It was also surrounded by larger neighbors—Indonesia, India, China, and Malaysia—from which, as a small city-state, it felt threatened, both militarily and in terms of population/immigration pressures. Singapore was said to live in a "dangerous neighborhood." In addition, Singapore's own internal society was torn by bitter ethnic rivalries between Chinese and Malays. For these reasons Singapore felt it could not afford democracy at that time and, instead, opted for an authoritarian regime under Lee Quan Yew, one of the most remarkable men of the late twentieth century.

Mr. Lee stood (it should sound familiar by now) for discipline, authority, and order. He and his party monopolized politics for the next thirty years. He established law and order, reduced crime, rapidly reformed education, and greatly improved the housing stock. He made Singapore (like Hong Kong) a safe, clean, peaceful, eminently livable city. He also went a little far: in Singapore you had better not spit or throw gum on the sidewalk or you will not only get fined but also do jail time! And he ran his political regime in an authoritarian, autocratic fashion, not really like a dictator but certainly as a tough, shrewd, no-nonsense leader. Interestingly, he maintained authoritarian control *even after* the possibility of external threat or internal social upheaval had passed, only *gradually* in the mid-1990s beginning to relax the controls and move toward democratization.

So there we have the "Asian model" and formula once again: economic development first, under an authoritarian or autocratic regime; gradual democratization; and later, once the economic base had been laid and the early traumas of new nationhood had been surmounted, new social pressures and pluralism in society meant the old authoritarianism wouldn't work anymore.

Other Asian Cases

Most of the other Asian nations have tried, in one fashion or another, to follow the model previously outlined. But they have not been nearly as successful as Japan and the "Four Tigers." Why is that? Only three answers are possible: (1) the model is wrong, doesn't fit them, or doesn't get at the key variables, (2) these other countries are somehow different from the five previously discussed; or (3) a combination of (1) and (2).

The variables that may be hypothesized as being important in explaining why these other Asian nations have been *less than successful* include the following:

1. Less U.S. attention, aid, and influence.
2. Inadequate or wrong implementation of the model.
3. Less efficiency, organization, and discipline.
4. Smaller markets for their products; fewer export opportunities.
5. An overall political culture less propitious for development.
6. Poorer natural resources.

Now let us look at some individual cases.

Indonesia was a Dutch colony for some four hundred years, achieving its independence after World War II. During its first twenty years of independence, its politics were dominated by the flamboyant, charismatic, nationalistic Sukarno who followed a nationalist policy, but from 1966–1998 it was ruled by dictator General Suharto–hence, the authoritarian model. Under Suharto the economy grew but not at the miracle rate of the East Asian tigers. Indonesia, despite vast natural resources, is a more divided nation, less well organized and disciplined than the tigers, and unable to utilize its natural wealth efficiently. In addition, Suharto, his family, and his cronies stole vast amounts from the public treasury, something the East Asian tigers with their Confucian sense of propriety did not do. Nor did the United States aid and pay as much attention to Indonesia as it did to Japan, South Korea, and Taiwan. Finally, Indonesia has a different culture than that of the tigers, less hard-driving, efficient, and motivated, and with lower levels of education.

The Philippines was a Spanish colony for four hundred years and an American one for fifty. As such, it is a mixture of indigenous, Spanish, and American influences. Becoming independent in 1946, it functioned as an imperfect democracy for twenty years before dictator Ferdinand Marcos took over in 1965, ruling until 1986. Marcos was like Suharto: an authoritarian leader governing a divisive, not well-organized or disciplined nation. There *was* considerable development under Marcos, but it was sporadic and uneven, often diverted to Marcos' family members, and nowhere near the level of the East Asian tigers. Although blessed with abundant natural resources, the Philippines, like Indonesia, has been unable to organize them efficiently as part of a coherent national development strategy. In addition, Philippine political culture, like the Indonesian, is not oriented toward the same disciplined, organized, hard-driving, developmental goals as are the East Asian tigers.[1]

Malaysia is a fascinating case for us: (1) its early, post–World War II independence history was checkered, unstable, and lacking sustained development; (2) U.S. assistance and attention have never been high; and (3) like Indonesia and the Philippines, it is not part of the East Asian or tiger, hard-driving, Confucian political culture. But over the last twenty-five years, under the energetic, able, efficient, dedicated Prime Minister Muhammed Mahathir, Malaysia really took off. Mahathir is interesting because, while an authoritarian and autocrat, he was a civilian prime minister, not a military dictator. Like Prime Minister Lee in Singapore, Mahathir ran a tight ship, did not suffer fools or the opposition (both the same, in his view) easily, was dedicated to his country's national development, and was not corrupt like Suharto or Marcos. Under his leadership Malaysia achieved impressive economic growth, not quite at the level of the tigers but not very far behind either, reaching a level of what the World Bank calls "upper-middle income."

India, like China, is a giant of a country, with a billion people, and obviously deserves far more detailed attention than we can possibly give it here. India is an exception in our series of cases, which nonetheless confirms the rule. It has been a *democracy,* not authoritarian, ever since it became independent from Great Britain in 1947, and with democracy comes a certain degree of chaos, disorder, and instability—all factors that have hindered India's economic development over the years compared with the East Asian tigers. Second, rather than allowing private sector development or a close alliance as in East Asia between business and the state, India has followed a socialist model that was often hostile to free enterprise. In the last few years, however, India has begun to allow greater free market activity, reduced the state's involvement in the economy, and allowed its private sector to flourish. The result has been faster growth, though not even close to the tiger countries, but without sacrificing India's often chaotic democracy. India, therefore, unlike the other Asian tigers, put democracy *before* economic growth, maintaining a free society but falling behind further economically in the process.

China is another anomaly, a giant of a country, with immense resources, 1.3 *billion* people, and like the other tigers a Confucian country (indeed, *the* center of Confucianism), but one which until recently was never able to get its act together or organize itself sufficiently to carry out a sustained development strategy. Dominated by warlords and colonial interventions (European, Japan), China had a communist revolution in the 1940s that brought Mao Tse-tung to power and forced the defeated anti-communist Chiang Kai-shek and his followers to flee to Taiwan. China's key problem is rather like that of Indonesia, the Philippines, India, Brazil, Russia, and others: how do you organize, under *whatever* political or economic system, a big, diverse, resource-rich country for integral national development? China's model has been the exact opposite of India's: whereas India put democracy first and only later emphasized economic growth, China put authority and discipline (Marxism-Leninism) first and only later began to relax the regime.

China's Marxist-Leninist regime was for a long time ruthless politically but inefficient economically. But over the last two decades the regime has evolved more in an authoritarian than a totalitarian direction, meanwhile freeing up parts of its economy and encouraging public-private sector cooperation. In other words, China now presents a model not all that different from Japan's or the Four tigers in their early, pre-democratic years: authoritarian politically but stimulating public-private cooperation economically. And with that model China has achieved phenomenal growth rates recently of 7 to 8 percent per year, among the best in the world. With its huge, productive population, China's GNP is third largest in the world, but on a per-capita basis it remains a poor country, at the level of Indonesia. Moreover, there are rising social and political pressures in China that may force the same kind of changes toward a freer political system (to go with the freer economic system) that we saw in the other tigers.

Other Asian Countries

Pakistan has alternated between democracy and authoritarianism, has never—because of the instability—been able to put together a sustained drive to development, and remains a poor country. *Vietnam, Laos,* and *Cambodia* were devastated by the wars in Southeast Asia in the 1960s and 1970s, were always poorer and less-developed than their bigger neighbors, and are only now beginning to put their societies and political systems back together to achieve economic development. *Burma* (now Myanmar) is a military dictatorship but not one that has achieved much growth. In the same neighborhood, *Thailand* has been doing remarkably well recently and may be poised to become the next Asian tiger.

Other NICs

For a long time the terms *Third World* and *developing areas* were used to describe the world's poor nations. These terms were used indiscriminately; *all* emerging nations were lumped into these categories. But by the 1970s it began to be noticed that some "developing countries"—precisely the Asian tigers discussed here—were developing faster than others, often at impressive, miracle rates. Hence, the term *Newly Industrializing Countries,* or NICs, was invented to differentiate the impressive success stories in the Third World from those that lagged behind.

Most of the NICs are located in Asia—the tigers, South Korea, Taiwan, Hong Kong, Singapore, China, Malaysia, maybe Indonesia, the Philippines, and Thailand. Certainly, the fact that so many NICs are in Asia must tell us that there is something unique, distinctive, and special about Asia, such as the political culture, the social structure, the Confucian values and work ethic of much of the region, the political and economic model used, and the international environment.

Outside of Asia there are few successful NICs. In the Arab world *not a single country* is classified as a NIC, although some of them are quite wealthy on a per-capita basis based on vast oil resources, even while their social and political systems remain retrograde and unmodern. Nor is there a single NIC in Africa, although Egypt, Nigeria, and South Africa are often mentioned as potential candidates because of their rich resources and large populations.

That leaves Latin America as the only other continent where one finds NICs. In general, however, even the Latin American success stories are less impressive than those of Asia, even while they often do better than the countries of the Middle East or Africa.

Argentina likes to think of itself as a European country (white, Western, wealthy, sophisticated) that happens to be located on the South American continent. It has vast resources, a large middle or consumer class, and the highest per-capita income in Latin America. However, Argentina is deeply divided socially and politically; its political system has been unsettled over a long period; and it has never lived up to its developmental potential. In recent years its economy has gone into a disastrous, downward tailspin from which it has not been able to extract itself; Argentina's per-capita income and standard of living are in a precipitous slide. It would not be accurate to call this country a NIC, or at least not any more.

Brazil is a giant, vastly endowed with resources, a "tropical China." Like the Asian NICs, its most successful development came under authoritarian rule in 1930–1945, and then again in 1964–1985. Growth rates in the latter period reached 8, 9, and 10 percent for a time—equal to or surpassing the Asian NICs—but then faded. Nor is Brazil as well organized, disciplined, and institutionalized as the Asian NICs. Its newly democratic political system remains unconsolidated, and it has alternated between rival economic models. The result is that it is difficult for Brazil to maintain consistent growth over a long period. Despite the ups and downs, Brazil is definitely in the NIC category, although it is somewhat less successful than its Asian counterparts.

Chile is one of the most successful NICs in Latin America. It, too, has rich natural resources and, unlike Brazil, a well-educated population, with a large middle class and a very sophisticated professional or technical class with vast international experience. Chile has a strong democratic and civic tradition, but it also had its authoritarian interlude, 1973–1989, under General Augusto Pinochet when a new, Asian-style, export-oriented economic model was put in place. Chile has also been extremely clever, like the Asian tigers, in finding and taking advantage of new niche markets abroad, even while diversifying both its internal economy and its exports. And, as it returned to democracy after 1989, it retained the essentials of its successful, private-sector-dominated and export-oriented economic model. Of all the Latin American countries, Chile is the closest to the Asian NIC success story.

Mexico is a very interesting NIC because it presents a variation on the main theme. From 1930–2000, a period of seventy years, Mexico was a *civilian* authoritarian regime. It was dominated by a single party, the Revolutionary Institutional Party (PRI), that provided remarkable stability all through this long period. The party integrated in corporatist fashion all social groups—peasants, workers, middle class—into its ranks and monopolized politics by means of patronage, corruption, and controlled elections. With that kind of political stability, the economy also flourished for many decades, achieving not the miracle growth rates of Asia but quite impressive rates at 4 to 5 percent per year. Unlike other Latin American countries, Mexico also followed an Asia-like, export-oriented economic model; and, of course, it helps in that regard to share a porous, two-thousand-mile border with the world's largest and richest consumer market, the United States. Over time—like the Asian NICs—Mexico gradually democratized to accommodate changed social and political conditions.

Venezuela was a NIC but is no longer. A country of vast resources, immense oil supplies, and great potential, Venezuela has fallen on hard times. Its economy has slipped backward, and its politics and society are deeply divided. Venezuela has an authoritarian past but, over the last forty years, it has been governed under democracy. Nevertheless, the democratic regime proved to be unstable, massively corrupt, and unable to carry out a sustained, long-term development policy. In recent years Venezuela has fragmented, polarized, and teetered on the edge of civil war. A once-promising NIC has fallen on hard times. In this it is more like Indonesia or the Philippines than the successful NICs of East Asia.

CONCLUSIONS

This completes our survey of the main NICs—those countries that have succeeded in breaking out of underdevelopment and into a pattern of self-sustained growth. What accounts for these success stories, which are still quite rare in the developing world? To begin to provide systematic answers to that question, we return to the list of hypothesized explanations offered earlier in the chapter.

1. *A long history of development.* Among our cases this factor applies only to Japan. *By definition,* NICs are *Newly* Industrialized Countries.

2. *Defeat in war and military occupation.* This applies to Japan, South Korea, Taiwan, and maybe Singapore. Ordinarily, we would think—and in most instances that is the case—war destroys countries and damages economies. But in the cases discussed previously (Singapore was threatened but not defeated), war may have concentrated the countries' developmental focus, destroyed old feudal institutions paving the way for bolder development, made them desperate to achieve growth in part to ward off other potential threats, enabled (or forced) these countries to modernize their industrial plant, and given inspiration to or desire to rise again and deter threatening neighbors. In the cases of Japan (by the United States) and Taiwan (by the Kuomintang), military occupation also led to development being stimulated by the occupation forces.

3. *U.S. aid and influence.* This is probably important but still marginal in all the cases studied. U.S. aid often helped prime the economic pumps; U.S. influence helped change traditional beliefs and led to an emphasis on development; open U.S. markets enabled these countries to concentrate on exports. But in *all* cases it is the local dynamic forces that were most important, without which little development would have occurred. The opening of U.S. markets to these countries' products was far more important than was foreign aid.

4. *The right economic model.* This is *crucial* in *all* cases. You *need* to get the economics correct. While the Import Substitution Industrialization (ISI) model was probably good for Latin America in the 1930s and 1940s, by the 1950s that model had run its course and was no longer useful; Latin America had stuck to the wrong model for too long. From mid-century on, meanwhile, it was the East Asian nations— the tigers—through their export-oriented model that were best able to take advantage of world economic conditions.

5. *Authoritarianism.* Undoubtedly, economic growth requires long-term political stability—thirty to forty years—to establish the conditions and get the motor force of development into high gear. Several sub-conclusions emerge:
   a. During the 1960s and 1970s, when the NICs really took off, authoritarian regimes (South Korea, Taiwan) proved more effective at economic growth than did democratic governments or countries (Brazil, others) that unstably alternated between democracy and authoritarianism.
   b. Successful authoritarian governments can be under either military or civilian (Mexico) control, or mixed systems in which trained technicians and professionals, both military and civilian, are in charge.
   c. But these authoritarian regimes need to be efficient, intelligent, and noncorrupt. That helps explain the differences between the successful

NICs, like South Korea, Taiwan, Hong Kong, Singapore, and Chile, and the less-successful ones like Indonesia, the Philippines, Brazil, and Venezuela. In other words, strong government *by itself* is not a sufficient answer; you also need strong, *honest, effective* government which *most* dictatorships fail to provide.

d. While the logic for strong, even authoritarian or autocratic government was powerful in the 1960s and 1970s, today, with so much emphasis, pressure, and international leverage in favor of democracy, it is doubtful if the older arguments for authoritarianism will work. This is a crucial factor to which we return in subsequent discussion.

6. *Institutional design.* You need to get your political institutions as well as your economic model correct. In today's world that means the rule of law, a system of checks and balances, transparency (so as to prevent corruption) in the handling of public funds and contracts, laws that protect property and the rights of companies to repatriate their profits, an honest and efficient bureaucracy and civil service, regular elections, and democracy. It also requires the institutions of an open, free-market economic system, oriented toward trade and exports as well as domestic markets, with few tariff barriers and only enough protectionism to preserve viable, growing industries, and limited subsidies to protect poor people's necessities such as basic foodstuffs and petroleum (for public transportation) prices.

7. *Culture.* Culture matters! It is not a coincidence that *all* of the most successful NICs are in the educated, hard-working, socially egalitarian, orderly, disciplined, efficient, mainly honest countries of Asia that are part of the Confucian ethos: Japan, South Korea, Taiwan, Hong Kong, Singapore, and now giant China. These countries may not only be contrasted on cultural grounds with the less-successful Third World areas of Africa, Latin America, and the Middle East, but also with the non-Confucian (and slower-growing) areas of South and Southeast Asia: Indonesia, India, and the Philippines. We need to know more about the specific cultural traits of the Asian success stories that have made their growth so dramatic.

8. *Resources.* Argentina, Brazil, China, Indonesia, Nigeria, and Russia all have immense natural resources but have never been able to organize themselves internally (or "get their acts together") sufficiently to achieve sustained national development. In contrast, Japan, South Korea, Taiwan, Hong Kong, and Singapore have few natural resources and yet are among the great economic dynamos of the modern world. Another contrast: Canada, France, Germany, and the United States are richly endowed *and* are among the richest, most developed countries in the world. So, it depends. On balance, it helps to have rich natural resources: Brazil has developed in large part because of its natural wealth even while its political system is often disorganized. But the

Asian examples listed seem to indicate that coherent national organization and a culture supportive of development can compensate for, and may be even more important than, natural wealth. On the other hand, suppose you're a Haiti, an Afghanistan, an East Timor, a Nicaragua, a Yemen, or an Ethiopia: almost no natural resources, disorganized and under-institutionalized politically and economically, *and* lacking a culture (Confucian or otherwise) strongly supportive of growth. *Then,* what do you do?

9. *The neighborhood.* It helps if you're close to wealthier neighbors and can benefit from the rub-off effects of their rich economies. The countries of Eastern/Central Europe benefit from being neighbors of rich, affluent Western Europe; South Korea and Taiwan gained advantages from being in wealthy Japan's orbit; and Mexico benefits enormously both from its trade with the United States and from that two-thousand-mile border which functions as an "escape valve" for excess Mexican population. Indeed, most of the Central American and Caribbean countries benefit in these ways from their proximity to the world's richest market, the United States; but the countries in South America are too far away to receive much benefit from that market.

Well, there we have it: to achieve development, a long history of prior development (Germany, Japan) is helpful; defeat in war and/or military occupation may be helpful; U.S. aid and influence, and especially markets, are often beneficial; having rich natural resources is helpful; and living in a wealthy neighborhood is advantageous. *Even more important,* however, among successful developers is having the right economic model, the correct institutional design, and a strong political culture supportive of development.

Two final—and provocative—comments are necessary. First, one of the most striking characteristics of the successful Asian NICs was the close, almost incestuous relationships for several decades among government ministries, banks, and private industries. But under the new international rules of openness and transparency, it may be that kind of tight, integrated, but also closed and secretive model may not be possible any more.

Second and related, it is equally striking that the most successful NICs achieved development under a stable, disciplined, *authoritarian* regime that ruled for thirty to forty years and provided a *climate* in which development could go forward, only *later* turning to democracy once the strong economic base had been established. But today, with authoritarianism discredited in much of the world and democracy seen as the only legitimate form of government ("the only game in town"), it may no longer be possible to replicate the Asian success stories. Unsettling though it may be, we have to recognize that democracy, advantageous though it is, often comes at the cost of *slower* growth in the Third World. We prefer democracy but there are also unmistakable, often unfortunate trade-offs between democracy and economic growth.

NOTES

1. The author was once on a plane flying between Singapore and the Philippines. My seatmate was a Singapore Chinese, married to a Philippine woman, with business dealings in both countries. I, therefore, asked him to explain to me why Singapore was so modern and developed, and the Philippines lagged behind. He looked around to make sure no one was listening and then whispered to me, "Because they're not Chinese!" In other words, in his view it was the Chinese or Confucian culture that explained the difference, not other structural or institutional factors.

5

Transitions to Democracy in the Developing World

The early 1960s had been a (brief) time of hope and optimism for democracy in the new nations of Africa and Asia and throughout the developing areas. But by the mid-to-late 1960s, as we have seen in earlier chapters, a great wave of authoritarianism, mostly under military dictatorships, had swept aside these earlier, hopeful, but weakly institutionalized democracies. The military regimes not only destroyed nascent democracies but were often vicious abusers of human rights as well. By the mid-1970s seventeen of the twenty Latin American countries were under authoritarian rule, as was much of the Middle East as well as Sub-Saharan Africa. Much of Asia, as we have seen, was under authoritarianism all along. Authoritarianism had replaced democracy as the dominant system of government and politics in the Third World.

Two important themes immediately command our attention. The first is that the trend to authoritarianism was so powerful during this period that scholars and policymakers alike began to argue that authoritarianism and the corporatism (state regulation and control of interest groups) that accompanied it might well be a *permanent* feature of Third World countries. The democracy model or paradigm was now supplanted by the authoritarianism-corporatism model. Many analysts all but gave up on the prospects for democracy in the developing areas—as it had been set forth in the developmentalist models of Almond, Lipset, and Rostow a decade or two earlier. And as might be expected, this shift in thinking also became a self-fulfilling prophecy: as scholars and others wrote gloomily about democracy's prospects and that authoritarianism-corporatism might be both inevitable and permanent, authoritarianism then became even more widespread.

The second fascinating feature of the new wave of authoritarianism was that there was an imitation effect. New authoritarian regimes sought to imitate other, earlier—and successful—authoritarian regimes. The primary examples or models of successful development under authoritarian auspices were, of course, the Asian tigers but there were other examples worth imitating as well. These included the authoritarian regime of Generalissimo Francisco Franco in Spain, which was both long-lasting *and* achieved growth rates in the 1960s of 7 to 8 percent per year; and the authoritarian regime of the generals in Brazil who, at least at the beginning of their rule (1964–1973), were scoring growth figures at least as large as Spain's. These are certainly impressive growth figures, worthy of emulation, whose methods and systems other authoritarian and would-be authoritarian regimes sought to emulate. Particularly for Latin America during the 1960s and early 1970s, a steady stream of authoritarian leaders and their finance ministers made their way to Spain to find out how Franco had done it. The "it" here refers both to his longevity in office (almost forty years) and the miracle growth rates (second in the world, for a time, only to Japan) achieved by the regime. Other Third World countries in Africa and the Middle East also had their favorite authoritarian models to imitate. So there was a "contagion effect": authoritarianism bred still more authoritarianism.

But then in the late 1970s and 1980s, the dam of authoritarianism broke. A "new wave" of democracy swept in.[1] The new wave of democracy began in Southern Europe (Greece, Portugal, then Spain itself, which had earlier been a model of authoritarianism) in the mid-1970s, then in the late 1970s and 1980s spread to Latin America, followed by several of the Asian countries (the Philippines, South Korea, Taiwan, eventually Indonesia, and others). The collapse of the Soviet Union in the 1989–1991 period enabled democracy to emerge in the Central and East European countries previously under Soviet control and, over time and at least partially, in Russia and members of the Russian Confederation of Independent States (CIS) as well. Democracy then found a foothold in Africa but in generally weak and not well-institutionalized form; in many African countries, democracy and authoritarianism alternated in power or else coexisted in an uneasy relationship. Even in the Middle East and the Islamic countries, perhaps the group least congenial to democracy, some political openings occurred—although it is difficult to classify any of these as full-fledged democracies—and fully three-quarters of the Islamic countries remained under authoritarian rule.

This chapter deals with what has now become a global transition in the Third World toward democratic rule. It begins by discussing the crises that started to affect the earlier wave of authoritarianism; then it defines democracy to make sure we are clear what we are actually discussing; next, it analyzes the transitions to democracy themselves, the still-present weaknesses and even crises of these new democratic regimes. It talks about the newer challenges to democracy as well as to U.S. policy in dealing with wobbly and often only semi-democratic regimes. Finally, we assess the future of democracy in the Third World.

THE CRISES OF
AUTHORITARIAN SYSTEMS

At the beginning of the 1970s, most of the authoritarian regimes discussed earlier looked strong, stable, and secure—maybe even permanently so if we accept the logic of much of the literature of the time. Look at Franco's Spain, the Brazilian generals, the Kuomintang in Taiwan, the South Korean military regime, the dictatorships of Marcos in the Philippines and Suharto in Indonesia, the Shah of Iran, the Somoza regime in Nicaragua, dictator Alfredo Stroessner in Paraguay, the Greek colonels, the authoritarian-corporatist regime in Portugal, Augusto Pinochet in Chile, and so on. None of these looked threatened in any serious way; all these authoritarian regimes seemed tough, efficient, and destined to last a long time. And yet within that same decade, half of these seemingly invincible regimes would be toppled and gone; during the course of the next decade, all the rest save one (Suharto) would be ousted.

What happened? Why did such seemingly strong, invincible, and long-lasting authoritarian regimes get swept aside so quickly? As usual, a number of interrelated factors were involved.

1. *Incompetence and inefficiency.*   Most of these authoritarian regimes came to power bragging that they could run their countries more efficiently than the (usually) elected, civilian-democratic regimes whom they replaced. But after a few years, in the absence of strong institutions (which is a characteristic of developing countries both democratic and authoritarian), most of these authoritarian regimes proved just as incompetent and ineffective as their predecessors.

2. *Corruption.*   The generals also promised to be honest in the administration of public funds. But again, in office the military-authoritarians were just as corrupt—or more so—than civilian politicians. Note Wiarda's law: when corruption on many business transactions in the Third World is only 5 to 7 percent, you can absorb it, write it off, and probably claim the loss as a tax-deductible business expense. But when corruption rises to a greedy 25 to 30 percent (what many dictators seek), that is beyond the profit margin of most businesses; opposition then mounts, and the regime quickly falls.

3. *Out of steam.*   Many of these authoritarian regimes lasted twenty, thirty, or even forty years. But that goes beyond the patience and even tolerance of most people who then demand a change. Remember Jefferson's dictum: governments need a radical restructuring every generation, or about every twenty to thirty years. People get tired, fed up, and want something new; that is what happened to many of these authoritarians.

4. *Aging dictators.*   Many of the same caveats apply. Suppose you came to power in your thirties, full of vim and vigor. After thirty to forty years in power (the cases of Franco, the Somozas, the Shah, Suharto, Pinochet, etc.), you're in your seventies, tired, set in your ways, and maybe sick. Sensing that the end may be near (watch the case of Fidel Castro in Cuba), the opposition and probably the general population will begin planning, even clamoring, for a change.

5. *Social change.*   If you've been in power for thirty to forty years and you've succeeded (as many of the authoritarians did) in stimulating economic growth, social—and often political—changes usually follow from that. Societies become more literate, educated, urban, long lived, and sophisticated; they begin to demand a say in political affairs. Similarly, new social groups (businessmen, labor unions, women, the middle class, farmers, indigenous or ethnic groups) emerge demanding a say in the political process—otherwise known as democracy.

Recall (from the previous chapter) that when the authoritarian regimes in South Korea and Taiwan faced rising pluralism and social change in this way, they gradually accommodated to democracy in a peaceful, evolutionary way. But most authoritarians try to resist these rising challenges through repression and greater human rights abuses, and they eventually get overthrown in violent upheavals.

6. *Resurgent opposition.*   Sensing that the end may be near, because of the rising social pressures previously described or the age and infirmity of the dictator, opposition groups, leaders, civil society associations, and political parties suppressed or dormant for a long time under authoritarianism get reactivated and reinvigorated. A hallmark of authoritarian regimes is that they suppress opposition, but as it begins to appear the old regime is on its last legs, the opposition resurfaces and begins clamoring for change.

7.   *Retreat to the barracks.*   Often a military regime, or an aging dictator, simply tires of the battle, seeks to avoid the confrontations previously indicated, and retires or retreats to the barracks. In the case of a bureaucratic-military regime, the armed forces may decide that staying in power longer than they are welcome will damage the integrity, stature, and professionalism of the military, and so they leave power peacefully. In the case of one-man dictatorships (Marcos, Suharto, Somoza, and others), the dictator may decide he's had enough, the line-up of forces is turning against him, and so he leaves office peacefully before the end, seeking a safe haven abroad where he can enjoy as much of the treasury as he can get away with.

8.   *Outside pressures.*   Most of these dictators came to power in earlier times when no one paid their internal activities close attention and they were applauded for keeping communists (and others) under control. But that was before nonstop CNN coverage, before the emergence of such human rights groups as Amnesty International and Human Rights Watch, and before the U.S. government's vigorous campaigns in favor of democracy and human rights. The collapse of the Soviet Union in 1989–1991 also removed a major reason to allow these anti-communist authoritarians to remain in power, since the communist threat was now gone. These outside pressures were undoubtedly influential in forcing some of the most notorious authoritarians (Marcos, Suharto, the Shah, Somoza, Pinochet, Duvalier in Haiti) from power.

9. *Times changed.*   This is a general explanation that includes elements from some of the others. The 1950s, 1960s, and 1970s were a time when one could still justify authoritarianism, either in the name of order and stability, anti-

communism, or the presumed need of underdeveloped countries for a strong hand. But by the 1980s, 1990s, and now, one can't make those cases anymore. Times have changed, people's consciousnesses have changed, and you can't justify authoritarianism and its accompanying abuses anymore.

So there we have it: nine reasons why in the 1970s and 1980s authoritarianism began to succumb to democracy. Authoritarian regimes that once seemed so hard and tough began to give way. Most of the authoritarian regimes gave way peacefully, moreover; few of them were overthrown in violent revolution. We are now, then, poised on the crest of the great "third wave" (earlier democracy "waves" occurred in the aftermath of World Wars I and II) of democracy.

DEMOCRACY DEFINED

In the West, and particularly in the United States, we tend to define democracy purely in institutional and procedural terms. In an early formulation, Prof. Joseph Schumpeter offered a classic definition of democracy as a system "for arriving at political decisions in which individuals acquire the power to decide by means of a competitive struggle for the people's vote."[2] Similarly, Harvard Professor Samuel P. Huntington echoes Schumpeter in his emphasis on competitive elections as *the essence* of democracy. Yale Political Scientist Robert Dahl, who has written more about democracy, at least in the United States, than just about anyone, amplifies this definition but still focuses almost exclusively on its procedural and institutional features: (1) organized contestation through regular, free, and fair elections; (2) the right of virtually all adults to vote and contest for office; and (3) freedom of the press, assembly, speech, petition, and association. In a later formulation, Prof. Dahl amplified this definition somewhat but kept its institutional focus.[3]

Most of us would not disagree very much with this definition. We all agree on the need for free, fair, and regular elections; the rule of law and constitution; separation of powers and a system of checks and balances; and basic human, civil, and political rights. Without these elementary institutional and procedural rights, democracy as we know it is not possible.

But now let us complicate the situation a little bit.

1. Many Europeans (and this sentiment is echoed in much of the Third World) believe in social and economic democracy (the welfare state) as much as in political or institutional democracy, as previously elaborated. Americans tend to believe these social and economic benefits should be decided in the policy process and through Congress, but Europe believes these (education, housing, health care, and social welfare) are fundamental *rights* every bit as important for democracy as elections or political and civil rights.

2. For a long time the Soviet Union and other communist countries (who called themselves "people's democracies") argued that political rights in the West were a hoax, and that what really counted was the people's (actually, the

state's) control of the means of production and distribution (i.e., economic democracy). We now know, of course, that was a sham, that communist regimes provide neither political nor economic democracy; but, despite the collapse of the Soviet Union and most other Marxist-Leninist regimes, that same sentiment is still heard sometimes—particularly in the underdeveloped Third World who are still hoping for a "magic formula" to leapfrog to the forefront of "advanced nations."

3. Many analysts believe that democracy is more than elections and institutions; it also involves attitudes and behavior based on tolerance, civility, respect for others, egalitarianism, equal opportunity, and a sense of social justice. This distinction between the *institutions* of democracy and the *attitudes* and *behavior* undergirding it helps explain, as we see in more detail later, the disillusionment with democracy setting in among Asia, Latin America, and elsewhere. For while many countries in these areas have the formal or legal institutions of democracy—regular elections, a constitution, separation of powers—they do not really practice democracy nor do they have democratic societies. Political scientists, therefore, distinguish between *formal democracy* (merely the institutions of democracy) and *liberal democracy* (the actual practice and attitudes of democracy).

4. Must democracy be everywhere the same? We also discuss this theme in more detail later. Here let it simply be said that the United States practices one form of democracy based on our British, Jeffersonian, Madisonian heritage; Europe practices another kind mainly based on its parliamentary practices. But when we get to the Third World we find even greater divergence: "Confucian" or state-bureaucratic forms of democracy in Asia, "organic" or "corporatist" (unified, centralized) democracy in Latin America, and Islamic forms in the Middle East. But there are many questions that need answering here: for example, when the king of Saudi Arabia goes out into the desert to consult with Bedouin tribes and leaders, is that democracy or is it still monarchy with a modern face? In other words, while we want to accept a variety of democratic forms and to suggest that democracy can vary from country to country, we will need to wrestle with the tough issue of what is truly universal in democracy and what, or how much, is culturally relative.

CASES AND PATTERNS

The earliest transitions to democracy in the modern era, or what Professor Samuel P. Huntington calls the "third wave," occurred in Southern Europe in the mid-1970s. Portugal had a revolution in the spring of 1974 that overthrew the long-time dictatorship of Antonio Salazar; a few months later the human-rights-abusing colonels in Greece were toppled, and in November 1975 Generalissimo Franco of Spain died after governing for nearly forty years. In all three of the Southern European cases, the overthrow or collapse of these authoritarian regimes was followed, although not always smoothly, by a successful transition to democracy. Southern Europe, especially the relatively smooth and peaceful Spanish case, became the model and inspiration for democratization in other areas, especially Latin America and East/Central Europe.

Latin America was the next area to democratize or re-democratize (it had been tried before, usually unsuccessfully). The transition began in Ecuador and the Dominican Republic in 1978, spread to the bigger countries of Argentina and Brazil by the early 1980s, and by the mid-to-late 1980s had enveloped nearly all of the countries. When Mexico elected an opposition candidate in 2000, it marked the culmination of that country's gradual march toward democracy. By this time, nineteen of the twenty countries (all except Cuba) are democratic. It was (and is) a quite remarkable turnaround, the most complete changeover from authoritarianism to democracy of all world areas, although at present democracy is in deep trouble in Latin America and, as we will see in more detail later on, many countries of the area seem to represent mainly *formal democracy* as distinct from genuine liberal democracy.

Next came Asian democratization in the mid-to-late 1980s. Japan is a special case, both because it is a developed country and because it has been gradually democratizing since the American occupation. The three main Asian democratizers in the 1980s were the Philippines in 1986, South Korea in 1987, and Taiwan in 1988. The Philippines is interesting, particularly as the first case, because it is the *least developed* of the countries listed and, therefore, one might have expected it to democratize later than the others. However, the dictatorship of Ferdinand Marcos was coming to an end; a widespread, democratically inclined People's Movement had sprung up; and U.S. and other international pressure was brought to bear in favor of democracy. In the South Korea and Taiwan cases, as we have seen, an emerging popular movement, mushrooming social change, and a conscious decision on the part of ruling elites that the system needed to change all helped lead during the 1980s to the demise of authoritarianism and the emergence of democracy. In 1998, with the ouster of dictator Suharto, Indonesia joined the democratic ranks, even while Malaysia and Singapore continued their quasi-authoritarian practices and China maintained its Marxist-Leninist regime.

By the time of the major changeover in Eastern/Central Europe in 1989–1991, democracy had become the only option, "the only game in town." Authoritarianism no longer had legitimacy as an option. We should say a few things about the transitions in East/Central Europe even though these countries, already mainly Western and at least semi-developed, are not the main focus of this book. First, although social and economic changes parallel to those in Latin America and Asia had been occurring in these countries, the main precipitating factor in East/Central Europe was the collapse of the Soviet Union, which freed up these countries to follow their own independent—and, as it turned out, democratic—path. Second, these countries are part of *Europe* and generally wealthier than most developing countries, although one still finds pockets of poverty there as bad as any in the Third World, and some countries—Albania, Moldovia, Georgia, and the Ukraine—are as poor as other underdeveloped countries.

Third, as one moves farther east, away from Western Europe and closer to Russia, which also corresponds to the transition from wealth to poverty and from development to underdevelopment, one finds countries—Belarus, Serbia under Milosevic, again the Ukraine, much of Central Asia, and even Russia itself—that are more akin to the Third World patterns observed here: poverty, underdevelopment, high unemployment, limited social changes, exceedingly weak civil society, and, therefore, an attraction to authoritarianism as a way to hold society together and relatively weak pressures so far for democracy. In other words, the patterns observed in the poorer countries of Eur-Asia (on the border between Europe and Asia) are not all that different from those in other developing areas.

The two areas of the globe that did not experience a large wave of democracy are the Middle East and Sub-Saharan Africa. The democratic openings and transitions to democracy that other continents and geographic or cultural areas experienced simply did not happen here. Of all the Middle Eastern countries, only one, Israel, is a full and complete democracy—and that is a special case because it is such a thoroughly Western country that happens to be located in a non-Western area. Of the remaining states, those with majority-Islamic populations (which includes fifty-two countries, some of them outside the Middle East), only a handful could be considered at least partly democratic. Of these, Turkey is the most democratic, seeking to improve its human rights situation, and trying to qualify for the European Union by improving its democracy, while also preserving its position as a bridge between East and West, Asia and Europe. Indonesia is also a budding democracy, but its political situation remains unstable and precarious. Of the others, Algeria, Tunisia, Jordan, Kuwait, Iran, and Lebanon have all had elections, have semi-independent legislatures, and may have some other *features* of democracy, but that is still not to say any of these are fully democratic either by the institutional or the political-cultural definitions offered. None of the other Middle Eastern countries, which represent 80 percent of the total, is even remotely or partially democratic.

The other big disappointment for democracy advocates has been Sub-Saharan Africa. Here, the authoritarian and bureaucratic-authoritarian regimes of the 1960s and 1970s were generally followed, not by democracy, but by renewed authoritarianism. Often there would be a brief, post-authoritarian opening that gave renewed hope for democracy, only to see that window of opportunity slammed shut again by a new military regime. Or else, authoritarianism would give way to ethnic conflict, civil war, bloody violence, looting, and lawlessness—which would pave the way for another round of authoritarianism. Not only did most of Sub-Saharan Africa not experience a sustained or consolidated transition to democracy, but it is hard in most countries to discern a clear trend *toward* democracy.

South Africa is a democratic state but it is, like Israel, an exception: a predominantly Western outpost in a mainly non-Western area. And today, under the governing African National Congress (ANC) Party, South Africa shows worrying signs—including the possibility of reverting to a one-party state—of moving away from the democratic camp. Other countries that might be considered partial democracies are Malawi, Botswana, Mali, Namibia, Nigeria, Senegal, Tanzania, and Kenya. A few other countries have briefly, often sporadically, tried democracy but without great success or long-term sustainability. However, as in the Middle East, a majority of African states, thirty-nine out of forty-eight, remain in the non-democratic category.

The end of the Cold War meant there was less reason for Western governments, primarily the United States, to support autocratic, anti-communist regimes. In addition, some African states—Nigeria, Kenya, Benin, Ivory Coast, Senegal, Tanzania, Botswana, Mauritius, Gabon, and South Africa—have experienced broader, long-term, socioeconomic change which provides a stronger base for democracy. Civil society has grown in many countries, and there is strong external as well as internal pressure for better human rights and democratization. Countering these favorable trends, however, are rising crime and violence throughout the continent, continued ethnic conflict, poverty, AIDS, and, not least, a rising Islamic presence in many countries that is not inclined toward democracy. The struggle for democracy in Africa is far from over.

Seeing the "big picture" in continental terms, we can say that much of Latin America, Asia, and East/Central Europe has become democratic in the last quarter century, while most of the Middle East and Sub-Saharan Africa has not. And even those areas that have become more-or-less democratic are often characterized by limited, partial, or incomplete democracy rather than full democracy (electoral democracy rather than liberal democracy). In the next decade, therefore, it will be interesting to see (1) if these partial democracies now become full democracies; (2) if the presently non-democratic areas begin to move definitively toward democracy; or (3) if, alternatively, we see a reversion to authoritarian rule. The key test cases would seem to be China, the Middle Eastern and Islamic countries, and Sub-Saharan Africa.

CAUSES OF THE DEMOCRATIC TRANSITIONS

While democracy has been established in some areas (Latin America, Asia, East/Central Europe) and is *beginning* to be felt in others (China, the Middle East, Sub-Saharan Africa), it is also important to discern the motivations and causes of these new democratic waves. Is this just a temporary trend liable to be reversed in the future or is it permanent, growing, and consolidated? By examining the causes and forces pushing for democratization, we can perhaps predict just how lasting it is likely to be and whether it is long term or only temporary.

Socioeconomic Change

In most developing nations, economic development and industrialization tend to give rise to new social forces that challenge older forms of tradition and feudalism. That is, in fact, what has been happening, often quietly and undramatically, in many developing countries over the last forty years. These include new business groups oriented toward globalization and the outside world; a new, urban middle class that is neither of the older peasant or elite classes; urban trade unions that can no longer be treated as serfs; farmer groups no longer content with traditional servitude; aroused ethnic or indigenous groups; new social movements of women and others; and civil society organizations that include human rights agencies, community groups, religious associations, and others. Eventually these groups began to demand changes in traditional structures and a voice in decisions that affect them most intimately. These rising demands can lead, as we have seen, to repression and authoritarianism in the short run but, as they become stronger, to democratization in the long run.

This is largely the pattern followed in Asia, Latin America, and East/Central Europe: rising social change, at first met with repression, later as these groups grew larger and stronger evolving toward democracy. For social change tends to give rise to greater pluralism and, with it, the *necessity* for a more complex, responsive, and adaptable political system which only democracy seems capable of providing. Both authoritarianism and Marxism-Leninism, by providing internal peace (albeit enforced), order, stability, discipline, and a strong state, are possible and perhaps even useful in the early stages of a Third World nation's development; however, the very development that they help generate gives rise to a pluralism that eventually undermines these regimes and stimulates the demand for democracy. In other words, democracy eventually comes to Third World nations both as an ideological preference and, perhaps more importantly, as a pragmatic, more effective response to the demands of modernization. But if this was a pragmatic choice rather than implying a heartfelt commitment to democracy, does that mean that other "pragmatic circumstances" in the future might call for an abandonment of democracy and renewed authoritarianism?

The Discrediting of Other Alternatives

By the end of the 1980s, which was the high point of the third wave of democratization, democracy's main alternatives had been completely discredited. Authoritarianism, which in earlier decades had seemed promising as a means to achieve development, had in most countries proved to be corrupt, inefficient, ineffective, and no more capable of achieving development than the civilian regimes whom the authoritarians had replaced. A similar pattern occurred with Marxism-Leninism: it had in the cases of the Soviet Union, China, and Eastern Europe seemed to provide the authority and discipline necessary to mobilize and regiment populations in order to achieve industrialization, but by the

1970s and 1980s the Marxist-Leninist alternative had largely run its course. It was proven corrupt and ineffective, was no longer capable of achieving economic growth—its main claim to legitimacy—to say nothing of its dismal human rights record and the stultifying effects it had on the spirits of those forced to live under its yoke.

The discrediting of its major alternatives, both authoritarianism and Marxism-Leninism, left democracy as the only solution. It is in this sense and in this context that Francis Fukuyama penned his famous essay on "The End of History"—not that all history had literally ended but that, in the great struggle of ideas between democracy, authoritarianism, and Marxism since the nineteenth century, the competition among these three great ideas and systems of rule had ended; democracy seemed definitely to have won out.[4] Or, so it seemed a decade or so ago.

End of the Cold War

During the period of the Cold War it had often been U.S. policy to support authoritarian regimes. This was certainly the case in South Korea, the Philippines, Indonesia, Iran, Egypt, the Congo, South Africa, Brazil, Mexico, Chile, Nicaragua, El Salvador, Guatemala, and numerous other regimes. It was not that the United States was enamored of authoritarianism; in most cases, the United States preferred democratic governments as long as they were effective and stable. But it is often the *very nature* of democracy, especially in the Third World where institutions are weak, *not* to be effective and stable but instead to be tumultuous, disorganized, chaotic, and divisive.

Authoritarianism, particularly of the long-term (thirty to forty years) kind that we analyzed in the previous chapter, seemed to solve all these problems of disorder and instability—conditions that seemed to favor communist and far-left groups. Plus, the authoritarians often were more vigorously anti-communist, which was *the main* U.S. preoccupation during the Cold War, than were their democratic counterparts, who as good democrats often stood for toleration even for communists. So given the choice between a stable authoritarian who often abused human rights but kept the communists in check, and a wobbly, unstable democrat who allowed freedom even for communists, the United States almost always opted for the "lesser evil" of the stable authoritarian.[5]

But this logic, whether one supports it or not, made no sense once the Soviet Union collapsed and the Cold War ended. One may still be (most of us are) opposed to communist or Marxist-Leninist regimes on political and/or ideological grounds, but at this stage—and this is the main issue in U.S. foreign policy—the *threat* is gone. With the Soviet Union now disintegrated, its once-large empire of satellite states and retainers gone (now, as in East/Central Europe, moving mainly toward democracy), and the threat of thirty thousand Soviet missiles raining down greatly reduced, who cares if there are still a few communists and communist groups active in the Third World?

Actually, we *do* care and we would prefer not to see communist regimes in very many Third World countries (for their sakes as much as for ours), but the truth is most of the communist groups still left are small, the guerrilla movements of previous decades have largely dried up, and many of them have reorganized as political parties and joined the *democratic* political process. But few of these groups any longer constitute a threat or a clear and present danger to the United States. The result, in the absence of a serious communist threat, is that the United States now much prefers democratic regimes as guarantors of long-term stability and good government in the Third World and no longer authoritarianism. We will have to wait and see, but surely think about, whether the war or terrorism and *that new threat* forces the United States to again accommodate to authoritarian regimes as the best guarantee of keeping the terrorists in check, just as they were once seen as the best safeguard against communism. The authoritarian regimes of General Musharraf in Pakistan or of Hosni Mubarek in Egypt suggest that, at least in some countries, the earlier logic for authoritarianism—effectively keeping the enemy in check—may apply again.

Globalization

Globalization helps the spread of democracy in a variety of ways. First, through globalized communications channels (radio, television, VCRs, movies, travel, the Internet) more and more people come to want the freedom, liberties, and rights now available through democracy. Second, globalization in the form of modern jet travel increases the possibilities for more people to see the outside world, see the benefits of democracy, and carry these ideas back to their home countries. Third, globalization tends to increase both social and economic development, as well as social mobility, modernization, and pluralism, all of which are advantageous if not prerequisites for democracy. Fourth, democracy is now in vogue, "stylish," what people want on a global basis, and certainly to be preferred to its authoritarian and Marxist-Leninist alternatives; globalization has been the agent of this transformation. Fifth, it is clear (see earlier discussion) that the United States and its allies now prefer a democratic regime that protects human rights; globalization has been the means by which this preference has been and is conveyed.

The sixth reason is a bit more complicated. It is not just that the United States and the international community, including now such international lending agencies as the World Bank and the International Monetary Fund, prefer democracy; so do business groups, the middle class, and government officials in the Third World itself. Linked to the outside world through such globalizing forces as trade, commerce, the need for foreign investment, and international loans, these groups see clearly that, unless their own governments practice honesty and transparency in the handling of public accounts, protect human rights, provide effective programs and opportunities for their people, and practice democracy, all this trade, investment, and these loans will be cut off. Under globalization, everyone understands perfectly well that, if a country is in violation of the norms previously listed, capital and investment can flee literally overnight to the two-hundred-odd other countries and political entities in the world, with disastrous consequences for the country abandoned. So these *domestic* groups in the developing nations themselves put enormous pressures on their own governments, which might otherwise be tempted to go the authoritarian route, not to abandon democracy, transparency, and human rights because otherwise their "water" in the form of loans and trade will be quickly cut off.

Military Retreat to the Barracks

The same set of reasons that forced the armed forces in many of the Third World authoritarian regimes out of power a decade or two ago are, so far, keeping them out of power today. The military was generally discredited by its corruption and inefficiency while in office, its human rights record was atrocious, and it often failed to deliver on economic development. The professionalism of the military was often damaged and, rather than accept any more discredit, many of these proud armies retreated to the barracks with their tails between their legs. As we saw earlier, almost none of these authoritarian regimes were actually defeated and *ousted* by rising popular movements; rather, they retreated in the face of rising humiliation.

As we will see in more detail in the next chapter, there is growing sentiment in much of the Third World for "strong government," but few people actually want the military with its repression and brutality back in power. Nor is the military itself eager to step back into power in most countries, knowing that it will be despised for doing so, that it cannot effectively manage the political and economic complexity of a modern state (most of these Third World countries are considerably more developed now than they were twenty years ago when the military was last in power), that the armed forces by themselves cannot *solve* national problems, and that they will be thoroughly criticized and *even more* discredited if they make a move for power. Plus, at the international level, all aid will be cut off; investment will dry up; and tough sanctions will be imposed, as occurred recently in Ecuador and Paraguay when the armed forces attempted a coup. And, in the present dismal economic situation of most Third World countries, why would the armed forces *want* to take over such a mess, which they cannot resolve and would result in even greater discrediting being showered on their heads? Who wants or needs that? Certainly not the military. In other words, there are few incentives at present for an authoritarian military regime to re-take power, and lots of bad things will happen if they do.

Elite Leadership

It is striking that, in almost all of the cases here mentioned of transitions from authoritarian to democratic rule, the initiative for such changes came from the elites and not so much from the masses. The push for democratization came mainly from the top, not from the bottom. It is true that in many of these cases there were people's movements, civil society groups, popular movements, and pressures from labor unions, farm groups, and other mass organizations; and it is also true that the elites who initiated the transitions were responding to the rising social changes which they observed globally and in their own countries.

Nevertheless, it is still the elites—businessmen, government officials, bankers, and the *bourgeoise*—that, pragmatically, initiated and led the changes that brought about democratization.

This seems counter-intuitive in some ways, for we usually think of elites as standing in the way of change and the lower classes as advocating it. But remember these are pragmatic elites who want to retain their power; they are practitioners of the old French adage that, in order to remain the same, things have to change. In this case, it was the elites that saw the end of authoritarianism coming, recognized that democracy was the wave of the future, and reasoned that it was better if *they* led the change rather than somebody else. In other words, from the elites' point of view, rather than being overwhelmed from below by the forces for democratization, it would be much better if *they* controlled the process, requiring some compromises on their part but understanding compromise was better than losing everything in a general conflagration.

Of course, it is always possible under democracy that the elites will lose their power (poor people tend to have more votes than rich people), and in the long run that is still possible. But in the short run it is striking in how many countries the elites (remember, here we are not talking just of rich people but also of elites in government, universities, armed forces, bureaucracy, etc.) are still in power even *after* democratization. The list includes the Philippines, Indonesia, South Korea, Taiwan, Brazil, Chile, Mexico, and Argentina—virtually all the Third World countries who have made the transition to democracy. In *all* of them the elites determined it was far better to accommodate to change rather than be overwhelmed by it, to *lead* the democratization process instead of being voted out of office by it. But if the elites were that pragmatic and calculating about democracy, it raises questions about their moral commitment to it and if in the future they might not, equally pragmatically, abandon it for some other easy solution. These are themes to which we return in the conclusion.

PROBLEMS OF DEMOCRACY
IN DEVELOPING NATIONS

A decade ago people were very optimistic about democracy and its prospects in the Third World. A large number of authoritarian regimes had given way to democracy; democracy was on the march; it was "the wave of the future." Scholars waxed eloquent about its possibilities, and policymakers made it the keystone of their policy.

But since then, hopes for democracy have gone into decline. Democracy in much of the Third World is not working very well. It is losing popularity. It is not delivering on its promises. In quite a number of countries, democracy has been overthrown or is in bad trouble. Public sentiment in favor of authoritarianism is again on the rise. Policymakers continue publicly to express confidence in it but privately they worry that the foundation of their policy is being undermined. What has happened? What has gone wrong?

Declining Public Support

Support for democracy is in sharp decline in just about every country that undertook a democratic transition in the last two decades. In the early 1990s, support for democracy as a *system* of government (not the more volatile issue of whether one approves of the way the current president is doing his job or not) was in the 85, 90, or even 95 percent range—about as high as one can get. In part this reflected the early euphoria of recent changes and the fact democracy had just been established and was still seen in a hopeful light. But now disillusionment has set in. Support for democracy has fallen to 60 to 65 percent in the majority of recent democracies, to under 50 percent in quite a number of them, and to below 40 percent in a few. It is safe to say, when support for the democratic system falls to below 50 percent, democracy is in deep trouble. Ecuador and Paraguay are in that category, and it is not coincidental that they have recently had coups or coup attempts, but big, important Brazil is also in the below-50-percent category.

While this declining support for democracy is worrisome, what may be equally troubling is the even more precipitous drop in support for what most political scientists think of as democracy's essential institutions. These include congresses or parliaments, political parties, labor unions, and other fundamental institutions of pluralist democracy. In most developing countries, support for these agencies is in the 10 to 20 percent range, and even lower in some cases. Plainly, people have little confidence in democracy's essential institutional structures. But can you have viable, functioning democracy without these institutions? Probably not. Significantly, these same public opinion surveys often show the support for the military institution to be higher than that for any other institution, at about 40 percent. That means that *no* institution has the support of the majority of the population—a worrisome sign for democracy—and that, of all institutions, the armed forces have the most popularity and legitimacy—another worrisome development if one favors democracy.

While support for democracy and its institutions is in decline, support for "strong government" is on the rise, coming close to 50 percent in many countries. Does "strong government" mean authoritarianism? And does that signal a new round, a "new wave," of authoritarian governments in the future? Actually, we think not necessarily, but the issue requires close examination.

First, much of the recent disillusionment with democracy stems from the fact that democratic institutions in Latin America, Asia, and Africa are not performing well. Corruption, special favoritism, cronyism, and patronage are widespread, detracting from the ability of democratic institutions to perform their main functions. A related point is that democracy has not been able to deliver social and economic reform and improvement as fast as people had expected. One can make the case that democracy is purely a *political system* of governance that has nothing to do with socioeconomic betterment, but that is a hard argument to justify to people in the poorest nations clamoring for better living conditions.

Third, despite the discouraging poll results, very few people in the developing countries want to return to the bad, old days of military dictatorship.

That means repression, brutality, absence of human and political rights, international ostracism, and sanctions leading to even worse conditions, and lack of freedoms of speech, press, assembly, and association. In other words, democracy may not always look good but, as compared with its alternatives, to most people it still represents the best option.

Finally and related to all of the above, the polls that seem to show a growing preference for "strong government" may be misleading. Probing deeper than a mere expression of preference indicates that what people in the developing world really want is effective government, not just "strong" or authoritarian government. That means a government that is honest and forthright, helps the poor, and delivers on its promises. In other words, a government must not just be democratically elected and constitutional but also *effective* in the delivery of public programs that actually help people.

All this is encouraging for democracy. Nevertheless, it *is* clear that (1) support for democracy is down, sometimes precipitously, in many developing countries; (2) democracy is not effectively delivering goods and services; (3) democracy is in deep trouble in many developing countries; and (4) there is some, probably growing but not yet majority, support for an authoritarian resolution to these problems.

Democracy Oversold?

Has democracy been overhyped and oversold? Is it a cure-all for all problems? Is it appropriate in all countries?

During the Cold War, 1945–1990, the United States and most of its allies were not much concerned with whether a country was democratic or not. Democracy was nice to have but it was a luxury. The main and overriding consideration during this period was whether a country was anti-communist.

But during the 1980s sentiment began to grow that democracy was not only morally good but that a decent democratic regime was the best way to solve internal or domestic problems and to serve U.S. foreign policy goals. After all, democracies tend not to go to war with each other, are best equipped to solve problems of rising pluralism, do not usually violate their citizens' human rights, and are better at providing honest, responsible government. These advantages are hard for policymakers to resist. Then, when the Cold War ended, the last remaining defenses for authoritarianism—stability and anti-communism—ended. At this point the earlier pragmatic reasons for favoring democracy gave way to official orthodoxy: history had "ended" and democracy was seen as "the only game in town." The rhetoric in support of democracy is now overwhelming, bipartisan, and nearly universal: how could any politician, or for that matter any American, be against democracy?

Two immediate problems arise. The first is that democracy usually requires a minimum social, economic, and institutional base. Democracy does not flourish or even have much of a chance in countries with low literacy rates, low educational levels, underdeveloped economies, and few associations or institutions (civil society, political parties, and honest and effective bureaucracies). Earlier this was put in terms of "prerequisites": unless a country had a certain level of social modernization, economic development, and institutionalization, its chances of establishing democracy were virtually nonexistent. Today we seldom talk of prerequisites for democracy any more, but it nevertheless remains true that countries at the lowest levels of socioeconomic and political development have almost no chance of establishing stable democracy. The base simply isn't there. Indeed, some scholars go even further and say countries with a per-capita income below $500 have almost no chance of becoming democracies, while countries in the $500–$2,000 range have possibilities but will likely still be unstable.

Only when a country reaches a per-capita-income figure of $3,000–$4,000 does it have strong possibilities for stable, democratic development. In short, as we argued earlier, there is a strong correlation between socioeconomic development and democracy, with middle-income to high-income countries having a *much* better chance of establishing *and consolidating* democracy than poorer countries. We should not, therefore, give up on democracy in poor countries but only recognize limits on what we can do to assist it and be realistic in our expectations. Such poor countries as Haiti, Somalia, Ethiopia, Uganda, Albania, East Timor, and Afghanistan are all testimonies to the difficulties, even impossibility, of establishing democracy in the world's poorest countries.

The second problem is cultural: some nations and some cultural areas are more amenable to democracy than others. Democracy, we have seen, was originally a Western construct. The question is: Is democracy universal and can it be constructed in countries that do not have the same history and culture as the West, without the Renaissance, the Enlightenment, the Industrial Revolution, and so on? The answer is: Yes, but with some difficulty.

Since World War II democracy has been established in Asia, but it often takes Confucian, statist, and paternalistic forms. Democracy in Latin America has a long but often frustrated history and, reflecting Latin America's culture, it tends to be more centralized, organic, and corporatist than in the United States. Both the Koran and the Shariah (Islamic law) tend to justify authoritarian rule, and it is no accident, therefore, that there is not a single, full democracy in the Islamic world. Realistically, recognizing this, when the George W. Bush administration proposed a democracy initiative for the Arab world as part of its war against terrorism (remember, democracies do not go to war against each other), it was careful not to exaggerate its possibilities and to propose only modest, pre-democracy programs such as working for a freer press, strengthening local government, and encouraging greater citizen involvement.[6] Finally, in Sub-Saharan Africa, because of colonialism, the artificiality of borders drawn by the colonial powers, the difficulties of new nationhood, the low socioeconomic levels, and the weakness of institutions, democracy has often been seen as a forlorn dream and no American administration has been willing to put much money, time, or resources into trying to build it.

There is a tendency, especially in America, to see democracy as the answer to all problems. Since the Cold War, the advancement of democracy has gained even more prominence in American policy, to the point of becoming an orthodoxy. Of course, we should try to encourage and build democracy where we can, but we also need to be realistic: successful democracy depends heavily on (1) levels of socioeconomic and institutional development and (2) cultural forces that lead to distinct kinds of political systems, not all of which are democratic.

Weak Institutions

Democracy does not spring up full-blown overnight. It requires long years, decades, even several generations of culture change and development of political institutions. Look at the United States: when it became independent in 1776, the thirteen colonies already had a century-and-a-half of gradually building democratic institutions and practices at the local, state, and regional levels that finally culminated in the federal constitution of 1789. Western Europe's experience of democratization was similarly slow and incremental. We should, therefore, expect the new and developing nations to also require considerable time to build the institutions of democracy; there is no easy way to shortcut the process.

The problem for almost all developing nations is not just that they have low levels of socioeconomic development but also weak institutions—especially those institutions that are supportive of democracy. Legislatures are weak and do not often serve as effective checks on excessive presidential authority. Courts and court systems are weak and often lack independence from police, military, or presidential power. Local government is weak and lacks independent taxing and policymaking authority. Public bureaucracy is often unprofessional and is dominated by patronage, cronyism, and corruption. Both presidential and legislative staffs are often weak, untrained, and inexperienced.

Society is often not pluralistic but dominated by narrow elite groups of government bureaucrats, religious leaders, military officers, and businessmen. Labor, peasant, indigenous, and women's groups are usually small and poorly organized. Political parties are weak and, as we previously saw, woefully unpopular. Civil society, interest groups, and associational life are frequently inchoate, poorly organized, and unable to make their members' voices heard. At all levels of society—and this is a hallmark of underdevelopment—disorganization and weakness of institutions prevail. It is not just that major groups lack input into the political system; it is also that often weak governments lack an institutional means to carry out policies at the local level in ways that have a positive effect on the grassroots population. So even if a well-meaning democratic government comes to power, it is often unable to make its writ heard or to implement programs effectively for the people most in need. Recall our discussion of the declining public support for democracy and the corresponding support for "strong" or "effective" government. But if the country lacks institutional infrastructure at all levels, no government, no matter if it is democratic, can be effective in carrying out public policy.

Economic and Social Problems

Underdevelopment is characterized by a series of vicious circles. Low social, economic, and institutional development serves as a hindrance to a country achieving democracy. But in the absence of a well-functioning democracy, it is often difficult, if not impossible, to carry out programs of social and economic development.

The problems, as would be expected, are acutest for the poorest of the poor countries. We tend to think, therefore, that once a country makes a breakthrough, either to democracy or to some minimum economic floor (perhaps our $2,000–$3,000 per person per year income), its problems are over. But development is an ongoing process; there are *always*—even in highly developed countries—residual problems or hangovers from the past and new challenges for the future. In most developing countries illiteracy remains high, and that is an ongoing problem. Health care is limited and life expectancy is low, and those features retard development. Poverty remains widespread; diseases like AIDS may ravage the population; and whole areas of the country (usually rural) and often the *majority* of the population remain locked in poverty even while the urban, modernizing sectors begin to change. What wealth exists is often terribly unevenly distributed between the rich and poor—although there are intriguing differences that are difficult to explain. Among the world's major geographic/cultural areas, Latin America has the world's worst distribution of income, while Asia has the most equitable distribution. There is no doubt that Latin America's unequal income distribution holds back development by excluding (varying by country) upwards of 50, 60, 70, and even 80 percent of the population from effective, full participation in the national social, economic, and political life.

Having closely watched developing countries over a 30–40-year period, many scholars find it useful to distinguish between a whole, widespread "culture of poverty" and the fact of remaining "pockets of poverty." A culture of poverty may be defined as a situation in which underdevelopment is widespread, illiteracy is high (over 50 percent), and poverty affects 70–90 percent of the population. That is *real* poverty and underdevelopment.

In contrast, quite a number of countries (South Korea, Taiwan, Chile, and Mexico) have over several decades made a concerted developmental drive and have succeeded in reducing poverty to 30–40 percent of the population. In other words, a culture of poverty affecting the vast majority of the population has given way to a far better situation in which most people are "making it" into the modern, developed world even while some are still left behind in their pockets of poverty. Those pockets of poverty still need to be dealt with and alleviated, but having only pockets of poverty (even though still large compared to developed countries) is far better than having a society-wide culture of poverty. Pockets of poverty can be dealt with, but cultures of poverty tend to look hopeless. When a country passes from a widespread culture of poverty to a situation of only having pockets of poverty, it can be said to have made it into the modern world.

Corruption, Crime, Lawlessness, and Narcotrafficking

Many of the developing nations are afflicted by widespread corruption, crime, lawlessness, and narcotrafficking. These activities siphon off sorely needed funds that could otherwise be used for development, lead to a disrespect for the law and government institutions, undermine public confidence and give rise to widespread fear and distrust, and scare off both foreign and domestic invest-ment without which no country can raise its standard of living, to say nothing of the losses of life and property.

The problem is that this is not just petty crime and corruption, which is prob-ably characteristic of most societies and cultures. Rather, it involves large-scale crime and corruption on a massive scale, which pervades all areas of life. In some developing countries the murder and crime rates are *many times* those of the worst American cities; corruption reaches into *all* government transactions, and narco-trafficking has been elevated to being the number one national export.

It is probably impossible to wipe out corruption entirely in any country, but with proper controls, transparency, safeguards, and laws of public disclosure it can probably be kept within a manageable range. But when corruption reaches substantially higher levels on every business transaction or government func-tion, the country cannot function: government grinds to a halt, investment dries up, business cannot operate because that is precisely their profit margin, and international lending agencies refuse to advance more funds. Some coun-tries are known as kleptocracies (literally, states dominated by thievery) because corruption may reach 90 percent on all transactions and because the *sole reason* for seeking political office is to rob the national treasury and use public posi-tions for private gain.

We need to make some distinctions here. It is likely that most of us are against all forms of corruption, but we also need to be realistic. A country in which cor-ruption is only a modest 5 to 7 percent can, as indicated, probably continue to function; countries where it reaches 35 to 40 percent are usually in bad trouble; kleptocracies at 90 percent (or more!) are hopeless. We also need to distinguish between patronage (a favor for a favor) and outright corruption or bribery. Most states and most governments in the world (including Arkansas, Louisiana, Chicago, or Washington, D.C.!) could not function without some reasonable, limited degree of patronage (rewarding of friends and supporters, jobs given in return for votes delivered, modest fees paid in return for services rendered); the problem emerges when patronage becomes the virtually sole reason for seeking public office or when entire government agencies are dominated by patronage considerations instead of providing services that truly serve the public.

Foreign aid donors (and the rest of us) will probably have to live with and learn to accept a modest amount of corruption and patronage. As the Brazilians put it, such "grease" (or *suborno, bakshish, coima, mordida,* or *pot-de-vin*—depending on the country you're in) is what makes the world go around and makes the often-creaking machinery of government function. The problem is how to prevent this from growing into larger-scale or society-wide corruption and kleptocracy.

Among development specialists, one way to do this is to put special em-phasis on the rule of law. For unless donors and investors, to say nothing of the general public, have some confidence that contracts will be honored, property will not be stolen, profits can be remitted, and courts and police will function more or less honestly, they will not get involved and the country will be writ-ten off as hopeless.

Another strategy is to insist on the privatization of large-scale government enterprises. For over the years development specialists have learned that, for the most part, because of the incentives involved, privately held companies tend to run more honestly and efficiently than large public corporations. Equally important is the obvious fact that, if you simply reduce government size, you also reduce the opportunities for corruption. The logic is: if you reduce the public sector opportunities for graft, you thereby reduce the graft. We should understand, therefore, that the emphasis recently by development specialists on privatization is not always primarily motivated by an ideological commitment to private sector capitalism but by a growing realization that (1) the private sector functions generally more efficiently and honestly than the public sector, and (2) reducing public-sector size also reduces government corruption.

A few words should be said about the issues of lawlessness and narcotrafficking. Crime and violence in most developing countries are mushrooming, reaching unprecedented proportions. Most of the crime is not directed primarily against foreigners, their investments, or government agencies; rather, the primary victims are the individual citizens of these countries. This is something new, a product of the last twenty years, because many traditional societies in the past, particularly under strict authoritarian rule, were among the safest, most law-abiding places on earth. Violent television, the movies, the ready availability of guns and drugs, the breakdown of historic norms of morality, desperation on the part of poor people, and simple greed and *machismo* have all fueled the rising crime and violence rates.

Crime, including violent crime (rape, armed robbery, murder, and kidnapping), is so pervasive and widespread in some countries that people are afraid to leave their homes, go about with armed bodyguards, buy expensive armored vehicles, and wall their neighborhoods off with security fences, dogs, and armed guards. Crime in these countries often reaches levels *many times* those of the worst U.S. neighborhoods, and has become increasingly vicious, mindless, and random. It goes without saying that such soaring crime rates are inimical to development, frightening away investment as well as the middle class (the "brain drain") in many developing countries. Rising crime is particularly prevalent as a development-retarding issue in Sub-Saharan Africa, Latin America, and Southeast Asia, but much less so in East Asia (the Confucian ethic?) and the Moslem countries (strict Islamic law?).

Narcotrafficking is also a major problem, closely linked to the rising crime rate, in many countries. In some countries (Colombia, Peru, Afghanistan, and Bolivia) drugs are the major export product; the drug barons that do the exporting from large gangs that intimidate judges, bribe and kill government officials, take over whole areas of the country, and destroy through violence and intimidation the fabric of society. Many are so powerful that they live like kings, above the law, even while maintaining local popularity by paying generous salaries and functioning like patronage politicians through sponsorship of churches, health clinics, and soccer teams.

But it is not just the poor producer countries that are victimized by the narcos; such countries as Haiti, the Dominican Republic, Mexico, and Central

America serve as transshipment points for drugs entering the United States from Asia, the Middle East, and South America; and there the corrupting influence of the drug trade is similarly corrosive. Meanwhile, the declared "war on drugs" is not succeeding and probably will not succeed until consumption habits in Western Europe and the United States change. And, while the drug trade is certainly corrupting and ruinous in long-range terms, short-term drug production undoubtedly has added to the producing countries' gross national product and to the income of their farmers.

Economic and Social Problems

The economic and social problems of the developing nations, and the vicious circles of underdevelopment, are often so overwhelming that they seem impossible of solution. Can you really have democracy when the literacy rate is under 40 percent of the population? How can you stimulate development in this high-tech age when most of the people have only a third-grade education—if that? How can people work hard and achieve a better life when the *majority* of the population is afflicted with debilitating disease that drains your energy and life expectancy is only in the forties? Where is the money for development to come from if foreign aid dries up; there is precious little foreign investment; and local capital, not trusting its own government officials—usually with good reason—sends its money to anonymous private accounts in New York, Switzerland, or Miami? In conditions of poor education, where are the agronomists, engineers, teachers, and technicians of all sorts who are absolutely necessary for development going to come from? How can you achieve development when the government is massively dishonest, fails to honor contracts, fills the public service with incompetent friends and cronies, and steals everything in sight?

We raise these questions both to show the difficulties of development and to reemphasize how all the issues are interrelated. You cannot achieve much more than formal democracy without a great deal (several generations' worth) of social change. You cannot have much social change unless you first have *massive* economic development and urbanization. It is highly unlikely that you'll achieve much economic growth unless you have a government that is honest and effective. But you're unlikely to have an honest, decent government unless you have real social change and pluralism, which in turn are dependent on prior economic growth.

And undergirding all of the social, economic, and political change is culture, value, psychological, and even religious change (i.e., the shift from a predominantly passive, accepting, fatalistic culture to a dynamic, more aggressive, more risk-taking, and entrepreneurial one). If one is conditioned to believe that only one's god or gods, fate, luck, chance, or maybe the lottery will help you get ahead, then little is likely to happen. But if one comes to believe that one's own initiatives, self-help, and pulling oneself up by the bootstraps are what help you get ahead, then good things are likely to happen. But how should you engender these principles in traditional, hide-bound societies, with limited educational opportunities? How do you break out of these vicious circles of underdevelopment? Where do you concentrate first? On social change? How do you do that? On economic development? Ditto? On achieving a decent, democratic government? Can that be engineered from the outside (as the United States has tried to do, with little success, in Haiti, Bosnia, and Afghanistan) or must it come from within? On changing the culture? Who knows how to do that? And, especially, changing the culture without ruining the country or countries we may seek to change.

The answer to all of these questions is: you need to do all of these things at once, and in a context of limited resources and never enough money. It is a dauntingly difficult task and requires many long years *and decades* of effort. Almost no one knows how to do it. In the United States we talk enthusiastically of "nation-building"—a happy, optimistic phrase but one that almost no one knows how to accomplish, certainly not the U.S. Defense Department or the State Department, or the U.S. Agency for International Development (AID), or the United Nations—although all of these may contribute.

Development and democratization are exceedingly difficult tasks. They will not be accomplished by resorting to easy, antiseptic words like *nation-building*. The whole process is much more complex than that. For more guidance, read on.

Traditional Attitudes

One of the assumptions of development theory is that once the change process begins, everything changes at once: socioeconomic modernization, political institutions (presumably toward democracy), and political attitudes and political culture. For some countries and people, this is undoubtedly true; but what is also becoming increasingly apparent is the lags that occur, the uneven and disjointed nature of the process, and the coexistence of both traditional and modern ideas in the same country or, indeed, the same person.

In much of the literature on developing nations, the assumption is that traditional attitudes will disappear and become modernized under the impact of development. Such "traditional" attitudes include loyalty to clan and tribe, loyalty to locality or region versus loyalty to the modern nation-state, and an emphasis on personal and patronage relations as compared to impersonal and institutional loyalties—the persistence of traditional ways of doing things. All these traditional behaviors are supposed to be confined to the dustbins of history once modernization begins. The assumptions are: once personalism and patronage disappear, corruption will no longer be widespread; or once tribalism, caste associations, patronage and clientelistic networks, and so on, fade, then loyalty will instead go to such presumably "modern" institutions as political parties, interest groups, and governments.

But it has not quite worked out that way. First, traditional attitudes and behavior remain very strong in most developing countries. Second, they persist even in the face of widespread modernization. Third, there seems to be no universal or inevitable evolution from traditional attitudes to more modern ones. Instead, fourth, most people balance both traditional and modern attitudes, in infinitely complex ways, even within their own persons. As a result, fifth, political institutions are similarly infused with both traditional and modern features at the same time, exhibiting complex, often confusing overlaps and fusions rather than a one-way, inevitable gravitation from the one to the other.

Traditional attitudes prevent and hold back democratization, it is often argued. But at the same time they enable people to maintain what they consider valuable from the past and worth preserving. And they enable people to filter out those aspects of Western modernization that they consider ill-fitting in their societies or inappropriate in their circumstances. Moreover, it is through such blends and fusions of traditional and modern that real change occurs, not through the wholesale abandonment of one set of attitudes and the complete acceptance of another.

Take the case of Japan, clearly one of the most interesting—and most modern—countries in the world. Part of Japan's genius is its ability to take what is valuable from the West, blend it with its own values and institutions, and produce a product *even better* than does the West, while simultaneously retaining its own national identity and ways of doing things. Other countries with strong indigenous cultures—China, India, Iran, Brazil, Egypt, and Nigeria—will seek to do the same: adapting to modernization (and Westernization!) while at the same time preserving what is deemed valuable in their own culture and tradition.

This is a quite different—and in my mind healthier—model and way of thinking than the one that sees all countries marching lockstep, universally, and inevitably toward some preconceived endpoint that looks remarkably like the Western countries. But what of those smaller, weaker countries whose cultures are insufficiently strong to filter out those Western ways they find unacceptable, nor capable themselves of serving as a base for home-grown modernization? Unfortunately and unhappily, they are liable to be swallowed up in the development process, destabilized by modernization but unable either to adopt Western ways entirely or successfully *or* to preserve traditional ways as providing a measure of stability once modernization begins. But even in these cases, local ways of doing things remain powerful.

Distinct Meanings of Democracy

Democracy means different things to different people, and it also occupies a different level of priority in different societies and cultures. In Iran *democracy* has come to mean "the rule of law," but that means Islamic law, government by the religious *mullahs,* exclusion of women, and widespread human rights violations; few of us would think of that as our definition of democracy. In Cuba *democracy* means absolute rule, without elections, by one man—Fidel Castro—who presumes to know and reflect the "general will"; but despite Cuba's accomplishments in the education and health fields, we cannot call it a democracy. In much of the developing world elections are the main criterion of democracy, but often elections are rigged or controlled and, as we have already seen, the mere holding of elections is insufficient to qualify a country as a democracy. Uruguayans often define democracy in terms of receiving the social and economic benefits of a welfare state, while Brazilians have in mind as their definition the idea of mutual favors, or patronage. None of these seems adequate as a proper understanding of democracy.

Let us go back to the basics—and to the discussion offered earlier. First, free, regular, competitive elections are absolutely essential if we are to call a country democratic. Second, a democratic country requires freedom of the press, speech, assembly, petition, and association. Third (and this is a political-cultural feature), a country should have a considerable degree of mutual trust, respect, tolerance, equity in the distribution of resources, and egalitarianism in its assumptions about society. Fourth (and these are crucial institutional variables), a country to be considered democratic should have the rule of law and some kind of institutional checks and balances to limit the possibilities of absolute power—although we can be flexible about what precise form that should take.

Here is the dilemma. In many official policy circles, as well as among American think tanks and U.S. foreign assistance groups, the notion is widespread that, to be democratic, a country must look just like we do, with the U.S.-style, three-part division of powers, strict separation of church and state, the military completely subordinated to civilian authority, strong and independent local government, and so on. But for most developing nations, these standards are impossible to achieve, or else their cultures are so different from our own that their countries cannot possibly function on that basis. At the opposite extreme is the idea of cultural relativism: that there are *no* standards; that every country can call itself a "democracy" if it wishes; and that we must accept the idea of a separate Asian, African, Islamic, and Latin American definition of democracy but with no common criteria. But this formulation is similarly unacceptable since it implies democracy is a meaningless term, that everyone can do their own thing and still call it democracy, and it gives rise to the phenomenon of strange and unfamiliar conceptions of democracy. What is needed, therefore, is a continued focus on the essentials (elections, freedom, etc.) as previously outlined, while allowing considerable, culturally based flexibility in how these institutions of democracy actually function.

This formulation offers the opportunity for a middle ground, and a way out of this dilemma. It insists on a clear definition and criteria of democracy: elections, freedoms, egalitarianism, rule of law, and checks and balances. But at the same time it allows *flexibility* in how democracy is institutionalized. That implies a country can have either an American-style presidential or a European-style parliamentary system. It means Latin America can have some degree of the organic-corporatist-statism that is reflective of its history, while East Asia can be communalist and "Confucian," and have the state and the private sector closely tied together. It suggests a place for tribalism in Africa, caste associations in India, and patronage networks there and elsewhere as legitimate political actors. For the Muslim and other countries it means the separation of religion and politics or the state does not have and *cannot* be exactly the same as in the West; for countries cast in the French model of centralized ministries and decision making, it implies strong local government on the American model may not always be appropriate.

In other words, we insist on universal *essentials* in our definition of democracy even while allowing countries and culture areas considerable leeway in devising an institutional system that suits them best. We return to these themes in the conclusion.

The Wrong Model?

During the last twenty years the main model in interpreting the Third World has been the transitions-to-democracy approach. Following the authoritarianism or bureaucratic-authoritarianism (BA) of the 1960s and 1970s, and as more and more countries began to move toward democracy in the 1980s and 1990s, the new focus in both policy and academic circles became the transitions to and consolidation of democracy.

In careful hands this was a useful focus, but in some minds and institutions the transitions-to-democracy approach became a rigid orthodoxy. First, in seeking not just to analyze but to *promote* the cause of democracy abroad, it ignored the long, slow (often two-three generations or more) processes involved, and the difficulties. Second, the approach was one-way or teleogical; it neglected the possibilities that in many countries the process of transition could be stalled, halted, or even reversed. Third, the approach assumed universality: it assumed that *all* countries would want democracy, or want it just as much, or would put it at the same level of priority—as compared with such issues as trade, stability, or economic development, for example. And fourth, it ignored the crucial cultural differences previously indicated, which would allow for greater flexibility and diversity in the approach and institutions that different countries took to democracy.

The result is that the transitions-to-democracy approach proved not very useful in explaining the present disillusionment with democracy, the rising call for "strong government," and the *coups d'etat* in several countries that reversed democratic trends. Nor, even more importantly, did it address or give us categories to understand what has become a main theme in this book: the mixed, overlapping, hybrid, crazy-quilt patterns in many developing countries that exhibit *both* democratic and authoritarian or corporatist features, the halfway houses that exist. We sorely need a nomenclature, a set of categories that describes and analyzes these various mixed systems, rather than seeing them all advancing on some mythical universal, one-way route to democracy.

In most developing countries what we presently have is not a pure or unadulterated form of democracy. Rather, what we have is democracy with adjectives: controlled democracy, limited democracy, regulated democracy, guided democracy, or corporative or Rousseauian democracy. Moreover, each regional or cultural area (East Asia, Southeast Asia, Sub-Saharan Africa, Latin America, and the Islamic world) seems also to be evolving its own, culturally conditioned form of democracy: organic in one place, bureaucratic in another, under strong leadership in some, partially reflective of the United States in others. Yet we lack a framework both for understanding these distinct forms of democracy or for assessing democracy's realistic prospects. In the conclusion we seek to fill some of these gaps in our knowledge.

THE END OF THE THIRD WAVE?

The 1980s and 1990s represented the high point in the "third wave" of global democratization. Southern Europe, most of Latin America, East/Central Europe, and much of East and Southeast Asia democratized during this period. But by now the great wave of democratization seems to have stalled, and neither in the Middle East nor in Sub-Saharan Africa has democracy established a very firm base. In a few countries democratization has been reversed; in a *large number* of others there is considerable disillusionment with democracy and declining support for it.

Does that mean the wave of democratization that swept over so many countries in the last two decades is over? At this stage we do not know definitively. There are both discouraging as well as more optimistic signs and trends. But since, because of globalization, the issue affects all of us as well as the developing countries, we need to watch these trends carefully.

NOTES

1. Samuel P. Huntington, *The Third Wave: Democratization in the Late Twentieth Century* (Norman, OK: University of Oklahoma Press, 1991).

2. Joseph Schumpeter, *Capitalism, Socialism, and Democracy* (New York: Harper, 1947).

3. Robert Dahl, *Democracy and Its Critics* (New Haven, CT: Yale University Press, 1989).

4. Francis Fukuyama, *The End of History and the Last Man* (New York: The Free Press, 1992).

5. Karl Meyer, "The Lesser Evil Doctrine," *The New Leader*, XLVI (October 14, 1963), 14.

6. *Washington Post* (August 21, 2002), A–1.

6

Neoliberalism
and Its Problems

I n the previous chapter we traced the evolution in the developing world from authoritarianism, or bureaucratic-authoritarianism (BA), to democracy, and the numerous problems encountered during this transition. In this chapter we trace a similar and parallel trajectory: the transition from closed, statist, or ISI (Import Substitution Industrialization) dominated economies to more open, market friendly, or capitalistic ones.

These two processes, in the political (from authoritarianism to democracy) and economic (from statism to free market capitalism) spheres, are closely interrelated. The ISI or statist model of economic growth was closely associated with the authoritarian regimes that championed it. Similarly, openness or democracy in the political sphere was closely associated with openness or free markets in the economic sphere. Presumably, these two transitions, from authoritarianism to democracy politically and from statism to open markets economically, went hand-in-hand. Countries that democratized presumably would also adopt free market policies, and by the same token countries that opted for open markets could also be expected to opt for open and free political systems, or democracy.

Both of these large, macro processes—toward democracy politically and toward open markets economically—were often assumed to be inevitable and universal. After the collapse and discrediting of both Marxism-Leninism and authoritarianism, there seemed to be no other options. Democracy and its handmaiden, free markets, or, if you prefer, free markets and their handmaiden, democracy, seemed the wave of the future. Recall our earlier discussion of the analysis of Francis Fukuyama and his famous proclamation that democracy and free markets, what is often termed *neoliberalism,* represented the "end of history." Recall also that Fukuyama meant that not in the sense that history had literally ended but in the sense that of all the great ideas and systems alternatives in modern history—democracy, capitalism, fascism, socialism, statism, communism, authoritarianism, totalitarianism—by the beginning of the twenty-first century only democracy and market capitalism were left standing, triumphant, without competition. Hence, history, the competition of ideas and great systems, had "ended."

It hasn't quite worked out that way, however. In the last chapter we showed that democracy, though seemingly triumphant, still faces so many hurdles, pitfalls, and problems that in many developing countries its popularity is fading and being undermined. In this chapter we focus more on the economic side, the transition from ISI to free markets, to see how successful that transition has been. We are interested in such questions as whether the transition to free markets is really complete and universal, where it has been successful and where not and why, how it has affected poor countries and their peoples, what the implications of the limits or failures of the current model are, and what alternatives to the prevailing neoliberalism there are—if any.

THE ISI MODEL

The liberal, free-market, or capitalist economic order has, of course, been in existence for some time. Described in positive terms by eighteenth-century philosopher Adam Smith and in negative terms by mid-nineteenth-century economist Karl Marx, the liberal model began in such capitalistic entrepreneurial countries as Great Britain and the Netherlands and then spread to other European countries as well as to North America. Capitalism or a liberal market economy superceded feudalism and was based on the premises that free and open markets were the best way of establishing wages and prices; that the state should not interfere overly in, let alone control, market mechanisms; that merit rather than birthright should determine one's place in the community; and that corporate feudal privilege (for religious bodies or elite groups) should be abolished. While the market philosophy and accompanying institutions (banks, financial institutions, stock markets) grew and eventually triumphed in the nineteenth century in Europe and the United States, they were also present, but attenuated, in the newly independent republics of Latin America. There, however, the liberal model was less successful and, hence, less popular, beginning to fade in most Latin American countries around the time of World War I and definitively crashing down in the Great Depression and world market crash of the 1930s.

Political liberalism (democracy) and economic liberalism (free markets) have long been closely associated. Of course, one wishes to have and to exercise one's political freedoms and the fundamental rights enshrined in the French declaration of the Rights of Man and the American Bill of Rights. But in order to be truly free, one also needs to have considerable economic freedom, to be able to change jobs or occupations if one wishes, to be independent from state economic as well as political controls, and to have some autonomy or space both politically *and* economically separate from the government. Only a free market system helps preserve those rights since, if you have political rights but not the economic rights and independence that liberalism provides, then you are not free at all. Liberalism is thus contrasted with totalitarianism of both left and right varieties where the state "totally" controls and snuffs out not only all political rights but all economic freedoms as well. Modern social democracy seeks, with mixed results, to avoid this dilemma by having freedom and democracy in the political sphere but an extensive welfare state economically.

While capitalism and free markets provided one model that emerged from the collapse of feudalism, another alternative model was mercantilism. Mercantilism also developed in the wake of feudalism's decline and fall, and was seen as an intermediary or transitional stage between feudalism and capitalism. It posited that the emerging, modern *state* should be the dominant force in the economy, not the marketplace. Mercantilism was more prevalent in France and continental Europe (and their Third World colonies) than in Great Britain or the United States where the free market model triumphed. Mercantilism was especially popular in states that wanted to escape from the shackles of feudalism but yet lacked the essentials (dynamic markets, an energetic entrepreneurial class, a widespread banking system, investment capital, or a business ethic) for full-fledged capitalism. Under mercantilism, the state would substitute for entrepreneurs and the marketplace, providing capital, banking, investment, and so on, as the most dynamic force in the economy.

One can, thus, see why the mercantilist model would be particularly attractive in the developing nations, one of whose characteristics is precisely the *lack* of those institutions of a free market system previously listed. In most developing countries, *only* the state can provide the investment capital and the infrastructure necessary for development. But while that sounds quite reasonable, let us also keep in mind the link made earlier between political and economic freedom. For many authoritarian regimes in the Third World, already in command of the political instruments of control (police, army, and government), the mercantilist model enabled them to extend their controls to the economy as well and, thus, further bolster their authoritarianism. Mercantilism or "statism" provided them with an attractive, even irresistible, model both to advocate development and at the same time increase the states' (their own) power. Nor should we forget that all this economic power concentrated in the hands of the state provided ample opportunity for graft, skims, and corruption by government officials on a massive scale.

Mercantilism or statism, or what later came to be called the Import Substitution Industrialization (ISI) model, came to Latin America in the 1930s. Recall that the earlier liberal economic model had not worked well there, had collapsed in the 1920s and 1930s, and had kept Latin America positioned as an exporter of primary (minerals, foodstuffs) products at a time of lower market prices for these goods compared to ever-more-expensive imported manufactured items. ISI, in such leading countries as Argentina, Brazil, and Mexico, was seen as a way to reverse this course: to use the resources of state-led development to stimulate industrialization that would lead to home-grown manufacturers replacing those previously imported—hence, the name *import substitution industrialization*. Initially, Latin America enjoyed considerable success with this model since it stimulated local industrialization, diversified their economies, and led to growth rates in many countries of 3 to 5 percent per year. It must also be said that most of these ISI policies were carried out under authoritarian auspices: the regimes of Juan Perón in Argentina, Getulio Vargas in Brazil, and the Revolutionary Institutional Party (PRI) in Mexico.

While Latin America led with the ISI model, other countries becoming independent in the post-World War II period followed much the same plan. They also faced rising demands for a better life on the part of their populations; at the same time, the absence of local markets, financial institutions, and entrepreneurs; and often the desire to use statism in the economic sphere as a complement to authoritarianism in the political. The 1950s and especially the 1960s (precisely when many new countries became independent) were the decades when mercantilism, statism, and ISI triumphed throughout much of the developing world (East Asia was the main exception). The military dictatorships of Argentina, Brazil, and most of the rest of Latin America, dictator Ferdinand Marcos in the Philippines, Suharto in Indonesia, and most of the new states of Africa, the Middle East, and South and Southeast Asia used ISI to try to develop their economies and move from being simple exporters of raw materials toward industrialization.

The preceding paragraph makes abundantly clear the point made earlier about the close relations between politics and economics. Just about every one of the countries and regimes previously named were authoritarian regimes; it is no accident that they also preferred ISI policies. Authoritarianism and a strong central state or dictatorship in the political realm went hand-in-hand with statism or ISI in the economic arena. Strong statist controls in the economic realm reinforced and strengthened the authoritarianism of the political regime—and vice versa. Mercantilism or state control of the economy gave these authoritarian regimes, which already exercised full control over the political and military realms, one more handle—the economic—by which to dominate their countries. No wonder these authoritarian regimes preferred the ISI model, even after it had clearly run its course.

The ISI model called for economic development but under state guidance, leadership, direction, and control. The statist model was preferred for several reasons: (1) suspicions of foreign capital and companies after long years of colonial exploitation; (2) the influence of socialist ideas and ideologies among the political leaders of developing nations; (3) absence of one of the key ingredients of economic growth, a dynamic entrepreneurial group or bourgeoisie; and (4) fear that losing control of the economy to the private marketplace might also result in these authoritarian regimes losing control of the political marketplace (i.e., yielding to pluralism and democracy).

ISI was a closed economic model which eliminated the pressures of foreign competition by raising tariffs so high that imported goods—from cigarettes, baby food, and canned soups to appliances and luxury automobiles—cost four or five times as much as locally made ones. Thus, the national industries that were products of this era had a privileged access to their domestic markets, thanks to high customs duties on imported items and other protective measures imposed by the state. Though ISI was often successful for a time in stimulating industry and manufacturing in various Third World countries, it also produced, in the absence of competition, inefficiency, corruption, and parasitism in the industries affected. These parasitic industries, both privately and publicly owned, were a haven for providing jobs to incompetent friends, family members, and political cronies of the owners or the regime in power. Over time they proved to be a severe drain on the economy.

The major goal of ISI was to assist "infant industries" by means of protectionism and high tariffs so that they could become strong enough to compete in world markets. However, as implemented, the policy had consequences quite different from those intended by the plan's architects, such as economist Raúl Prebish and the United Nations-sponsored Economic Commission for Latin America. There was little attempt by these infant industries, especially those that were run by the state, to become truly self-sufficient, efficient, and competitive; instead, the state often used them as gigantic patronage "dumping grounds" for all manner of incompetent political hangers-on, which over time made them even less competitive. In addition, in many instances, instead of aiding new and infant industries, the plants involved continued to rely on imported parts, merely assembled them at home, and then dumped them into the domestic market. There were almost no incentives to increase the quality or quantity of the products or decrease the dependency on imported parts, machinery, or capital goods. Protectionism guaranteed that these industries could be as inefficient as they wished since it was assumed (correctly) that the state would make up for their deficits, and there were no deadlines, guidelines, or timetable regarding the opening up of the system to international competition.

ISI worked for a time in some countries but by the 1970s and 1980s it was clear that the ISI model was no longer working well. Among the reasons for its discrediting:

- It had led to immensely bloated and inefficient state sectors.
- Corruption was widespread and endemic within these large, out-of-control state industries.
- In many developing countries the amount of GNP generated through the state sector climbed to 60, 70, or 80 percent, reaching nearly to the level of the socialist economies and progressively squeezing out the private sector.
- Most of the ISI-inspired state-owned industries turned into gigantic patronage agencies filled with the incompetent supporters and hangers-on of the party or regime in power.
- The ISI system proved incapable of adjusting fast or flexibly enough to adapt to changing international transformations or changed markets.
- ISI made the local products, shielded from competition by high tariffs, shoddy and expensive at the same time.

- The ISI model was discredited by the economic downturn in most developing nations in the 1970s and by the Third World debt crisis of the 1980s.

- ISI was further discredited by its association with so many authoritarian regimes, themselves discredited by the late 1970s and 1980s by corruption, inefficiency, human rights abuses, and lack of democracy.

By the early 1980s, therefore, the ISI regime had been thoroughly discredited. Economic liberalism or open markets and free trade were about to take its place. These trends were reinforced by the growing realization of the economic failures of the Marxist-Leninist regimes, and then by the collapse of the Soviet Union and its satellites in the 1989–1991 period. Yet it would be a mistake to think that Third World economists, businessmen, and government officials, who had been the chief supporters of ISI, were entirely convinced that ISI was bankrupt and that economic liberalism should take its place. In the United States, the emergence of an open markets/free trade regime has been celebrated as a complete victory and the triumph of "our" model, but in the Third World that supposed triumph was far more ambiguous.

Many remained skeptical of open, capitalistic markets and free trade; opinion polls at the time showed the political and economic elites about evenly split between ISI and free markets. We emphasize these points because in the present difficult economic circumstances of the Third World, many are now saying, "We told you so"; proponents of the ISI model are again coming "out of the woodwork" (and out of the international lending agencies—World Bank, IMF—where many of them worked after their years in power); and many Third World regimes, disillusioned with free markets, are now preparing to return—once again—to greater statist economic controls.

NEOLIBERALISM AND THE WASHINGTON CONSENSUS

As set forth by its main critics, there were two major problems with the ISI model: (1) too big and inefficient governments, and (2) too much state control (fixing of both prices and wages) over the marketplace. Having formulated the problems and causes of Third World economic failures in this way, it was easy to see what the solution had to be: reduce state size and allow markets to operate freely. These policies, called "neoliberalism" or new liberalism, since they represented a revival of earlier theories of the free, liberal, unfettered market, came together in a package called the "Washington Consensus."

But whose "consensus" was it; what groups and/or governments bought into the consensus? Initially, as with so many other ideas in American policy-making, the formulation and setting forth of the plans behind the Consensus came out of the Washington think tanks, which often have an enormous impact on policy. The American Enterprise Institute for Public Policy Research

(AEI) is a right-of-center think tank that was and is close to the Republican Party and provided many of the key ideas to the Reagan and Bush administrations, which had long championed open markets, free trade, and private direct investment over public foreign aid. For Democrats, the key think tank on this issue was the Institute for International Economics (IIE), a liberal but moderate research institute, and particularly economist John Williamson. While AEI had long supplied advice as well as personnel to Republican administrations, by the time the Democrats won the election in 1992, the ISI or statist model had clearly run its course and Democrats were also searching for a new model. That is what the IIE and Williamson provided, in the form of the Washington Consensus: a quite remarkable basis of agreement between otherwise rival think tanks and between both Republican and Democratic administrations.

The success of the free market model was bolstered, not only by the failures of ISI, but also, precisely during this period, by the failures of socialism in the Soviet Union, Eastern Europe, and throughout the Third World. Hence, although sometimes reluctantly, the Democrat Clinton Administration also embraced the Washington Consensus, and its free-market ideology became the basis of U.S. foreign policy. Since the United States is the biggest donor and tends to strongly influence the policies of the big international lending agencies, the World Bank, the IMF, the Inter-American Development Bank, and other regional development banks also came to accept the Washington Consensus—even though often reluctantly, once again, because many of their personnel are statists and were the main designers of the ISI model. Thus, the "Washington Consensus" came to encompass: (1) the main Washington think tanks, (2) both Republicans and Democrats, (3) the U.S. government and its foreign policy, and (4) the big international lending agencies.

The three main elements of the Washington Consensus, all interrelated, were:

1. Democracy and human rights
2. Open markets
3. Free trade

Here we focus mainly on the economic aspects of the Consensus, turning later to its political effects.

Elements of the Free Market Model

Four main economic policy thrusts constituted the reform agenda of the Washington Consensus. First, since excessive statism (both ownership and interference in the marketplace) had been diagnosed as the primary cause of the Third World's poor economic performance, it followed that the state's restrictive economic practices would have to be reduced or eliminated. The Washington Consensus advocated fully open markets, free trade, and liberalization of all financial and capital markets. The Consensus believed that, if statist and mercantilist restrictions were removed, a dynamic entrepreneurial class would emerge and the economies of the Third World would flourish—both of these being big assumptions.

Second, the Consensus demanded macroeconomic stability. This had two main components: controlling inflation and reducing the fiscal deficit. Inflation had to be brought under control because it was ruining the purchasing power of consumers and driving prices out of sight; inflation had stemmed from the fact that governments (the state again!) had gotten into the bad habit of covering their often elaborate and wasteful (corruption, patronage, extravagant entitlements) policies by printing more and more paper money not backed up by tangible worth.

A second technique for financing corruption, patronage, and politically popular entitlements was to borrow extensively abroad, mainly from private banks. The result was foreign indebtedness matching and then surpassing that of the great debt crisis of the 1980s when numerous Third World countries borrowed themselves into insolvency. They had assumed that their debts could be periodically rolled over and paid for with new loans in a never-ending cycle. The strategy was supportable as long as these countries' economies and the world economy were growing, but if a downturn occurred they would quickly be in bad trouble with payments on their debts, often totaling 50 percent or more of their national budgets, exceeding their ability to pay. For many countries, such deficit financing proved ruinous. The formula for solving the problem or at least making it manageable was to curb their expenses and prevent new inflationary pressures or foreign indebtedness.

The third leg of the Washington Consensus was privatization of state-owned economic enterprises. In many Third World nations the state's share in the economy had come to total 60, 70, or 80 percent, almost as much as in a socialist country. This remarkable development had been justified on the grounds that (1) the private entrepreneurial sector in many of these countries was weak and, therefore, the state had to step in and develop industry, (2) the enhancement of the state sector would provide a nice balance (a "middle way") between the private and public sectors, and (3) it vastly expanded the power and patronage of the government in power.

But many of these state-owned enterprises had grown to be enormously corrupt, bloated, inefficient, and noncompetitive. In many countries they were seen as gigantic "watering troughs" for corrupt politicians and employees to rip off to the maximum extent possible. Often at the same time, they became gigantic patronage operations by which politicians and government officials paid off their political debts by putting hundreds, even thousands, or sometimes whole ethnic groups on the public payroll. These were not just handfuls of patronage positions, as in your local city hall, but literally a means to pay off whole classes, enemies as well as supporters, by giving them access to public positions for which they seldom showed up to work, only to collect their paychecks. The state-owned enterprises in all countries were shot full of corruption and inefficiencies often requiring thirty to forty employees to do the work of three or four, and thus making them uncompetitive on world markets. Particularly as the super-efficient East Asian economies geared up for maximum production in the 1960s, 1970s, and 1980s, the corruption- and inefficiency-riddled statist enterprises of Latin America, Sub-Saharan

Africa, Southeast Asia, and the Middle East could not compete and—to complete this vicious circle—had to rely on ever larger state subsidies, deficit financing, and protective tariff barriers to survive. The situation was untenable and only getting worse.

The fourth pillar of the Washington Consensus was austerity. To overcome all this corruption and waste and to get back to fiscal responsibility, governments in the Third World would have to tighten their belts. Not only would they have to eliminate corruption and inefficiency but they would also have to cut back on social programs, subsidies for the poor, and major development and construction projects that put people to work. For example, many Third World countries subsidized the costs of such "poor people's foods" as rice, beans, and cooking oil, as well as the price of gasoline. Since most people in the Third World do not own cars but rely on public transportation (buses, jitneys, trucks) to get to work, the cost increases sparked by the removal of the gasoline subsidy was often disastrous, the difference between getting to work and not getting to work. Unfortunately, the belt tightening that had to be imposed under the pressures for austerity hit poor people as well as the rich, and its effects on the poor were even harsher. In most countries austerity packages could have been designed that exempted gasoline and basic foodstuffs, but for the most part they were not—until it was too late, after austerity had produced food riots, bus burning, grocery store looting, *and* (see the previous chapter) the undermining or discrediting of democratic governments that had recently come to power in much of the Third World.

The Washington Consensus was an all-or-nothing package. A country could not accept only part of the package; it had to accept the whole thing. Otherwise, it would not receive the loans from the World Bank, the IMF, the United States, and the private banks that it desperately needed to stay afloat, let alone *grow* economically.

Second, the Washington Consensus represented a solution to which *all* countries had to conform—what came to be called the "cookie cutter" approach: "One size fits all." In practice, there could be slight variations in the steps taken and some, limited negotiations between the country involved and the World Bank, IMF, and U.S. "doctors" that prescribed the "medicine." But essentially, the overall package looked the same in all countries: deregulate, downsize the state, privatize, and austerity. As John Williamson of the Institute for International Economics, who was instrumental in drafting the Washington Consensus, wrote, these prescriptions were *the* path to follow since they were "embodying the *common core of wisdom embraced by all serious economists,* whose implementation provides the minimum conditions that will give a developing country the chance to start down the road to the sort of prosperity enjoyed by the industrialized countries" (emphasis added).

It must be said initially that there *was* indeed consensus by almost everyone concerned with the developing nations on the main ingredients in the Washington Consensus package. (Almost) all agreed that the developing countries needed, *to some degree,* to deregulate, downsize the state, privatize, and tighten belts. The questions would be, how to do that and how much to do.

Second, it should not be thought that these were simply policies formulated by the United States, the World Bank, the IMF, and the private banks, and *imposed* on the poor, hapless developing areas. True, the Washington Consensus was a product, as the name suggests, of Washington, D.C., but it was also widely accepted by the main governmental, business, and political sectors in the Third World. They saw, particularly in the wake of the Cold War when foreign aid was drying up and the ability to maneuver advantageously between the superpowers had ended, that in order to remain competitive in global trade, they would have to streamline, eliminate waste, cut out corruption, honor contracts, enforce the rule of law, and move toward open markets and free (unprotected) trade. They, too, saw that they could no longer rely on subsidies from the First World, deficit financing, the printing of worthless paper money, the endless rollover of foreign loans, and local corruption and inefficiencies covered over by protectionism and foreign assistance. But while the elites in these countries were mainly in agreement on the Washington Consensus, as usual no one had bothered to consult the lower classes both rural and urban on whose shoulders the burden of austerity's sacrifices would inevitably fall.

Free Trade?

Meanwhile, the free trade agenda that had been set forth in the 1980s was also running into some problems. However, we need to offer some comments by way of introduction.

In a sense, it can be said that the United States has long stood for free trade. The United States has long been an importing, exporting, trading nation; free trade thus serves our interests. Particularly nowadays as by far the world's most powerful economy, the United States is in an advantageous position not only of standing for free trade but also being in a position to profit the most from it.

Second, we should keep in mind that the regime of open markets discussed earlier and free trade go hand-in-hand. Open markets and free trade—they seem to fit like hand-and-glove. Both seem to occupy the moral high ground—"open" markets and "free" trade—and how can one argue with these lofty principles? But also recall that, as the globe's dominant economy, these principles also serve our own self-interests.

By the 1970s and 1980s, thirdly, the United States was beginning to worry that, with the rise of the closed protected market of the European Community (later rebaptized as the European Union or EU) on the one side, and the rise of the powerful Japanese economy and its Asian trading partners on the other, the United States might over time be excluded from both of these large, dynamic markets. Hence, the United States began to think of forming its own common market in Latin America. The United States and Latin America are in some senses "natural" partners: the United States is a highly educated, industrialized, highly technological, increasingly service-oriented economy, while Latin America has the raw materials, primary goods, manufacturing and assembly plants, and cheap labor supplies that the United States needs.

But herein lies a dilemma. If the United States stands for free trade, isn't it contradictory to have a special trading relationship with Latin America and then to erect protectionist barriers against the goods from other nations? As a global power with a global economy, the United States needs to be able to trade with *all* nations. Would it be possible to have both a special relationship with Latin America *and* at the same time profitable trade relations with the rest of the world?

The stimulus to organizing a free trade zone with Latin America came from the fear of instability in Mexico and other neighboring countries torn by conflict and civil war. In 1983 Mexico had triggered the "great Third World debt crisis" by indicating it could not pay its foreign loans. Then in 1988, after sixty years of stability, came the first hints of potential political instability in Mexico and the prospect that a leftist Marxist might win the presidency. The prospect of a destabilized Mexico either economically or politically and, if that happened, millions of Mexicans fleeing across that porous, two-thousand-mile southwestern border sent fear into the hearts of U.S. political leaders who determined they had to do something to alleviate the threat; hence, the development of the plans for NAFTA (the North American Free Trade Agreement) involving the United States, Mexico, and also Canada, as well as for a free trade agreement (FTA) encompassing all of Latin America.

It is important to emphasize that NAFTA was not primarily an economic plan but a strategic one. It used the free trade strategy to help create jobs and prosperity in Mexico but the main purpose was political and strategic: to head off the potential for instability and revolution which would also have devastating consequences for the United States. Even though its ultimate purposes were strategic, NAFTA was always debated in the United States as an economic policy: whether it produced *U.S.* jobs or lost them. The off-track nature of this debate made it harder to pass future FTAs with other countries.

NAFTA passed the U.S. Congress only with great difficulty and the handing out of political plums and patronage to congressmen in return for their votes. Big Labor was opposed to NAFTA (and other FTAs) on the grounds that it cost U.S. jobs; environmental groups were also worried about pollution in U.S.–Mexico border areas. The result is that NAFTA remains controversial to this day and FTAs with other countries or groups of countries in the Americas have been slowed almost to a halt.

Since the issue is so controversial politically, politicians are often unwilling to champion it; hence, most of the negotiations for free trade take place at lower levels in the bureaucracy. Negotiations are presently ongoing or nearing completion for new FTAs with Chile, Brazil, the Andean region, Central America, Sub-Saharan Africa, and the Caribbean. President George W. Bush was able to get the Congress to give him fast-track authority (as had Presidents George G. W. Bush and Bill Clinton before), which means he can negotiate these agreements freely without fear of endless congressional amendments to scuttle the agreements later on. Quietly and without great fanfare, such agreements are moving forward inch by inch.

But there have also been major setbacks, leading the Latin American (and other) developing nations to say, in a reversal of arguments, that, while *they* stand for free trade, the United States does not. New tariffs and other restrictions have been placed by the United States on the import from the Third World of steel, cotton, orange juice, textiles, and numerous agricultural products. Such restrictions are the result of the power and political clout of lobbyists representing the interests of these industries in the United States. The government argues that it needs to compromise on these issues in order to build political support for other bigger trade agreements later on, but others are not so sure. While free trade negotiations are ongoing, they are also difficult, controversial, and often stalled in the U.S. political process. The overall result seems to be that another leg of the three-legged Washington Consensus—free trade—has been undermined and faces an uncertain future.

MISTAKEN ASSUMPTIONS OF THE WASHINGTON CONSENSUS

The Washington Consensus was based on quite a number of very large assumptions about the economies, societies, and political systems of the Third World that in the end proved not to be true—or perhaps only partly true. Here we examine what those assumptions were and why in the developing world they did not work out as expected.

1. That the freeing up of these economies would give rise to a dynamic entrepreneurial class that could substitute for the state's role in the economy, seize the initiative, and stimulate economic growth. But dynamic entrepreneurial groups don't emerge out of thin air; they take a long time to develop and their emergence is related to other changing elements in society—for example, growth of the rule of law, honesty, and transparency in the administration of the public accounts, protected property rights, and so on. In most developing countries, however, there is no dynamic entrepreneurial class or it is very small. What passes for entrepreneurs is usually the friends, relatives, and cronies of the regime in power; they often have special access to government contracts and monopolies. They are parasites whose goal is to rip off the system to line their own private pockets, not to provide jobs and growth to the economy as a whole. The worst case is Russia where some 90 percent of the former public patrimony—under socialism owned by the state—has been ripped off in this way, with little or no benefit to the public-at-large. We may *wish* that a dynamic private sector would emerge to replace the state in the developing nations, but the facts are that what *passes* for a private sector is usually in it mainly, even exclusively, for themselves and not to benefit society as a whole.

2. That a host of financial institutions would emerge as these economies were freed up that would assist in the development process. But banks, lending agencies, financial service agencies, capital markets, stock exchanges, and so on, in developing countries tend also to be weak and cannot be created quickly.

Generations are required for these institutions to grow, and not just a few years. In addition, the few banks and financial institutions that exist in most developing countries tend not to be in business to give loans to small businessmen and dynamic start-up companies; rather, they are holding companies, often tied up closely with the regimes or elites in power, profiting from insider connections and monopolistic government contracts; *not* seeking to change the system but protecting their stake in it.

3. That the freeing up of the economies in the developing world would produce growth, jobs, and benefits that would trickle down to the lower and middle classes. But this assumption ignored the class structure and class attitudes in most developing countries. These tend to be very rigid, elitist, hierarchical, and inegalitarian. In fact, what has happened in too many cases under the new neoliberal economic order is that the elites, who already have the money and the political connections previously described, have become enormously richer; the small middle classes in the developing nations have been squeezed by salary freezes or job losses in the face of inflation; and the restless lower classes have received few benefits at all and have often become worse off.

One of the best illustrations of this is Brazil, whose multimillionaire class has grown enormously richer in recent years and has gone strenuously into the helicopter market so they can fly over the poor shantytowns on their commute from suburban mansions and that way never have to see or experience the poverty that exists at ground levels. Or in Mexico where a recent presidential candidate asked one hundred of his friends and cronies to secretly pony up $25 *million* each to support his candidacy, a figure that makes the United States and its campaign finance laws seem pristinely clean by comparison. In other words, the freeing up of the economies of the developing nations did not necessarily produce the greater opportunities and equalities expected; instead, it provided even greater wealth to the already rich and left a good part of the rest of the population, in the face of rising prices, even worse off.

4. That privatization would lead to greater honesty and efficiency in the running of major, formerly state-owned industries. The logic behind this proposition seemed unassailable: it suggested that, since many governments and state-owned industries in the Third World were bloated and riddled with corruption, the most sure-fire way to end the corruption was to take the money away, and, therefore, the opportunity for graft, by vastly cutting back the size of the state. And the way to do that was through privatization of all the major state-owned industries. The solution sounds clever, even ingenious, but it ignores several very important facts: that only the elites or foreign companies in the Third World have the money to buy these industries; that military officers and crony officials close to the regime in power would have inside knowledge and thus an inside track to take over the former state-owned firms; and that in Russia, Eastern Europe, Southeast Asia, and Sub-Saharan Africa, it would be mainly corrupt mafias that would use strong-arm methods and corrupt techniques to capture these important economic

sectors. In addition, privatization usually resulted in higher prices for the goods produced, shortages (of electricity, foodstuffs, other products) and often greater inefficiencies and corruption than before, and higher unemployment. Privatization proved to be no panacea, and those in charge should have known that from the start.

5. A related issue is that of patronage. Presumably privatization and government downsizing would not only end corruption but also patronage. Patronage was perceived, accurately, as leading to bloated bureaucracies; friends, relatives, and political supporters of those in power being put on the public payroll; and, hence, enormous inefficiencies. But patronage also put people to work in countries where jobs are scarce, provided the only source of income to hundreds of thousands of families, served to reduce unemployment, helped to "grease" the machinery of government and make it work, provided the wherewithal for political parties to operate, and was an important factor in making the delivery of public policy programs possible. If corruption and patronage were ever completely eliminated in much of the Third World, it would probably cause their governments and entire public policy programs to collapse. *Of course,* you need to have honesty and efficiency in the implementation of public policy, but a too precipitous and too thoroughgoing "cleansing" of this sort could have dire destabilizing consequences for the countries affected, especially if carried out by well-meaning but naive and nonunderstanding international aid officials.

6. In almost all the texts by the World Bank, the IMF, and the advocates of neoliberalism, the issue of economic development was viewed as a technical and a managerial problem. It was based on the assumption that economic growth would flow automatically once the correct laws, procedures, and market forces were put in place. That is how it (mainly) worked in the United States, so why would it not work in the developing world? But a technical and managerial solution such as this disregarded all cultural, social, political, and historical factors. It ignored that these changes take *time* to work out; that elites and corrupt officials would rip off the system to their own advantage; that the social structure and mores in most developing countries are not the same as in the West; that the rational, enlightened behavior on which the policy was based took hundreds of years to develop in the West and was grounded on social and cultural changes (the Renaissance, the Enlightenment, the Protestant Reformation, the Industrial Revolution, the movement toward limited, representative, participatory, pluralist government) built up over centuries. These could not be seen as just technical, managerial changes but revolutionary ones affecting *all* areas of life; it was wrong and self-defeating to ignore all these larger cultural *and* contextual factors.

7. Political considerations and sensitivities were cast aside in favor of a one-size-fits-all approach. All countries would use the same model; presumably, the policy outcomes would then be the same as well. But that is pure nonsense; it comes from allowing economists and economists only to design

your development program. Economists tend actually to believe that their models fit all cultures and societies, that what works in one country will certainly work in all others, and, furthermore, that it is economics that triggers and then drives all social and political considerations. Unfortunately, economists have dominated the discussion of development for the last sixty years, but anyone with an ounce of experience in the Third World knows it doesn't work that way.

Cultures, societies, geographic regions, and countries vary enormously; what works in one may or *may not* work in others. Distinct cultures and social structures will vary the outcome, governments intervene in the process at all levels, corrupt regimes and politicians may distort the process, and democratic governments must make everyday calculations on what will work and what is impermissible in their environments. In some countries the process of economic reform can proceed rapidly; in most, it requires greater time, often several generations. People need to be socialized into new habits and practices; institutions take a long time to develop and become accepted. In some countries the changes can be thoroughgoing; in others, government subsidies, protectionism, and patronage positions must be phased out ever so slowly. Austerity and belt-tightening can similarly be imposed only gradually depending again on the government's calculations of how far it can go, how tight to turn the screws, before it has mass discontent and a rebellion on its hands. Note that *all* of these are preeminently *political* considerations, and any recommendations proceeding from international economists and the lending agencies that ignored these factors would be both fadish *and* self-defeating.

These represented quite fundamental flaws in the Washington Consensus. The goals were often noble and usually well-intentioned, but the assumptions on which they were based were faulty, grounded on wrong, naive, and misguided assumptions about Third World countries and their politics, cultures, and social structures. But if the assumptions were all wrong, why should we be surprised by the mistaken policy initiatives they produced?

ECONOMIC CRISIS

From the mid-1980s through the mid-1990s, the neoliberal economic model and the Washington Consensus that surrounded it seemed to be paying dividends. Not only were more and more countries democratizing but their economies were growing as well. East Asia, Latin America, and—more modestly—the Middle East and Sub-Saharan Africa experienced growing economies. Foreign investment was pouring in, jobs were being created, quite a number of Third World economies were taking off, and things looked hopeful. The fact that democracy and economic growth were correlated seemed to suggest that the earlier developmentalist models of Rostow and others from the 1960s, in eclipse for the previous twenty years, might come back into favor. That, after all, is what the Washington Consensus, with its emphasis on democracy, open markets, and free trade, suggested.

The great motor forces of this economic resurgence in the Third World were two: the strong international economy (United States, Europe, Japan) and the dynamism of the Third World itself. This was also a period, the 1990s, of economic recovery and then of a *tremendous* boom in the First World, particularly the United States. Flush with funds, U.S. companies and investors poured billions of dollars into Third World countries. Brazil alone was receiving $30 billion per year in new investment; other Big Emerging Markets (BEMs), such as Argentina, Mexico, Venezuela, Egypt, Nigeria, India, China, Indonesia, South Korea, and Taiwan, also received huge infusions. This unprecedented infusion of capital stoked the boilers of Third World economic growth.

This was also a period of great hope, optimism, and enthusiasm within the Third World itself. Democracy had just been established in many countries; political and economic reform was in the air; and local businessmen as well as foreign ones were investing heavily in their own countries' futures. Jobs were being created, new opportunities arose, energies were being unleashed, and some of the money even trickled down.

But then came a series of downturns and crises that sucked the enthusiasm out of these booming markets. In Russia, a combination of corruption, the ripping off of the former public patrimony that had existed under socialism, and a weak government under the sickly Boris Yeltsin led to a souring of the investment climate, a run on the currency, and the devaluation of the ruble to the "worthless currency" status. In emerging countries Thailand and Indonesia, similarly overheated currencies coupled with fears of political instability led to runs on those currencies, devaluations, the slowing or withdrawal of investment, and left governments and private sectors unable to cope. Economic troubles soon spread to such previous high-flyers as South Korea, Taiwan, and even Japan.

Latin America was the next to be hard-hit, and in the weaker economies of the Middle East and Africa the devastation was even greater. Let us focus on Latin America for now since that area was considered a "model" for the Washington Consensus, for U.S.-directed reform efforts, and is more or less intermediary between thriving East Asia and backward Africa. In Latin America, the figures showed that, despite strenuous efforts over twenty years, the area was no better off in 2000 than it had been two decades earlier. World Bank reports indicated that in Latin America the gap between rich and poor was the worst in the world, that *80 percent* of the region's indigenous people lived in poverty, and that forty million *more* people lived below the poverty line now than in 1980. *All* the countries of the region were being affected by the economic downturn. The World Bank warned that the potential for social instability stemming from poverty was great and that it could "kill" long-term growth.[1]

Many Third World economies soon teetered on the brink of collapse and their economic reform efforts were stymied and in big trouble. Most countries were afflicted by a triple bane: low domestic savings rates, high government borrowing and debt, and an over-addiction to foreign capital. Borrowing and debt in many countries soared to all-time highs, surpassing the levels reached during the Third World debt crisis of the 1980s. Interest rates in these countries remained prohibitively high, slowing growth, and turning off the enthusiasm for investment and reform that had reigned earlier. A large number of countries went into a prolonged slump with chronic current account and budget deficits. Recession or slow growth in the developed countries (the United States, Western Europe, Japan) exacerbated the crisis in the Third World.

The reforms trumpeted as part of the Washington Consensus largely ground to a halt, or else they produced consequences that the architects of the Consensus failed to anticipate. Many Third World leaders had used the earlier prosperity not to push for reform but to stuff their governments and myriad official agencies with friends, relatives, and political supporters. Corruption and patronage often expanded rather than being reduced. Privatization efforts too often meant the provision of insider cushy deals to cronies and family members rather than cost savings and more efficient services. In Brazil, botched energy privatizations led to higher prices, lower supplies, and widespread public discontent. Many of the reform and privatization efforts produced not greater efficiency and rationality but, as prisoners of the social and political structures and systems of special favoritism of these countries, greater corruption, patronage, and inefficiency.

Approximately a decade after much of the developing world embraced democracy and free markets as part of the Washington Consensus, much of the Third World was bankrupt and on the rocks again. Both foreign and domestic investors had grown weary of putting their money into potentially unstable and unsafe countries; indeed, many were disinvesting and sending their money elsewhere (capital flight). The potentially huge consumer market in the form of an emerging Third World middle class that they had counted on was becoming impoverished and drying up. Most countries had not developed sufficient earnings from either exports or domestic savings to wean themselves away from debt and/or foreign capital. Continued deficit financing as in the 1980s was leading to such large debt payments that there was little left over to provide basic services, let along investment funds for growth. The ghosts and demons of the past were returning: dangerous dependence on foreign loans and capital; bloated, inefficient, patronage-dominated governments; and an ineffectual political class unable or unwilling to make necessary reforms. In addition, during the boom years, most of these countries had vastly expanded their social programs and entitlements, putting everyone (or everyone who counted) on the public payroll, and now they were politically unable to cut back on the benefits.[2]

By 2003 economists were referring to the period since 1997 as "half a lost decade," as compared with the full "lost decade" of the 1980s. In the Third World this meant large foreign debt, absence of growth, and failure of economic reform. Growth in most "developing" countries was an anemic 1 to 2 percent, or else zero, or in the negative column. Despair was in the air. In contrast to the earlier time when the Washington Consensus seemed to offer a way out of the crisis, now no one is certain what to do.

SOCIAL AND POLITICAL CONSEQUENCES

The economic downturns of the past few years, the continued social and economic inequalities, the stalling of the movement toward free trade, and the inability of democratic governments to provide the goods and services their populations had come to expect have led to widespread disillusionment with the Washington Consensus. After its early successes, the Consensus had lost its luster.

Throughout the Third World, popular frustration has been rising. This can be seen in such increasingly fragmented countries as Indonesia, the Philippines, Egypt, India, and much of the Middle East, Central Asia, Nigeria, Argentina, Venezuela, Ecuador, and others. Even elected governments are under siege and sometimes succumbing to corruption, drug trafficking, income inequalities, AIDS, crime, civil conflict, and ineffective bureaucracies. Many of these problems are closely related to the disappointments of economic development. As U.S. State Department official Peter Romero has stated, "It doesn't take a clairvoyant to predict that democracy will wane in the face of economic privation." He went on to say that the recent wave of democratization cannot be taken for granted.[3]

Growing popular discontent, massive social and popular movements, frustrated Islamists, vast numbers of unemployed persons, dissatisfied middle classes, peasants squeezed by lower prices for their goods, workers losing jobs, and rising inflation—all of these social and economic frustrations are combining to threaten civilian authorities and democratic rule. Countries have made transitions to elected or constitutional governments but they have been weak in dealing with the underlying problems of poverty, inequality, and joblessness. They are "formal democracies" but not yet "liberal" or "just" democracies. U.S. officials point out that there is a danger that, if people don't soon see the results of free trade and economic reform, then the free-market/democracy model as a whole will be discredited.

In such countries as Ecuador, Argentina, Peru, Paraguay, and Venezuela, coups d'états have already occurred; but so far constitutionalism has been precariously maintained and democracy has survived, though just barely. Economic development in these and other Third World countries has slowed to the vanishing point or turned negative; disillusionment with not only the existing government but also the *system* of government (democracy) is growing. Nor have there been sufficient changes in the distribution of income. In Latin America, for instance, the top 10 percent of income earners receive 40 percent of total income, while the bottom 30 percent get 7.5 percent. Distribution of income is getting worse rather than better.

Much of the Third World is living in dangerous and precarious circumstances. Economic growth has slowed worldwide; it negatively affects the developing world far more than the developed world; and within the Third

World, it affects the poor far more than others. This carries over into the political sphere. In South America, presidents in four of the ten countries have been forced to resign since 2000. Africa is awash in violence, ethnic strife, civil war, and national disintegration after some earlier signs of democratization a few years ago. Indonesia, with over three hundred ethnic groups on thirteen thousand islands, hovers on the verge of breakup and national disintegration. Such giants as Brazil, China, and India may fall into disarray.[4]

While democratic elections were held in many developing countries in the 1990s, they were unable to deliver on their promises of prosperity and higher living standards. This may well doom the Washington Consensus. When governments do a good job and *do* deliver, the electorate often allows them to stay in power even if it means changing the constitution to do so. "But the moment the economic performance weakens," says *Foreign Policy* editor Moisés Naím, "the electorate doesn't give a damn about elections and starts throwing governments out."[5] The message is: Deliver or else!

In the meantime, practices that hopefully were supposed to disappear with the arrival of democracy are reappearing. Crime, violence, and cynicism about the political process are all up. Street demonstrations, civil conflict, and human rights abuses are increasing. The armed forces are once again being pulled into the political process as the ultimate arbiters of national politics. Division, fragmentation, and polarization are pulling countries apart. Extra-constitutional plots, coups, and rumors of coups are everywhere. In some countries the armed forces are again taking power to restore stability or are thinking of returning to power.

Economic downturns and political disintegration are closely linked. For most Third World countries are based on extensive patronage networks. As long as the economic pie is expanding, there are always more pieces—more "goodies," in the form of jobs, programs, and patronage favors—to hand out to the clamoring social groups. These patronage networks reach all the way from top leaders to their lieutenants, to local leaders, and to people at low levels. But when the economy is stagnant or turns negative, there are no more patronage plums to hand out. This disrupts the entire chain of patronage from top to bottom. And in countries heavily based on patronage, this can be terribly disruptive, resulting in the unraveling of the entire political system. Such political unraveling may be accelerated by the fact that privatizations and state downsizing have already reduced significantly the patronage opportunities available. Unlike in the United States and other developed countries whose political systems can easily survive economic downturns, in the Third World economic recession can quickly and easily lead to coups, upheavals, or full societal and political disintegration.

This process of democratic-free market decay and accompanying possible political collapse presents a quandary not only to the countries involved but also for U.S. policy. The United States and the international community have said they will not recognize any government that comes to power through a coup or unconstitutional methods and will impose sanctions on any such regime. But the United States also wants order and stability as well as democracy, and it has winked its eye at several unconstitutional takeovers recently so long as the country at least maintained a democratic facade. But that is a very dangerous precedent to set, especially after the United States and others came out so publicly for democracy and the Washington Consensus. Moreover, the growth of the "civil society" that the United States so much hailed (and aided) in the 1990s as a substitute for corrupt bureaucracies, governments, and political parties is now deeply divided, at each other's throats so contentiously in countries like Indonesia and Venezuela that it risks precipitating civil war and national breakdown.[6]

The recent undermining of the Washington Consensus has led to a great deal of hand-wringing in United States policy circles. The strategy—free trade, open markets, and democracy—that has dominated U.S. policy for over a decade is under strong attack and may be breaking down. The breakdown of Third World political systems may be exacerbated by the disruptive fallout of the war on terrorism. There is much uncertainty, doubt, and anxiety over the policy—as well as questioning and even finger-pointing over what or who has gone wrong. Is it the United States that got it wrong or is the Third World to blame? Are the problems with "the Consensus" a result of international factors (the decline of the world economy) or do they lie at the feet of the Third World countries themselves? Were the *basic assumptions* of the program flawed or were good policies *badly implemented?* The answer is: both and all of these, but passing out blame like that does not help the developing world to solve its problems.

The Third World is presently facing a terrible dilemma. On the one hand, the predominant model, the neoliberal model as represented by the Washington Consensus, is not working at all well and is under strong attack. But there is no viable alternative. No one wants to return to authoritarianism, mercantilism, and statism; the Marxist alternative is similarly discredited and in disrepute. At the same time, most Third World economies are too weak and too small to go it alone in international affairs or to rely exclusively on domestic markets to provide economic stimulus. And that means the choice sometimes posed between open markets/free trade and protectionism, or between democracy and something else, is a non-choice. It is either open markets or accept slower growth; it is either democracy or international ostracism.

In today's interdependent world, as we see in more detail in the next chapter, you *have* to trade, you *have* to have open markets, you *need* to compete, and you *have* to have democracy. There are no other options. But that does not mean, as the earlier formulation of the Washington Consensus had it, a cookie-cutter approach: one size fits all. Countries can and do differ in their histories and cultures, in the practices and institutions of democracy, and in their economic systems. Each country's natural resources and export potential are different. Privatization and economic reform programs will differ depending on circumstances. In the give-and-take of a democratic political process, some countries may choose to exempt basic foodstuffs, electricity, gasoline, and cooking oil from the ups-and-downs of the market. Each country must find its own precise balance in all these regards, and must be sensitive to its own internal political pressures, which they undoubtedly know better than IMF missions or U.S. economic advisers. The neoliberal model, of course, has its problems and inequalities and requires adjustments and interventions by the state. No model is perfect, of course, so until a better formula is presented, democracy, free trade, and open markets still look—despite their problems—like the best bet for the Third World.

NOTES

1. *Financial Times* (February 4, 2000), 5.

2. *Wall Street Journal* (July 25, 2002), 1.

3. *Washington Post* (January 30, 2000), A21.

4. *New York Times* (April 13, 2002), A9.

5. *Ibid.*

6. See Howard J. Wiarda, *Civil Society: The American Model and Third World Development* (Boulder, CO: Westview Press, 2003) for an overview of civil society pointing out its negative as well as positive consequences.

7

Globalization and its Critics

Globalization has been with us for a very long time, indeed since the dawn of time. If Sub-Saharan Africa was the locus of the first human beings, then the gradual dispersion of the human species to the far corners of the earth was the first globalization. The domestication of animals, the development of agriculture, the invention of primitive tools like the wedge or the wheel, and the spread of these beyond the places where they were invented are all hallmarks in the history of globalization, as are steam engines, the invention of printing, telephone and telegraph, radio and television, computers, and the Internet.

Confucianism, Hinduism, Buddhism, Christianity, and Islam—the world's great religions—have all been agencies of globalization as well as, sometimes, in conflict with each other. Greek civilization, the Roman empire (which spread the use of a single language, law, sociology, and politics), and the Roman Catholic Church, which spread Christianity throughout Europe, were also instruments of globalization. So were such great military conquerors as Alexander the Great, Darius of Persia, Philip of Macedonia, and Genghis Khan. Globalization can, it must be said, take peaceful as well as violent forms.

Moving into the modern age, the Renaissance, the Enlightenment, the Scientific Revolution, and the Industrial Revolution were all agencies of globalization. So was the age of European expansion in the sixteenth and seventeenth centuries, which enormously expanded mankind's knowledge of the rest of the world and brought European ideas and institutions to far-flung regions, the area we would now call the Third World. But this Europeanization and Westernization of the globe, while clearly beneficial in some major respects, was also sometimes devastating in its impact on local cultures and indigenous peoples.

Let us summarize the discussion so far:

- Globalization is not new; it has always been with us; it is part of world history and the process by which things change.

- Globalization takes many different forms: cultural, social, economic, military, religious, technological, and political.

- Globalization is always contested and controversial; there are always going to be winners and losers.

- Globalization is ubiquitous, always present; it cannot be stopped (though it may be modified), nor is it likely to be reversed, nor would most of us want to do so.

- Globalization is most often peaceful, but it can also be disruptive and violent.

- Some countries and/or cultures are able to handle globalization better than others, absorbing its useful features while rejecting the rest; however, other countries and cultures, generally the smaller and weaker ones, may be overwhelmed by it.

Globalization is thus a complex, ambiguous, and mixed concept. It carries many different meanings. As a concept, it subsumes many different forces, which need to be carefully sorted out, under its umbrella. Globalization can be good or bad, depending on one's priorities, values, and morals. Above all, globalization is *always* with us, so we need to be careful about what we mean by the term, to sort out its many, often overlapping aspects, and only then can we draw balanced conclusions about it.

GLOBALIZATION IN THE PRESENT CONTEXT

In the present context, globalization takes a variety of forms and carries a variety of meanings. In their most controversial aspects, these include the following.

1. *Culture.*   *American* culture in particular is pervasive on a global basis. The elements of culture that have spread to the rest of the world include blue jeans, rock music, McDonald's, consumerism, big, fast cars, movies, and entertainment, as well as American ideas of justice, freedom, human rights, and democracy.

Almost every country in the world now has McDonald's restaurants—often dozens or hundreds of them. Many of these have become hangouts for young people, providing an opportunity to get away from their parents or stifling authority, a place to meet their girlfriends or boyfriends, and a liberating refuge in an otherwise authoritarian society. Similarly with rock music and its message of liberation (from parents, school, and government) and "do your own thing"; in a rigid authoritarian or Islamic regime, that message can be extremely subversive of established authority and even of governments, which is why authoritarian regimes seek to censor it. The same applies to the movies: movies can teach young people how to escape from their parents, sexual liberation and codes of conduct that are particularly American, and movies of the Arnold Schwarzenegger/Bruce Willis (the "Die Hard" series) kind probably promote anti-Americanism and, abroad, a perverted vision of America through their portrayal of excessive and gratuitous violence. Americans are often used to all these messages and partly inoculated against taking them too seriously, but in other countries the power of American culture can be overwhelming, subversive, and potentially destabilizing. And that helps explain why it can be both loved as well as resented.

Some countries and some people have reacted against this heavy American cultural influence. But television, VCRs, radio, compact discs, tapes, and the Internet enable people in these countries to bypass the censorship and, often, to rally against the regime in power. Most of us would consider these forms of globalization to be good, liberating, and democratic things.

Among Western countries, France has been the one that has sought most assiduously to defend its own culture and keep out what it thinks of as an American onslaught. It has tried to put limits on American movies, on American television, and the use of the English language. It fights vigorously and constantly to maintain the use of French as an official international language on a par with English. It seeks to maintain the purity of the French language while banning such Americanisms as "sandwich," "lunch," "French fries," and other such "perversions." A French farmer, José Bove, became a national hero for a time when he rammed his farm tractor into a McDonald's restaurant; however, he later went to jail and lost his luster when it was revealed that he held some truly crazy ideas. It is also the French who most often use the terms *hegemony, behemoth,* or *bully* to describe America. Yet the power of the American cultural influence is so great that even France has been forced to back off on many of these restrictions; while the French language and culture are quite glorious, they cannot keep the American influence from rising. Furthermore, while the French elite is often resentful of the American influence, public opinion surveys show that the French public likes American movies, television, and music and is quite level-headed in its views.

2. *Language.* Forty or more years ago, French was still considered the universal language of politics, international relations, and social interchange. Now it is English. In Europe, almost every educated person speaks English as a second, third, or fourth language; in much of the rest of the world, English has now replaced French, German, or Russian as the language that young people learn. In many countries, street signs are in English as well as the native language; television and radio are often heavily dominated by English-language expressions and even broadcasts; airports, airlines, and other modes of transportation use English as their official language; and in most museums and other facilities that attract international visitors, English is the main foreign language used.

While the globalization of the English language is great for American officials operating, or tourists traveling, abroad, it also means, because seemingly everyone else speaks English, Americans are even less inclined to learn other languages than was true in the past. It also breeds resentment throughout the world in that Americans expect everyone else to speak their language while only rarely do they learn other people's languages. Of course, the ability to use your own language while abroad while others have to struggle to keep up in their often-still-imperfect English gives you enormous advantage in any business transaction or diplomatic negotiation being carried out. Recall also that in foreign countries people are quite literally being bombarded constantly with English-language music, commercials, and political messages.

3. *Technology.* In many areas, but not all, American technology is the best in the world; one thinks of computers, software, biomedicine, the Internet, the special effects in the entertainment industry, prescription drugs, food processing, and many other areas. One can get statistics on numbers of U.S. patents, Nobel laureates, and copyrights—all overwhelmingly dominated by the United States. For a time in the 1980s, it was thought that Japan or perhaps other nations might surpass the United States, and in certain technologies (television sets, VCRs, maybe even luxury automobiles like the Acura and Lexus) they do. But the *overwhelming majority* of new or enhanced technologies in the world are dominated by the United States. Even in those industries—such as steel—once thought moribund, new technologies have been used to revive and make competitive a flagging U.S. industry.

The technological gap is especially large in the military sphere. U.S. military technology has become so advanced that it has not only left America with no serious rivals in the world but it has left U.S. allies behind as well. An enemy country would be foolhardy these days to seriously challenge the U.S. militarily, as shown by Iraq after its invasion of Kuwait, the Serbs in Bosnia and Kosovo, the Taliban in Afghanistan, and Iraq again in 2003. But the gap also produces tensions with U.S. allies because it is now so large that America feels it can wage war, if it has to, better and more effectively by itself rather than in concert with erstwhile allies. The allies often resent this and criticize the United States for its "unilateralism," even while relying on the United States to do global peacekeeping chores and relieving themselves from spending the money to keep pace with U.S. military technology. In *many* fields, civilian as well as military, the technological gap between the United States and other countries breeds resentment, jealousy, and sometimes anger.

4. *Economics.* The United States has the most powerful economy in the world—by far. There are no other rivals at present, nor any on the horizon. The U.S. gross national product is two or three times that of its nearest rivals, Japan and Germany, and with a living standard that is, or among, the highest in the world. The American economy is not only big, but also one of the wonders of the world in terms of its dynamism, innovation, and ability to create jobs.

As the world's biggest and most powerful economy, America's economic power and ability to dominate others sometimes breeds resentment. Among those countries that lie on or close to America's borders (Canada, Mexico,

Central America, and the Caribbean) the fear is often powerful that the strength and reach of the American economy will simply suck them up (make that slurping, sucking sound!) into the American orbit whether they or we wish it or not. In some quarters that may be called "imperialism," but it is also the inevitable consequence of a huge, dynamic, globalized economy located right next to smaller, weaker economies. Not only is such dominance characteristic of the United States and its neighbors but also powerful Germany in relation to the weaker, poorer Eastern European countries, or Japan and China in relation to their smaller Asian neighbors.

In the developing countries generally, there is often great fear of American economic power and the ability of U.S.-based companies or multinationals to take advantage of local conditions, to pressure (or bribe) government officials to get what they want, to exploit local resources, and to "rip off" the country. After all, many of these companies have bigger budgets, have better Wall Street connections, can mobilize more lawyers, and exert more influence, as well as having the enormous power of the U.S. government behind them, than do most of the countries in which they operate. These inequities, this imbalance, this asymmetry has given rise to the theory of "dependency" which suggests that the poorer countries will always be subservient to and "dependencies" of the bigger countries, although the smaller countries often have their strengths and their ability to manipulate the bigger countries. Hence, most scholars, while recognizing that dependency is a fact of life (big, powerful countries tend to dominate smaller, weaker ones), also emphasize *interdependence,* the complex relationship that suggests both big and small countries can benefit from trade, investment, and commerce.

In the developed countries there is also resentment of U.S. economic superiority. Many European countries are envious and, therefore, often resentful of the ability of the U.S. economy to create jobs, adapt to new circumstances, and recover from recession better than their own economies can. At the same time, they often resent the U.S. bragging about its accomplishments and presuming to tell the Europeans how to do things better. Most of the European economies, in response to constituency political pressures, have, in fact, opted to protect their so-called "social economies," which means elaborate and expensive social welfare provisions, rigid labor markets that make it difficult to fire anyone, taxes roughly double those of the United States, and considerably higher state involvement in the economy than is true in the United States, in exchange for slower economic growth. That is their choice and it is a trade-off many if not most Europeans have accepted, but it *does* mean slower growth and a less-flexible economy than that in the United States.

Resentment is also directed at the large international lending (World Bank, International Monetary Fund) and trade agencies (World Trade Organization), which the United States is presumed to dominate. Both the World Bank and the IMF are often insensitive politically; they frequently advocate a one-size-fits-all lending policy that is not appropriate for all countries; and it *is* true that the United States is the most influential voice in their deliberations. But both agencies have become more flexible and politically conscious over the years, allowing for exceptions, being willing to postpone austerity in crisis times, and, while advocating privatization and free markets, being flexible about them and allowing state subsidies of such essentials as rice, gasoline, and cooking oil to continue. Still, they believe that Third World countries can't fundamentally alter the laws of economics, that they have an obligation to pay back their loans, and that they do need to put their economic houses in order. The U.S. government has used its influence to advocate *both* the orthodox and the flexible sides of the international lending agencies' policies. Likewise the WTO stands for free trade but it is also flexible, adaptable, and not insensitive to the needs of the unfortunate whose jobs and livelihoods are sometimes sacrificed as free trade comes to dominate.

5. *Politics and international affairs.*   The United States is at this stage the only surviving superpower. It is a *hegemon,* to use the French term. The Soviet Union has collapsed; Japan has economic but not strategic might; Europe is only in the beginning stages of developing a common defense capability; and China, still a Third World country, is not there yet. The United States, therefore, stands alone in the world as the only country with economic, political, military, and cultural ("soft") power, as well as the ability to project ("to touch someone," as the Pentagon puts it) that power to all corners of the earth.

The overwhelming dominance of the United States inherently breeds resentment, hostility, and jealousy mixed with envy on the part of those not so richly endowed. Moreover, in international relations theory, whenever there is a "unipolar [one country-dominant] moment," other countries tend not only to pick on the dominant country but also to gang up to do so.

The resentments engendered by this overwhelming U.S. dominance take a variety of forms. U.S. allies are often resentful of U.S. power and they may seek, as France or Germany did with their refusal to go along with the United States on a war strategy toward Iraq, to try to change or undermine the policy. Potential rivals to the United States like China refuse to officially recognize U.S. superiority and insist on being treated as equals. Because the United States is so powerful and its culture so pervasive, it also offers a tempting target to terrorist groups who may try to bring it down. Many Third World countries are resentful of the U.S.'s dominance but prudence dictates that they cooperate with the United States in their own interests. Among the proverbial men (and women!) in the street, attitudes are often mixed: admiration for the United States and its successes but often at the same time resentment at its power, occasional arrogance, and even lifestyle.[1]

The United States is often resented not just for what it does but also, often more importantly, for what it *is.* Of course, the United States is sometimes disliked for its policies with which other countries or people may disagree. But equally important, the United States is often resented for what it is: a big, rich, powerful, and *successful* country (in contrast to so many others) both economically and politically. If the United States were only resented for its policies (such as in the Middle East), the problem would be easy to fix: change or modify the policies. But it is far harder for the United States to change what it *is,* and indeed most of the public and, by reflection, U.S. politicians would not want to change that anyway. In other words, some of these resentments the United States can alter, but the more deep-seated roots of anti-Americanism—based on who Americans are as a people and what they stand for—will not go away and are likely to be with us for a long time. One country's success breeds other countries' resentments. And, as with the traditional Russian peasantry, if one person (or country) does better than the others and gets a little "uppity," then the others gang up to bring him down.

6. *Preachiness.* As many foreigners see it, if the United States were only bigger, richer, and more powerful, that would be one thing; however, the United States, as a "beacon on a hill" and a "missionary nation" in the Woodrow Wilson–Jimmy Carter tradition, also seems compelled to want to bring the benefits of our obviously "superior" economic and political institutions to other poor, "benighted" people throughout the Third World. In these respects, the United States is often seen as preachy, patronizing, and condescending, and such attitudes are often deeply resented abroad. The trouble is, Americans really believe, often with good reason, in the superiority of their political (democracy) and economic (immense prosperity) institutions. And Americans feel they have an *obligation* to teach others how to achieve their successes; namely, by imitating and following the United States and its institutions. Such preachiness is not usually as a result of arrogance, much less a desire to dominate the world, but because Americans truly believe that the conditions of the Third World will be vastly improved if it imitates us and our institutions.

We therefore have the National Endowment for Democracy to teach American-style democracy abroad; the Center for International Private Enterprise (CIPE), to say nothing of a host of private U.S. businesses and corporations, to teach American-style capitalism abroad; and a variety of other quasi-private, quasi-official agencies to teach American-style local government, American-style public administration, American-style family planning, American-style land reform, American-style central planning, American-style property law, American-style legal training, American-style justice, American-style elections (never mind the controversial year 2000 election!), American-style legislative staff work, American-style executive staff work, and so on. Often ignored are the facts that America's own institutions are seldom perfect in these regards, and that other countries have different ways of doing things, that American institutions may not always be the most desired, appropriate, or even workable in other cultures and countries. It is small wonder that these U.S. efforts often breed resentment abroad, and that the United States is often disliked for its constant preaching and often heavy-handed meddling in the internal affairs of other nations.

Most countries, however, eventually go along with such U.S. efforts, in part because they have little choice (foreign aid and investment funds often depend on agreeing to such reforms), in part because their own institutions are not working well, and in part because they also believe the U.S. institutions and ways of doing things to be superior. In today's world, given such immense U.S. power and no real alternative to it, most prudent governments will eventually come around to doing pretty much what the United States wants them to do.

To oppose the United States, beyond mild criticism, is imprudent—and there are bad consequences. That is why, after the initial inaction, private misgivings, and even criticism by some governments, many U.S. allies came around to supporting President George W. Bush's war efforts against Iraq. To do otherwise is foolish; in this day and age you do not want to antagonize the United States. It is better to go along with the United States on one issue in the expectation that will help you win points on the next issue, which may be more important to you than is Iraq. It sounds cynical but that is the way it works. In the present-day world of the United States as the only superpower, it makes no sense to cross America.

It is clear from this analysis that globalization takes many different forms—ideological, technological, economic, political, cultural, and military. It is clear that many if not most of the globalizing changes underway emanate from the United States. While globalization is not quite synonymous with Americanization, it comes close to being so. That helps explain why so many of the anti-globalization demonstrations also carry anti-American messages. The United States is the chief advocate for, agent of, *and* beneficiary of these new global currents. And in some quarters that provokes a vigorous response and even outcry.

THE INSTITUTIONS OF GLOBALIZATION

Globalization is all around us. It is almost literally in the air we breath (pollution and acid rain—now both globalized) and the words we speak—particularly if these go out over telephones, fax machines, e-mail, radio, television, or the Internet. Who among us, in the name of anti-globalization, would want to shut down any of these?

Hollywood and the film industry are institutions of globalization. So are CNN, MSNBC, FOX News, ABC, CBS, and NBC. But then, so are the British Broadcasting Corporation (BBC); Sky News (also British); and the Italian, French, Spanish, and German international broadcasting agencies, to say nothing of Al Jazeera, the international Arab news channel. All airlines that fly internationally are agencies of globalization; so are the international hotel chains, banks, and restaurants that cater to travelers. The Ford, General Motors, and Chrysler automobile companies, as well as BMW, Volkswagen, Volvo, Toyota, Honda, Nissan, and Hyundai, are all institutions of globalization. So are the English, French, German, Portuguese, Spanish, and Chinese languages, among others. Every company that either buys abroad or sells abroad (up to 30 percent of the U.S. economy now depends on foreign sales), and that in the process creates jobs, provides goods and services, keeps prices low, and raises standards of living, is also an agency of globalization.

The points are obvious: globalization is all around us; most of us benefit enormously from globalization; almost everything we do has global implications; globalization is woven into our culture and lifestyles; we are all parts of a global society whether we wish it or not, and few of us would want to give up the benefits we receive from globalization. So if all this is true, where lies the beef?

The fact is that none of us, including the protestors, is totally against globalization. We receive too many benefits from it and we could no longer live without it. And those countries that have tried to completely insulate themselves from globalization's effects—North Korea, Vietnam, Cambodia, and Cuba—are not only pretty sad, even dismal places to live, but even they found they cannot entirely shut themselves off from the outside world, nor do they wish entirely to do so. The question, therefore, is not whether we are for or against globalization but which aspects of it we oppose and which we favor, and which of its many agencies and institutions we favor and which we oppose.

In actual fact, protests against globalization have come to center on only a handful of institutions: multilateral corporations, the World Bank and the International Monetary Fund (IMF), and the World Trade Organization (WTO). Let us see what the complaints are.

Multinational Corporations (MNCs)

Multinational Corporations are frequently accused of polluting the environment, of running sweatshops in Third World countries, of exploiting these countries, and of putting profits ahead of people.

One ought to begin by distinguishing between the Marxian critique of all multinational corporations, because they are a part of international and world capitalism, as inherently bad and evil, *and* the more reasonable (and responsible) critique that says that multinational corporations, like all human institutions, sometimes make mistakes, are self-serving, sometimes try to cheat or skirt the law, then try to cover up these mistakes, and, in general, act in their own self-interest. The Marxian critique is a minority one, except perhaps on some college campuses and among some, radical groups of protestors; "true believers" of this position are usually immune from rational, reasoned persuasion to any other point-of-view because, for them, Marxism is like a religious faith that is not subject to empirical verification. Here we focus on the more reasonable critique that *is* subject to the marshaling of evidence and, hence, a more balanced view.

Let us face the facts: MNCs do muck around in the internal affairs of other nations (less now than in earlier eras), *do* have profit as their primary motive (that, after all, is why they are in business), and do sometimes (but now rarely) engage in nefarious, illegal activities. But let us balance this view with the facts that (1) most MNCs try, in *their own* interests, to be Good Neighbors in the countries where they may locate; (2) the MNCs generally provide higher salaries and better benefits than do local firms, and often housing, health care, and meals to their workers; (3) fearing the consequences (nationalization of their properties), most MNCs scrupulously obey the laws of their host countries and try to accommodate to local norms (which may also involve payoffs and bribery, but then, "everybody does it"); and (4) most importantly, the

MNCs provide sorely needed investment, jobs, and a stimulus to the economy which almost all Third World countries are desperate to receive.

The issue, therefore, is not that all MNCs are evil and all developing nation governments are always right and pure of motive. Rather, the issue is one of balance. The facts are that the largest MNCs can mobilize more influence and political connections than can many Third World countries; that gives them immense bargaining power. On the other hand, skillful Third World countries, including small ones, can also have considerable influence in the negotiations that take place. They have the resources and primary products the MNCs want, the expanding middle-class markets, the labor supplies, the favorable tax advantages, and the *knowledge* that MNCs wish to come into their country. Plus they wield the ultimate threat: the possibility of nationalizing the company, or its technology, that invests in their country—although most Third World countries nowadays are so desperate for capital that they don't want to risk future investment by nationalization.

These advantages show that developing countries are not without influence in dealing with big companies. The result is usually a genuine bargaining situation, one of *interdependence* as well as dependence, in which both the country and the company negotiate to get more of what they want. It is true, of course, that companies try to get the best deal possible out of these negotiations, but then so do the countries involved. A country with a skilled, adept leadership can often get much of what it wants from these negotiations. In most cases, it becomes a *partnership* based on mutual interest that emerges, not a one-way street in which one party holds all the best cards.

So, is there a "race to the bottom," as some have alleged? By that is meant that MNCs "shop around" to find the country with the lowest wage rates and then go there—but only until they find a country with an even lower wage scale. The answer is, not really. There are a few cases of this, and recently we have seen a handful of MNCs in Mexico move to Southeast Asia because environmental laws, labor laws, and wage rates are lower or less enforced there. But many things factor into a company's decision to locate, including proximity to the big U.S. market, transportation costs, banking and financial institutions, honest government and future stability, as well as wage rates. Plus, most MNCs, once invested in a country in the form of a factory or assembly plant, have a huge stake there and cannot just pull up and relocate elsewhere on short notice. So while, of course, there is a tendency for companies to go to the places that offer them the most advantages, that also involves a bargaining process with the Third World governments that are not without their own advantages in these talks; and once established in a particular country, most companies are reluctant to leave and would only do so under extreme circumstances: political instability in the country involved, severe economic pressures, such high levels of corruption that it proves impossible to generate there, or a complete breakdown in the dialogue with the host country. The picture is thus not black or white; instead, the image we should have of most MNC–Third World country relations is one of constant, ongoing bargaining and negotiations.

The World Bank and the International Monetary Fund (IMF)

Both the World Bank and the IMF were established after World War II to maintain the global economy and the world's economic systems. In many quarters it was feared that World War II would be followed by a severe economic downturn just as World War I had been followed by the Great Depression, and the Bank and the IMF were designed to prevent that from happening. The Bank was established to function rather like a global central bank (or like the Federal Reserve in the United States) to oversee global economic trends and perhaps, in limited ways in a world of sovereign states, make modest correctives or adjustments to them, while the IMF was intended to be a lender of last resort if a country got into desperate financial trouble. Initially, the Bank and the IMF were meant to monitor the economies of the developed countries, but since the 1960s and the increase in new and poor nations in the world, both of these sister institutions have come to focus on loans and programs for the Third World. And instead of being lenders of "last resort," they have become the primary agencies in providing funds to the developing nations.

Voting and influence in both of these global institutions is weighted, according to the amount of donations that a country makes to them. As the largest donor by far, the United States has the biggest voice in how and where these institutions spend their money. That means that the U.S. view of development, of foreign aid, and of lending almost always prevails, although other major countries also have influence and, as with MNCs, Third World countries are not without their own bargaining power in dealing with the Bank and visiting IMF missions. Informally, the Bank is always headed by an American while the IMF is headed by a European, although with an American subdirector.

As with MNCs, these are not inherently evil institutions, as many of the protestors claim, aimed at exploiting the Third World. Often misguided or mistaken, yes; but "evil," no. Let us explain.

First, the overwhelming American influence means that both institutions adhere to essentially the American or Western model of development, a model fashioned over fifty years ago and, by now, woefully out-of-date—even though still followed by the U.S. government and its aid agencies. That model, as shown in Chapter 2, was patterned after the American and European experiences with development, is terribly ethnocentric, and has limited relevance to the Third World. Although the model has had different emphases over the years, it has been remarkably consistent in emphasizing raw economic development over considerations of social, cultural, and political conditions. It is an economic determinist approach, paying little attention to whether a country is honest or corrupt, democratic or authoritarian, civilian or military-led. Emphasizing economics and economic growth above all else means the Bank and IMF gave loans to some pretty bloody, authoritarian, corrupt, human rights-abusing regimes, who often pocketed the money rather than using it for honest, worthwhile development purposes.

The model followed by the big lending agencies assumes that sheer investment or "pump-priming" is the sole, virtually only factor in development, without taking into account the nature of the regime in power or the many cultural differences in the world. It *assumed* that the American model of economically driven technocratic change devoid of all political, societal, and cultural considerations could simply be transplanted to the Third World, where, of course, the conditions were quite different. The model was not based on any empirical knowledge of the Third World but on the historical record of the United States and Western Europe, whose experiences and processes of development were thought to be both inevitable and universal. But that model does not fit the Third World very well as the experience of the last fifty years has taught us; nevertheless, with only modest adjustments of its assumptions, that is still the model that the Bank and IMF try to impose on the Third World.

Second, and reflecting the first point, the Bank and IMF are overwhelmingly staffed by economists and financial officials, not by anthropologists, sociologists, and political scientists. Quite naturally, by training and background, these officials see economics as the main driving force in development, again ignoring the cultural, sociological, and political differences among nations. They argue that cultural and political conditions cannot repeal the "laws" of economics, which is, of course, true but ignores that those laws need often to be adjusted to fit the situation and culture of the affected country. The World Bank/IMF formula is thus a rigid, "one-size-fits-all" model that fails to take individual histories, cultures, values, or politics into account. But that is an indefensible position; one would think that after half a century the Bank and IMF would have learned something about the distinct countries where they operate. However, unfortunately, they have not. I find these institutions still holding to an outdated, narrowly focused, discredited development model that has seldom helped the Third World and often hindered it.[2]

The third consideration is of Bank/IMF missions to the developing countries to assess their creditworthiness, *and* the *conditions* ("conditionality") that these missions place on their loans. Almost always, these conditions involve belt-tightening on the part of the applicant countries: fiscal austerity, a balanced budget, inflation under control (no printing of worthless paper money!), cutbacks in social services (to achieve that balanced budget), and state shrinkage or the privatization of usually inefficient, patronage-bloated, state-owned firms. While this is the formula (and "one-size-fits-all"), I have found these IMF missions to be increasingly flexible and, surprisingly, more politically sensitive over the years. In other words, as with MNCs and the issue of private investment, these relations, between an IMF mission and a host country government, are increasingly driven by bargaining and negotiations, and not by the Bank or IMF simply dictating economic policy.

Here is what happens. An IMF mission comes into a country, usually for a brief two- or three-day visit. It is wined and dined by the host country government, which floods it with data and reports and seeks to put its best foot forward. The IMF then puts forward its one-size-fits-all model involving austerity, privatization, reduction of subsidies, and so on. The host government then responds, "Of course, you are correct at the macro level and in the long term. But in the short term, if we remove subsidies on gasoline and the price goes up, buses and public transportation will have to raise fares and people cannot get to work [few working people have cars in the Third World]; if we remove subsidies on rice and beans [the staple diet of the poor], we will have food riots, looting, and mass starvation; if we remove subsidies on kerosene, people cannot cook; if we privatize electricity, rates will go up and poor people cannot afford it." And so on, and so on. In the days of the Cold War, Third World governments would argue additionally that, if they did all these things, we would have revolution and the "commies" would take over, which proved often to be an effective argument; nowadays they say democracy will be reversed—also an effective argument but not as effective as the "communist" one.

In other words, when faced with one of these IMF visitations, local Third World governments are not without their own influence and bargaining power, because no World Bank or IMF mission, let alone the U.S. government, wants to see the countries they are responsible for destabilize or have their democracy overthrown. And that gives developing countries considerable leverage. Whether they use that leverage wisely and cleverly is, of course, up to them. But the point is, as with MNCs, this is a bargaining relationship, not a wholly one-way process of the IMF "dictating" policy for the Third World. The relationship may still be uneven, but a clever Third World country can often get much of what it wants out of this bargaining. We may still conclude that the IMF and World Bank sometimes follow misguided, ethnocentric policies; but it is also true that Third World countries have considerable leverage in these negotiations. One, therefore, should see this as a political relationship of give-and-take and not simply one where the IMF or World Bank can impose entirely inappropriate solutions on the countries involved.

The World Trade Organization (WTO)

Created in 1995 and headquartered in Geneva, Switzerland, the WTO is the youngest and least well-known of these international organizations. It has just under 150 members, or approximately three-quarters of the nations in the world. Just as the IMF and World Bank were charged with maintaining global economic probity and stability, the WTO has as its mission to regulate, normalize, and *expand* global trade. For trade has a multiplier effect on economic development: for every $1.00 invested in international trade, a country gets back approximately $2.00 in income. That is why so many countries want to join the WTO: trade is in everyone's interest. The rising tide of free trade tends to lift all boats and to expand *all countries'* economies.

As compared with the World Bank and the IMF, the WTO is still a relatively small organization. It was created because earlier efforts to expand and regulate global trade were done largely on an ad hoc basis, usually at brief meetings of developed countries' economic ministers and trade negotiators; and it was thought that having a permanent organization with a central office and director would help institutionalize the trade regime. It was also seen as a way to bring Third World nations into the process. But while the WTO has a certain life of its own and some degree of independence, it remains, like the international lending agencies, largely a creation of the wealthier, bigger, more powerful nations. In other words, the United States, which provides most of the funds, chooses the organization's president (an American), and has the biggest say.

Negotiating trade policy is detailed, slow, often boring, slogging work, which helps explain why few people know much about the WTO or pay it serious attention. In this age of globalization and vastly expanded international trade, it is also extremely important, which helps explain why so many of our foreign policy officials (Warren Christopher, Sandy Berger, Charlene Barshevsky) have been trade lawyers. But trade policy is seldom dramatic or on national television like war with Iraq or North Korea's nuclear program, and yet most of us know in the back of our minds how important it is, affecting jobs and the overall international economy. Moreover, most WTO agreements are reached in private (secretly, opaquely), which to some makes it an object of suspicion. The WTO's very secretiveness is what has aroused the interest of globalization protestors who believe that decisions affecting the core of people's lives—food safety, environmental concerns, jobs, and so on—are being made behind closed doors.

Everyone agrees that the WTO needs to be more transparent, but getting to that point has proved to be more difficult than expected. Both the legal briefs submitted by the parties to dispute and the followup oral arguments are kept secret (the United States is one of the few countries that releases these to the public), and the trade judges' decisions are also kept private, usually for several months. The counter-argument is that, if the hearings, briefs, and opinions were publicized, they would invite a flood of interest group activity, lobbying, and lawsuits, and thus overwhelm the (still) small WTO bureaucracy. Small, poor, Third World countries also fear that, in an open environment, they will be either embarrassed by revelations of corruption or incompetence, or overwhelmed by the lawyers and powerful interest lobbies of the developed countries.

But a strong case can be made that greater openness is beneficial to all parties in the long run, even while recognizing that some of the horse-trading that goes into any trade agreement can best be done in private. Negotiations *do* need to be insulated somewhat from private lobbying in order to hammer out mutually productive deals, but the current system carries secrecy too far. The best analogy may be to a parliament where positions are staked out publicly but often finally negotiated privately; similarly, in parliamentary bodies, private interest group input is often beneficial to the process so long as it is the broader *public interest* that gets served in the end. Anything less than that only provokes suspicion on the part of member nations and hostility on the part of anti-globalization protestors who (usually falsely) assume that secretive deals are being hatched that are prejudicial against the poor and against Third World nations.[3]

SUCCESSES AND FAILURES
OF GLOBALIZATION

Globalization has *always* been with us since, really, the dawn of humankind. We cannot stop globalization, nor would we want to do so since globalization brings us many of the things that make our lives enjoyable and worthwhile: television, movies, the Internet, cell phones, computers, VCRs, food supplies, automobiles, technology, cheap prices, and a high standard of living. Stopping globalization is not an option; instead, the only question is whether we can ameliorate some of globalization's harmful effects. Trying to stop globalization would be like trying to stop the world, and that cannot be done. Globalization is with us, around us, a part of us; the only question remaining is whether we adjust to it well or badly.

Under the impact of modern communications, technology, and transportation, globalization's pace has now accelerated. That is why it has been in the news so much recently. We are more aware of globalization and its profound impact than were earlier generations. Our awareness of globalization has grown precisely because of the very technologies previously listed that are among the strongest agents of globalization: television, movies, the Internet, and so on.

Globalization sets loose powerful cultural, social, economic, and political forces, and inevitably as part of such a powerful global movement of change it produces both winners and losers. Most of us benefit enormously from globalization and, frankly, could not live without it (which is why so many countries wish to join the WTO); but we need to recognize that there are losers in the process and that we need to pay attention to them also. Here we try to sort out the relevant positive *and* negative things about globalization, and to draw a balance. First, the positive:

1. Globalization increases international trade, and for almost all countries and peoples that's a good thing.

2. Globalization increases international prosperity; ditto.

3. Globalization makes our lives richer: television, movies, computers, automobiles, foods, flowers, and so on.

4. Globalization promotes diversity, multiculturalism, and international understanding, through immigration, the media, and cultural exchanges.

5. Globalization assists the Third World through international trade and, hence, greater prosperity; globalization lifts (almost) all boats.

6. Globalization undermines authoritarian regimes and advances democracy and human rights because democracy is now the only legitimate system of government, and countries that violate those norms are subject to severe sanctions and ostracism.

7. Globalization keeps prices low for almost everything and provides us with a great diversity of products.

8. Globalization in its emphasis on freedom, human rights, and democracy helped defeat the Soviet Union and enabled the United States to win the Cold War.

9. Globalization is good for working people by creating new products, technologies, and, hence, jobs and higher living standards.

10. Globalization is synonymous with development, modernization, and the future.

Those who oppose globalization prefer the world to stop so they can get off, but we know that is impossible. In Tom Friedman's terms, globalization is a Lexus; those who oppose it prefer a world of taking siestas under an olive (or coffee or banana) tree.[4]

But globalization also produces losers, mainly people who cannot adapt to new currents and, therefore, get left behind. To be truthful, no one knows what to do for those left behind, although doubtless politicians will come up with palliatives that may partially relieve their plight. It may sound a bit heartless but the fact is one either adjusts and adapts to globalization or one gets left behind, and for those left behind the choices are not bright: retraining, subsidies, or early retirement. Who, then, are the big losers in this process?

1. *Indigenous peoples.*   The lands, villages, and cultures of indigenous peoples are being encroached upon by the forces of globalization. We can try to protect them, establish special preserves for them, and use the police or army to keep out interlopers. But all these steps are hard to enforce, and inevitably the march of modernization is going to force indigenous peoples to adapt or be swallowed up by the larger society.

2. *Traditional cultures.*   Traditional cultures are often harmed by globalization. It would be nice if all traditional cultures, their cute costumes, and often quaint ways could survive. But many of us have a romantic and false picture of traditional cultures: "happy" peasants dancing gaily in the streets, living in a lush-green countryside, and taking long siestas in large hammocks under the coconut trees. The nonromantic reality, however, is usually poverty, disease, bloated bellies (from malnutrition) in the children, and hopelessness. Some societies (more on this later) will be able to preserve, hopefully, the best aspects of their traditional culture in the face of globalization; in others, traditional culture will fade or disappear—except as it reappears in homogenized forms for the benefit of junketeering tourists—and maybe that's not all bad!

3. *Small farmers.*   While globalization *tends* to lift all boats in the long run, in the short run many small farmers, who cannot compete with the large, globalized agri-industrial concerns, must either change their crops or go out of business. A third option, increasingly followed in the Third World, is to migrate to the cities or abroad.

4. *Small shopkeepers.*   The Third World is dotted with tiny "mom'n'pop" stores that cannot compete with the Wal-Marts or Targets of this world. Their options, like those of small farmers, are to find a new specialty, migrate, or go out of business. None of these is a very happy alternative.

5. *Older workers.*   In much of the industrialized world, old industries (textiles, shoes, steel) are noncompetitive and going out of business. The solution most often suggested is to retrain the workers whose jobs are lost in new technologies. But can you take a fifty-five-year-old worker and retrain her/him enough in new computer skills to be able to compete with a young eighteen-year-old? Not likely. The other options are to subsidize the noncompetitive industry involved (usually a dinosaur) so it can survive for a time, or offer early retirement to its workers—both expensive and unattractive alternatives.

6. *Unionized workers.* Today's globalized economies require flexible, adaptable workers who may have to change jobs many times in their lifetimes. But that flies in the face of a unionized shop whose primary interest is in job permanence and security. The unwillingness or inability of unionized shops to adapt to these new, more flexible job markets helps explain the decline of union membership in almost all industrialized societies.

7. *Third World workers.* Third World workers *of all kinds* are particularly vulnerable. They are mainly nonunionized, do not enjoy the protections or social safety nets of workers in developed countries, and are subject to the whims (factory closings, new product lines, moves to another country) of multinational corporations. While precarious, however, their lives and opportunities would be *far worse* if there were no MNCs or globalization.

8. *The poorest countries.* The poorest countries tend not to reap the benefits of globalization. The following "law" generally holds: the poorer the country, the less it benefits from globalization. The poorest of the poor countries tend not to have the resources, the infrastructure, the products, or the skilled workers or trade negotiators to take advantage of globalization. But their sad plight is not the result of globalization per se; rather, it is a product of the more general vicious circles of underdevelopment in which these nations are caught. Globalization would undoubtedly help these poor countries—if only they could become a part of it.

9. *The environment.* The environment undoubtedly suffers as a result of the greater crowding, pollution, and environmental degradation brought on by globalization. But what are the options: going back to the "sleepier," nonmodern, nonindustrialized nineteenth century? Preventing the Third World from industrializing (and thus remaining backward) so they don't pollute as much as the First World did and does? Both of these are untenable positions. We cannot tell Brazil or another Third World country that they must refrain from industrialization, not participate in globalization, and thus remain poor so that we in the wealthy countries can enjoy the pure oxygen generated by a roadless, undeveloped, factory-free Amazon rainforest. No, the solution must come from elsewhere (clean factories, scrubbers on chimneys, automobile and truck emission controls) and not from telling the Third World to stay poor so that we in the rich North can enjoy clean air.

The conclusions that stand out from this analysis are obvious:

1. *On balance,* globalization is a good thing.

2. It *tends* to improve living standards worldwide and to benefit peoples and countries in both the First and the Third Worlds.

3. The losers from globalization tend to be those peoples and institutions who would be disadvantaged by *any* modernizing changes: indigenous peoples, small farmers and shopkeepers, older and unionized workers, traditional cultures, and the poorest countries.

4. Society or the international community needs to find ways to help these marginalized sectors or countries, but opposing globalization or trying to turn back the clock will not do it.

THE ANTI-GLOBALISTS

In recent years, meetings of the World Bank, IMF, and WTO, as well as those of high-level business and finance ministers, have been the subject of headline-grabbing protests in such cities as Seattle, Washington; Davos, Switzerland; Prague, Czech Republic; Nice, France; Gothenburg, Sweden; Salzburg, Austria; Genoa, Italy; and Washington, D.C. The protests have nowhere been able to close down these meetings, but they are disruptive as well as expensive, in terms of the police overtime and cleanup required. The protestors tend to be small in numbers, but they reflect a broader, popular unease with globalization.

At one level there are serious issues involved, but at another these rallies are like campus protests that occur according to the seasons, usually in the spring. They provide an opportunity to take a break from classes, to have a lark, to demonstrate against the establishment, and to sow some wild oats, seemingly without penalty except, perhaps, brief arrest and a small fine. Many of the leaders involved are professional protestors who float breezily from issue to issue; some have been doing this for years, even *decades,* going back to the Vietnam War. Protesting is often viewed as fun, a chance to meet other young people, and to do this in the name of a cause. One is tempted to say to the protestors (and government and bank officials often do): "Get a life!"

But the issues and makeup of the protest groups are more complicated than that. The groups are diverse, consisting of some serious persons and others who are frivolous. In the United States the groups tend to consist of both the Old and the New Left: Marxists, old Vietnam War protestors, radical student leaders, activists and liberals who can be mobilized around specific issues, "Trotskyites" (whatever that means these days), and anarchists. In Europe the protestors tend to come more out of political party ranks: Greens, Socialists, Social-Democrats, and Communists, but also with Trotskyites and Anarchists thrown in. Most of the protestors are young, in their twenties, and still in college or graduate school; in Europe many of them are young and working class, fearful of losing jobs to foreign competition. Most are peaceful, but some use violent methods, a faction that is usually known and often condoned by the organizers.

The protests have brought together others from even more diverse backgrounds and made "strange bedfellows" out of otherwise opposed groups. The groups include environmentalists, anti-capitalists (a new name for Marxists?), radicals, labor groups, "sovereigntists" (the new name for those opposed to lifting trade and immigration barriers), human rights activists, and others who feel aggrieved or injured by the sheer growth of modern business and international trade. The "strange bedfellows" opposed to globalization include conservative, nationalist Pat Buchanan on the Right, and another former (minority party) presidential candidate Ralph Nader on the Left.

While the antics of the anti-globalization forces are often comic-opera and not very effective, it would be a mistake to dismiss them too quickly. For surveys show that, while they have little sympathy for the mainly upper-middle-class and sometimes violent young protestors, the American public is deeply suspicious of globalization.[5] The protestors are thus only the most visible presence of what is an often vague sense of unease on the part of the public.

Depending on the survey, a large plurality, and sometimes a majority, of Americans are opposed to further trade liberalization, to additional immigration, and to globalization in general. These same surveys show that Americans understand the benefits of free trade, but they tend to see the costs in loss of jobs and lower wages as outweighing the benefits. Similarly, in the Third World, various publics understand the advantages of lower trade barriers but they are opposed to privatizations, removal of subsidies, and government belt-tightening that adversely affects their living standards.

In the United States, Democrats, women, union members, and African Americans tend to be more opposed to globalization than other groups. The reasons for this are two-fold: these are the groups whose jobs are most threatened by globalization (either by the competition from immigrant labor or by the fleeing of American factories to countries of lower labor costs); or, if they are employed, have seen their wages stagnate on a long-term basis. Perhaps the most striking finding of these surveys is that attitudes toward globalization are closely correlated with the skill and educational level of the respondents: the better educated and most skilled among the public tend to favor globalization (they are the ones who benefit from it), while the less skilled and less well educated—precisely those groups previously noted—are most opposed. It is likely that *both* these groups are correct in assessing their own self-interest: those better educated and better skilled who benefit from globalization tend to support it, while those less skilled and less well educated and thus most threatened by it tend to be opposed.

While that may be an accurate reflection of divided public opinion on this issue, most professional economists see it differently. They say that, when total wages and benefits are calculated, the wages of almost all American workers have not been stagnant but have increased over the last twenty years. In addition, the jobs of only about 3 percent of American workers are threatened by foreign competition; plus, the number of jobs created from increased U.S. exports through globalization *way* outnumbers the job losses from imports. Their conclusion: globalization has a net positive impact both on wages and jobs. And, as part of the multiplier effect of trade, globalization also creates jobs, higher wages, and economic growth in the Third World. In other words, people's *fears* about the effects of globalization are out of line with the economic benefits. But then, in politics, what people believe is frequently more important than what actually is reality.

It is not clear that the (mostly) young, (often) radical protestors represent public opinion on these issues. No one elected them to organize protests or to serve as spokespersons about globalization; most of those who have doubts about globalization would be appalled at the (sometimes) violent street tactics used; and the radical ideology and often the lifestyles of the protestors are way outside the mainstreams of American politics. On the other hand, the protestors have undoubtedly tapped into the widespread unease that exists among the public, especially on issues like jobs and wages. It is clear the World Bank, IMF, and WTO all recognize this because they have responded to the protestors far more positively than the latter's small numbers would merit. These international agencies have invited the protestors in for discussions; have listened to their complaints; have issued news releases expressing their concern for indigenous peoples, the environment, and the poor; and have modified their policies accordingly. It is interesting that these agencies which claim to be completely nonpolitical are, in fact, reacting to the protests in completely political ways.

There *are* important issues out there: pollution, acid rain, global warming, the environment, labor rights, the deleterious effects of globalization on indigenous peoples, small farmers, and the lower classes in the Third World. All these issues need to be dealt with at both the national and the international levels. The question is, in a democracy, whether the protestors have either the technical expertise or the public legitimacy and representativeness to speak for the country and the world on these issues.

CONCLUSIONS

This chapter has highlighted that globalization has *always* been with us; it takes many different forms (cultural, technical, economic, religious, political, and strategic); and it cannot be stopped, nor the clock turned back, nor would we want to do so. Very few of us would want to turn in our foreign cars, our cell phones, our computers, our televisions, or our VCRs—all of which are part of globalization. Nor would we want to sacrifice our cheap gasoline, high living standards, abundant goods, and low prices for most things—which are similarly the result of globalization. It is telling that even the protestors mainly use the instruments of globalization—the Internet and cell phones—to organize their anti-globalization networks.

Globalization is here to stay and, *on balance,* most of us benefit enormously from it. The issue is not rejecting globalization or seeking to return to an earlier, "sleepier" time, but whether we can adjust to globalization and amplify its beneficial effects. *Of course,* we need to protect the environment, but being against globalization will not do that. *Of course,* we need to worry about indigenous peoples, small farmers and shopkeepers, and working-class persons in the Third World, but opposing globalization will not solve those problems either—and since it is globalization that creates jobs, raises wages, and lifts the standard of living in the Third World, stopping it will make these people worse off rather than better off. The question is not whether we can turn back globalization—we cannot—but whether we can adjust its powerful forces to benefit more people rather than fewer.

Much the same applies to countries as to individuals. There are some countries that are so poor, so underinstitutionalized, and so underdeveloped that they are unable to take advantage of the investment, growth, and development opportunities that globalization provides. Some countries (often the same ones) have such weak and fragile cultures that they are *overwhelmed* by globalization rather than selectively borrowing from and adjusting to it.

In contrast, such countries as Japan, China, India, Iran, Mexico, Brazil, and others have strong indigenous cultures and ways of doing things and are able to selectively borrow from Western-led globalization even while preserving their own customs and traditions—the preferred way to deal with such changes.

Look especially at Japan: it is one of the most modern, most industrialized, and most prosperous nations in the world, and yet by *selectively borrowing* from the West and from globalizing influences, it has maintained its special Japanese character; no one visiting Japan for the first time would think she/he was in Chicago, London, Paris, or Berlin. And yet, many poor countries which lack the strength of a powerful culture like the Japanese are likely not to be able to take advantage of globalization but to be overwhelmed, maybe even smothered, by it. Those countries, just like the unfortunate peoples mentioned earlier who have been left behind by globalization, need special assistance, special consideration, and special help. There are signs that even the World Bank, the IMF, and the WTO now recognize that fact.

NOTES

1. Many foreigners have never been to the United States but nevertheless have strong opinions about it, mainly shaped by the unreal images of television and the movies: the lavish lifestyles portrayed in "Dallas" or "Beverly Hills 90210," or the "Wild West," violent, and gangster films like those of Bruce Willis, Clint Eastwood, or Arnold Schwarzenegger. When I lived in Europe last year and lectured widely on U.S. foreign policy, I was repeatedly asked questions about capital punishment, which Europe has abolished and now feels morally superior about. Unfortunately, when I studied international relations, I never thought I'd have to respond to questions about capital punishment, about which I have no expertise.

2. In the interest of truth in packaging, and also because the story illustrates well the point made, the author needs to say that he was once interviewed for a World Bank position. The Bank mistakenly thought I was an economist. When I told them that I was a political scientist, they said, "Oh no, we cannot take political considerations into account when making loans." That is, in fact, forbidden by the Bank's charter, but what is meant by that prohibition is that the Bank is not supposed to take *partisan* considerations into account. In other words, the Bank could not distinguish between *partisan considerations* (Republican or Democrat) and my work as a *political scientist* in assessing whether a particular government was creditworthy (honest, democratic, and dedicated to genuine development rather than just the private enrichment of its own officials) or not, or in weighing the political *effects* of Bank loans on the receiving country. That interview took place in the 1980s; I have since learned that the Bank has more recently hired a handful of anthropologists (because it belatedly "discovered" its policies often had effects on indigenous peoples) and even a "couple" of political scientists to judge democracy/human rights issues—a tardy step in the right direction but not nearly enough.

3. *Washington Post* (December 26, 2002), A-38.

4. Thomas Friedman, *The Lexus and the Olive Tree: Understanding Globalization* (New York: Farrar, Straus, Giroux, 1999).

5. See the analyses in *International Herald Tribune* (March 16, 2001), 15, and (July 6, 2001), 4; and in *Washington Post* (September 5, 2001), B-1.

8

Conclusion: The Future of the Developing Areas

The rise and emergence of the developing nations onto the world stage has to be—along with the unification of Europe and the collapse of the Soviet empire—one of the most incredible stories of the last half-century. Beginning in the 1940s and 1950s, when many of the new nations threw off the shackles of colonialism, the number of countries in the world doubled—and then doubled again. Many of these countries have assumed important roles in the world: Brazil has the world's ninth-largest economy; Mexico, the twelfth; China is becoming a world power; South Korea and Taiwan, along with Hong Kong and Singapore, have achieved miracle growth rates; and India, Indonesia, Iran, Egypt, Nigeria, and South Africa, as well as Argentina, Brazil, and Mexico, have emerged as important regional powers. The developing nations play important roles in the United Nations and other international forums; at the same time, quite a number of them—Pakistan, Afghanistan, Iraq, North Korea, Ethiopia, Ruanda, Somalia, Haiti, Colombia, and Venezuela—have become important flash points in international conflict.

In this book we have sought to explore the main ideas and policies that have animated the Third World over the last half-century. There are many books, usually focused on a single country or small group of countries, that describe the poverty and often miserable living conditions in the developing countries, but here we have sought to do more than that. Our purpose has been to wrestle with the concept of development itself, to look at the big picture, to try to understand the programs and policies that have been directed toward the Third

World over the last fifty years. One of the more interesting conclusions of the book is that, while the theory of development has often lagged woefully behind, many developing countries have in the meantime done quite well for themselves. At the same time, among the least developed of the "developing" nations—what are often called "failed states"—we still do not know after a half-century of experimentation how to relieve their endemic poverty, or how to lift them up and get them on the road to self-sustained growth.

THEORIES OF DEVELOPMENT

The first real, sustained effort both to try to understand underdevelopment and to do something about it came in the 1950s. By that time a number of important and newly independent nations had emerged onto the world scene—India, Indonesia, Pakistan, and Egypt; during the following decade a *host* of other newly independent countries in Africa, Asia, the Middle East, and the Caribbean would join them.

Scholars as well as government officials of the already industrialized nations, principally the United States, were vitally interested in this explosion of new nations onto the world scene. The scholars were fascinated by the phenomenon of new nationhood and genuinely wanted to help these countries achieve successful development and modernization. The U.S. government was mainly interested in the foreign policy implications of these changes: with the example of Communist revolutions in China, Burma, Vietnam, the Philippines, and later Cuba in mind, and fearing that India, Indonesia, and others might follow the same path, U.S. foreign policymakers sought desperately to find an alternative model of development that would provide a non-communist route to growth.[1] These two motivations—to help the emerging nations achieve growth and to fashion a non-communist model for achieving it—came together in the early development literature. Moreover, these two purposes were widely viewed as mutually complementary; at the time few perceived that the developmental goals of the emerging nations and U.S. foreign policy might come in conflict or prove contradictory. Much of the policy legacy and assumptions of that early era remain with us today in the U.S. foreign aid program and the assumptions of development advocates.

The earliest formulations for achieving development were fashioned by economists, not sociologists or political scientists.[2] Development economics became a main subfield in virtually all U.S. economics departments; and even today, when we look for expertise on development, we tend to turn to economists. But, as we have seen in the book, that focus ignores that development is at least as much a process of cultural, social, and political changes as it is of economic growth. For without a dynamic entrepreneurial group willing to work hard, invest, and move the society along (culture), without social modernization (literacy, health care, education, etc.), and without an honest, efficient, representative or democratic government genuinely interested in society-wide development (political), no amount of economic pump-priming will do much good.

The first economists to write on development half a century ago had few models and little firsthand information on which to draw. Almost none of them had ever been to a developing nation before, let alone carried out serious research in the Third World. So they drew upon the only information and case studies they had: the experience of the United States and other already developed nations.

There, it *seemed* to be the case that economic development came first and political development or democratization followed. But an equally plausible case can be made that it is the culture that changes first (toward rationality, enlightened thinking, a work ethos, and capitalist risk-taking) and that economic development follows on that.[3] Along with culture change comes political change, the development of honest, efficient, representative government institutions that ensure that economic development occurs rationally and efficiently; is shared widely among the population; and is not just siphoned off into the pockets of corrupt politicians, oligarchies, and military dictators. But these latter views concerning the importance of prior cultural, social, and political change did not find their way into the early development literature where it was assumed that economic pump-priming by itself was sufficient to stimulate development and that cultural and political change would *follow* economic growth. But most of us think that they got the formula backward; nor could more be expected from economists who tend, naturally, to think that it is economics that constitutes the chief driving force in development and that all these other cultural and political factors were secondary.

The emphasis on economics alone helps explain the early direction of development policy, its many false starts, and its many permutations over the years even to today. Thus, the earliest development assistance took the form of economic pump-priming, the building of huge dams and other infrastructure programs, and the pouring in of foreign aid, with the assumption and hope that, once a country reached self-sustained growth, democratization and policies of social justice would follow. Later the emphasis shifted to what was called "basic human needs" and then "sustainable development," but all of these programs continued to emphasize the economic aspects of development to the exclusion of other factors.

What, however, if the government through which the development aid was being funneled was corrupt, unrepresentative, and dedicated more to enriching itself and its cronies than in developing the country? Unfortunately, that was the case during much of the 1960s and 1970s where, recall, the early democratic leaders had been replaced by a wave of corrupt, brutal, authoritarian governments: Marcos in the Philippines, Suharto in Indonesia, and many military-dominated dictatorships in Sub-Saharan Africa, the Middle East, and Latin America. In these countries, economic assistance went mainly to benefit the regime in power and seldom to the people as a whole. Development aid in many of these countries was squandered and wasted and, particularly in the short run, did little to benefit the country or the mass of the population. For some fifty years now and continuing often to today, the emerging countries have been the victims of mistaken assumptions and failed development policies.

When these early development policies failed to work, intellectuals and political elites in the developing nations turned to other strategies that *seemed* to offer greater hope—or to deflect the blame. These included dependency theory, which provided a rationalization to blame underdevelopment on the already developed nations; corporatism, which often justified top-down, statist and authoritarian rule; Marxism, which seemed for a time to offer an alternative to the U.S.-favored model of development; and indigenous or homegrown models of change, which rejected all outside formulas. *None* of these models worked out very well either; none of them provided the magic bullet that many developing countries were looking for. They—and we—need to face the facts: there is no magic formula. But, as we see later, there is, nevertheless, much that can be done to encourage development.

The theory of development has always lagged behind the actual processes of development in the emerging nations. While scholars, intellectuals, and government officials were debating the several models previously noted, many Third World countries were, in fact, developing. Much of this development took place out of sight of the model builders and without regard to the grand designs that development planners had formulated. It occurred at lower levels, at the levels of often ordinary people, millions of them, working hard, starting small businesses, going to school, improving themselves, and raising themselves up by the bootstraps. As the Brazilian aphorism puts it, "development occurs at night while the government [and the planners] sleeps."

This development was most strongly experienced in East Asia: first in the "tiger" economy of Japan, then in the "little tigers" of South Korea, Taiwan, Singapore, and Hong Kong, more recently in Malaysia, Thailand, China, and other countries, too. There was, as we have seen in Chapter 4, a distinct *model* evolved: one that emphasized order, authority, state-led development, and a close and intimate connection between government ministries, banks, and large companies. But behind this model was also a powerful Asian *cultural tradition* that emphasized education, hard work, honor and pride, and obligations to family and society. More recently we have come to see that an opening to democracy, pluralism, and social justice, some degree of freeing up of autarkic or mercantilist economies, and an open trading system that responds to globalization are also valuable ingredients in the development process.

WHAT WORKS IN DEVELOPMENT

Despite the obvious failures, the ups and downs, and the great debate over distinct theories of development, a great deal of *actual* development has occurred over the last forty years. Per-capita income in the developing countries has nearly quadrupled between 1960 and 2000, going from approximately $300 per person per year in 1960 to nearly $1,200 today. Life expectancy has risen from forty-six to seventy-three years, while infant mortality has dropped from 150 per one thousand births to about fifty. Primary school enrollments are the highest they have ever been in the developing world, and literacy rates worldwide have jumped from 25 percent to over 50 percent. World food production has risen dramatically; populous China and India, both of which faced mass starvation in the 1970s, have seen food production quadruple and have become self-sufficient in foodstuffs. Radios per capita, televisions per capita, telephones per capita (all agents of globalization), urbanization, literacy, and life expectancy—all of these providing measures of modernization—are all up quite dramatically to twice, three times, or four times the level they were at our base point of 1960. Meanwhile, birth rates have also dropped dramatically in almost every country, from six births per woman in the 1950s to approximately 3.2 today, thus reducing family size, bringing birth rates into line with economic growth, and helping to reduce joblessness, poverty, and social pressures. All these figures show that, despite the pessimists and doomsayers, there has, in fact, been a great deal of development over the last half-century.

The most successful area of development has been East Asia, or (to emphasize the cultural factor) those countries that are part of the Confucian culture area. These countries also employed a model of export-led growth managed by an efficient, bureaucratic state that guided and channeled development, kept corruption low, and also maintained a large degree of social equality. Besides Japan, which we can consider a developed country, the best examples are South Korea, Taiwan, Hong Kong, and Singapore. *Alone among developing countries,* these four were not only able to overcome underdevelopment but, in a short, four-decades-long period, to leapfrog over other countries and arrive at a position that made them as wealthy on a per-capita basis as many of the European countries. It is a truly phenomenal accomplishment; *never in the history of the world* had such a mammoth, dramatic leap to developed status occurred in such a short time. It is significant that these great success stories employed a frankly authoritarian and statist model of development, only later turning to democracy and pluralism; but in today's climate where democracy is the internationally required formula, it is unlikely that the East Asian model could be repeated in quite the same form—although huge China, the world's most populous country, seems determined to follow that model.

After Asia, Latin America has been the second most successful developing area. In the same 1960–present period that we have been talking about, Latin America has gone from 70 percent rural and agricultural to 70 percent urban and modern, from 70 percent illiteracy to 70 percent literacy, and from an average per-capita income of about $400 to one approaching $2,000—a five-fold increase. In addition, Latin America has gone from seventeen out of twenty countries authoritarian to nineteen out of twenty democratic; to a much better situation of human rights; and from closed, mercantilist economies to much freer, more open ones. Countries like Argentina, Brazil, Chile, Costa Rica, Colombia, Mexico, Panama, Uruguay, and Venezuela led the way (some of these have since fallen on harder times), but the other, smaller, less well-endowed countries have not been doing too badly either, and over the last five years the Dominican Republic had the highest growth rates in the world!

The two most laggard areas for development are the Middle East and Sub-Saharan Africa. The Middle East contains a mix of some very rich countries (mainly based on oil) and many very poor ones. The Middle East has also lagged on democratization, although Turkey has made great strides toward democracy, and six or seven other countries in the area are also moving in that direction. In terms of both democracy and development, the main factors retarding growth seem to be culture (including religion), which has not adjusted adequately to modernization or to representative, pluralist government; low socioeconomic development which further retards democratization; and the machinations and manipulation of outside powers and international or "dependency" forces (including the Israeli-Palestine conflict) which impede development. Nevertheless, some of the Middle Eastern countries are making progress, a few have even applied for admission to the European Union, and over time much of the Middle East can be expected to develop as well.

Sub-Saharan Africa contains more of the world's poorest countries and poorest peoples than any other area. Looking at the poverty, the corruption, the AIDS, the violence and civil strife, and the instability and lack of effective governmental and private sector or civil society institutions, many are inclined to throw up their hands in a gesture of helplessness and give up on the area. But that would be a mistake for a large number of reasons, including not just humanitarian ones but also the fact that in this era of globalization (including immigration) we, too, are affected by the poverty, the disease, and the state disintegration that occurs in Africa. It is not in *our* interest to abandon the continent; in addition, some eight or nine African countries are now doing fairly well in terms of both development and democracy. The barriers and difficulties are higher here than in any other world area, but that is not to say that the prospects are hopeless.

We do not wish to present an overly optimistic and pollyannaish view of the Third World, since many problems remain and the threat of ungovernability and state and society breakdown is a real one. First, the *distribution* of wealth in many developing countries—less so in Asia, more in Latin America and the Middle East—is terribly uneven, adding to the social and political tensions that already exist. Second, although it has been reduced, mass poverty still exists in many countries, most notably in Sub-Saharan Africa and parts of Southeast and South Asia, Latin America, and the Middle East. Mass poverty affects approximately one-third of the population in the developing world, but that is *down* from two-thirds forty years ago. Moreover, only in Sub-Saharan Africa and parts of Southeast Asia and Latin America do we still see whole cultures of, or society-wide, mass poverty; in most of the developing world what we now see are pockets of poverty—"islands" of persons left behind or bypassed by the new wealth of many developing nations. It is these inequities that the forces of globalization will exacerbate if they are not dealt with adequately.

This does not exhaust the list of problems in the developing world, although maldistribution of wealth and continuing mass poverty in some countries are the main or macro problems. Other problems include corruption, dictatorship, violence, disease (which mainly stems from or is made worse by poverty), patronage, traditional cultures and ways of thinking that often retard modernization, weak institutions (governments, courts, bureaucracy), absence of transparency in the handling of public accounts, weak civil society (those intermediary groups that stand between the state and the individual), and absence of legal protections for property as well as individuals. The list of problems, particularly among the poorest of the poor, seems to go on and on.

Having surveyed the last fifty years of development policy, and recognizing that there are no panaceas, no magic bullets, what can we now say about development, about what works in development and what doesn't? My working list of the major ingredients follows, but let us recognize that other specialists may want to add to the list and that each country or area may have special needs in these regards.

- Above all, you need *capital* for growth. Capital can come from foreign investment, foreign aid, or through local investment—usually from a combination of all of these. Without capital, a country cannot grow economically or provide any of the needed social programs. Therefore, you should not nationalize or harass foreign investments, which will possibly frighten away capital forever.

- *Family planning* is important. Most countries need to limit population growth so as to increase per-capita income. If your economy is growing at 2 to 3 percent but population is growing at 4 to 5 percent, you do not need to be a nuclear scientist to figure out that at these rates you will forever be getting worse off.

- *Agricultural research and development* is needed so that most countries can basically feed themselves and become self-sufficient, as India and China have done.

- A *political culture* is needed that supports and is conducive to growth. Most experts believe this is what has enabled East Asia to surpass other developing areas in terms of development.

- *Honest, effective, noncorrupt, efficient government* and public administration are essential at all levels.

- Elites, leaders, and middle classes that favor development, and that are willing to share it with all groups of society rather than monopolizing it for themselves.

- *Democracy* is a tricky one. Recall that many of our most successful earlier developers—South Korea, Taiwan, Singapore, Mexico, Brazil, and now China—achieved growth under the long-term stability provided by authoritarianism, turning to democracy only when social change forced them to. But now the pressures, domestic and international, for democracy are so powerful that few countries can resist. Democracy is now required, but the messiness that is democracy will in some cases mean slower economic growth. Viewed positively, democracy helps improve human rights, provides a mechanism for resolving conflicts and adjusting to change and growing pluralism, and in the long run helps provide the stability in which economic growth can occur.

- Production goes down under agrarian reform but in some cases it may be necessary for social and political reasons of equity. In any case, avoid nationalization of private land as it will kill investment.

- A gradual evolution from patronage-based politics to more *merit-based* systems; *transparency, openness,* and *"sunshine"* are now required in government contracts and business transactions.

- *International trade* has a multiplier effect on economic growth, but this must be managed skillfully and effectively—South Korea, Taiwan, Chile, and Singapore are examples.

- *Free markets* are needed. You can't run an efficient, productive economy on a Marxist-Leninist (communist) or authoritarian, mercantilist, and statist basis anymore. The overwhelming consensus among economists is that you must have free markets, with some government regulation and oversight. For example, China still has a Marxist-Leninist political system but it has increasingly freed up its economy.

- *Social programs* are needed. Economic growth has to be combined with social justice (programs of health, housing, and social welfare), but there is a trade-off: every dollar or peso invested in social programs means one less dollar or peso devoted to investment for growth. Hard choices have to be made.

- In today's high-tech world, education and a skilled labor force are absolutely essential, including mass education, adult literacy programs, and technical training.

- Absolute *avoidance* of *war* and international conflict is key. War (including civil war, terrorism, and war between states) is absolutely ruinous of development efforts; witness Vietnam, Cambodia, Afghanistan, the Balkans, Rwanda, Liberia, the Congo, and Colombia. Other countries are similarly at risk to falling into violent civil conflict and ungovernability.

What is remarkable is the degree of consensus on this agenda that now exists among economists, foreign aid officials, bankers, businessmen, government officials, and the public. That consensus would not have existed thirty or forty years ago. But now, with the collapse of Marxism-Leninism in so many countries, along with the decline of authoritarianism worldwide, the main alternative models have been vanquished. *Everyone* now agrees that in order to get balanced, sustained growth, with social justice and all groups benefiting from the process, some form of democracy, pluralism, and honest, accountable government is absolutely necessary.

To say that there is consensus on the main engines of development policy, however, is not to say that there is agreement on all specific decisions in all circumstances. Different persons can legitimately disagree over the precise balance between dollars/pesos spent for development and growth, and the funds spent for social programs. We can also disagree over the exact balance between private sector initiatives versus the degree of regulatory role of the state or government. Privatization of bloated, corrupt, inefficient, patronage-dominated, money-losing state industries is necessary; but the timing of these steps is open to disagreement, as is the extent of privatization, and those decisions cannot be based on some universal formula but should be left to elected officials in these countries who know their own political situations and possibilities for effecting change better than do outsiders. It should not bother us that there are disagreements over some of these issues; after all, that is what democratic give-and-take and a democratic political process is all about: to resolve issues over which there is conflict.

Glasses are always half full or half empty, depending on your position or point-of-view. It was exactly forty years ago that this author went off to the developing world for the first time. Since then I have lived, traveled, and done research in all of the developing areas: Latin America; North Africa and the Middle East; Sub-Saharan Africa; East, South, and Southeast Asia; and Russia and Eastern Europe. In my *lifetime* of work in these areas, I have seen tremendous progress in health care, living standards, literacy, human rights, economic growth, stability, democracy, infrastructure, and international awareness. I look at those figures for Latin America and other areas over this forty-year period that show a change from 70 percent illiterate to 70 percent literate, from 70 percent rural and agricultural to 70 percent urban, from 70 percent uninvolved in or unintegrated into national life to 70 percent integrated, and a *quadrupling* or *quintupling* of per-capita income in quite a few countries, and I am enormously encouraged. Clearly, there has been progress, often irregularly and by fits and starts, and often independently of the models that we and development planners present, but *enormous, impressive progress* nonetheless. To me, then, the glass of development looks half full—actually, about 70 percent full.

More recently I have done research in southern Africa, India, China, and Southeast Asia (Indonesia, the Philippines, East Timor). In these areas one is forced to come to grips with just how far development still has to go. In East Timor, for instance, which may be the poorest, least-developed country I have ever worked in, with 90 percent unemployment and few natural resources, the glass is not 70 percent or even half full; it is about 90 percent empty. Nor should we forget that 30 percent or so of the population in *relatively successful* Latin America and East Asia are not yet integrated into national life, either economically (not a part of a modern money economy), politically (no democratic participation), or in other ways.

The developing world has come a long way in my lifetime but it is obvious that it—and we, in our understanding of and assistance to it—still have a long ways to go. We now know much better than we did, in terms of the list of policy ingredients presented earlier, what works in development—and what doesn't. But sympathy, empathy, understanding, and a considerable degree of modesty as to the certainty of our recommendations as well as our ability to effect change is still required of those who study and work in the developing world. Development remains a long journey but an eminently worthwhile one.

NOTES

1. Donald L. M. Blackmer, *The MIT Center for International Studies. The Founding Years, 1951–1962* (Cambridge, MA: The MIT Center for International Studies, 2002). The book is mistitled; it is really a history of U.S. efforts to deal with development issues.

2. Especially W. W. Rostow, *The Stages of Economic Growth* (Cambridge: Oxford University Press, 1960).

3. Lawrence E. Harrison and Samuel P. Huntington (eds.), *Culture Matters: How Values Shape Human Progress* (New York: Basic Books, 2000); David Landes, *The Wealth and Poverty of Nations: Why Some Are So Rich and Others So Poor* (New York: Norton, 1998).

Suggested Readings

Aguero, Felipe, and Jeffery Stark, eds. *Fault Lines of Democracy in Post-Transition Latin America*. Boulder: Lynne Rienner Publishers, 1998.

Alagappa, Muthiah, ed. *Political Legitimacy in Southeast Asia: The Quest for Moral Authority*. Stanford: Stanford University Press, 1995.

Almond, Gabriel A., and James S. Coleman, eds. *The Politics of Developing Areas*. Princeton: Princeton University Press, 1960.

Apter, David. *The Politics of Modernization*. Chicago: Chicago University Press, 1965.

Baloyra, Enrique, ed. *Comparing New Democracies*. Boulder: Westview Press, 1987.

Banfield, Edward C. *The Moral Basis of a Backward Society*. New York: Free Press, 1958.

Bauer, P. T. *Dissent on Development*. Cambridge, Mass.: Harvard University Press, 1976.

Beling, W. A., and G. O. Totten. *The Developing Nations: Quest for a Model*. New York: Van Nostrand, 1970.

Binder, Leonard, James S. Coleman, Joseph LaPalombara, Lucien Pye, Sidney Verba, and Myron Weiner, eds. *Crisis and Sequences in Political Development*. Princeton: Princeton University Press, 1971.

Black, C. E. *The Dynamics of Modernization: A Study in Comparative History*. New York: Harper and Row, 1966.

Bratton, Michael. "Beyond the State: Civil Society and Associational Life in Africa." *World Politics*, 41 (April 1989): 407–430.

Braveboy-Wagner, Jaqueline A. *Interpreting the Third World*. New York: Praeger, 1986.

Brown, David. *The State and Ethnic Politics in Southeast Asia*. London: Routledge, 1994.

Brynen, Rex, Bahgat Korany, and Paul Noble, eds. *Political Liberalization and Democratization in the Arab World* (Volume 1). Boulder: Lynne Rienner Publishers, 1995.

Camp, Roderic Ai, ed. *Democracy in Latin America: Patterns and Cycles*. Wilmington, DE: Scholarly Resources, 1996.

Cantori, Louis J. "Civil Society, Liberalism, and the Corporatist Alternative in the Middle East." *Middle East Studies Association Bulletin*, 31, 1 (1997).

Chazan, Naomi, et al. *Politics and Society in Contemporary Africa*. Boulder: Lynne Rienner Publishers, 1992.

Cheng, Tun-Jen, and Brantly Womack. "General Reflections on Informal Politics in East Asia." *Asian Survey* (1996): 320–333.

Cornwell, Richard. "The Collapse of the African State." In Jakkie Cilliers and Peggy Mason, eds. *Peace, Profit, or Plunder? The Privatization of Security in War-Torn African Societies*. Pretoria, South Africa: Institute for Security Studies, 1999.

"Culture in Development: New Perspectives." *The Fletcher Forum of World Affairs*, 13 (Summer 1989).

Dealy, Glen. *The Public Man: An Interpretation of Latin America and Other Catholic Countries.* Amherst, Mass: University of Massachusetts Press, 1977.

DeBary, W. T. *Asian Values and Human Rights, A Confucian Communitarian Perspective.* Cambridge, Mass.: Harvard University Press, 1998.

DeCalo, S. *Coups and Army Rule in Africa: Studies in Military Style.* New Haven, Conn.: Yale University Press, 1990.

Deutsch, Karl, and William J. Foltz, eds. *Nation Building.* New York: Aldine, 1963.

Diamond, Larry. *Developing Democracy: Toward Consolidation.* Baltimore: Johns Hopkins University Press, 1999.

Diamond, Larry, ed. *Political Culture and Democracy in Developing Countries.* Boulder: Lynne Rienner Publishers, 1994.

Diamond, Larry, Juan J. Linz, and Seymour Martin Lipset, eds. *Democracy in Developing Countries.* Boulder: Lynne Rienner Publishers, 1988–1989.

Doyle, Michael. *Empires.* Ithaca, New York: 1986.

DuToit, Pierre. *State-Building and Democracy in Southern Africa: Botswana, Zimbabwe, and South Africa.* Washington, D.C.: U.S. Institute of Peace, 1995.

Edie, Carlene J. *Politics in Africa: A New Beginning?* Belmont: Wadsworth Press, 2003.

Eickleman, Dale, and James Piscatori. *Muslim Politics.* Princeton: Princeton University Press, 1996.

Eistenstadt, S. N. *Post-Traditional Societies.* New York: Norton, 1974.

Field, George L. Comparative Political Development: *The Precedent of the West.* Ithaca: Cornell University Press, 1967.

Finkle, Jason L., and Richard W. Gable, eds. *Political Development and Social Change.* New York: John Wiley & Sons, 1966.

Freund, B. *The Making of Contemporary Africa: The Development of African Society Since 1800.* London: Macmillan, 1961.

Friedman, Thomas. *From Beirut to Jerusalem.* Farrar Strauss and Giroux, 1991.

Fukuyama, Francis. *The End of History and the Last Man.* New York: The Free Press, 1992.

Gamer, Robert E. *The Developing Nations.* Boston: Allyn and Bacon, 1976.

Gerner, Deborah, ed., *Understanding the Contemporary Middle East.* Boulder: Lynne Rienner Publishers, 2000.

Geiss, I. *The Pan-African Movement.* Londen: Methuen Press, 1974.

Ghadbian, Najib. "Political Islam and Violence." *New Political Science,* 22, 1 (March 2000).

Gordon, April A., and Donald L. Gordon, *Understanding Contemporary Africa.* Boulder: Lynne Rienner Publishers, 2001.

Grugel, Jean, ed. *Democracy Without Borders: Transnationalisation and Conditionality in New Democracies.* London: Routledge, 1999.

Harbeson, John, Donald Rothchild, and Naomi Chazan, eds. *Civil Society and the State in Africa.* Boulder: Lynne Rienner Publishers, 1992.

Harrison, Lawrence E., and Samuel P. Huntington, eds. *Culture Matters: How Values Shape Human Progress.* New York: Basic Books, 2000.

Hartz, Louis, et al. *The Founding of New Societies.* New York: Harcourt, Brace, 1964.

Heegar, Gerald A. *The Politics of Underdevelopment.* New York: St. Martin's Press, 1974.

Heilbroner, Robert. *The Great Ascent.* New York: Harper and Row, 1963.

Holt, Robert T., and John E. Turner. *The Political Basis of Economic Development.* New York: D. Van Nostrand, 1966.

Horowitz, Irving L. *Three Worlds of Development: The Theory and Practice of International Stratification.* 2d ed. New York: Oxford University Press, 1972.

Hunter, Robert, and John Reilly. *Development Today: A New Look at U.S. Relations with the Poor Countries.* New York: Praeger, 1972.

Huntington, Samuel P. *Political Order in Changing Societies.* New Haven: Yale University Press, 1968.

_____. *The Clash of Civilizations and the Remaking of the World.* New York: Simon and Schuster, 1996.

_____. *The Third Wave: Democratization in the Late Twentieth Century.* Norman: University of Oklahoma Press, 1991.

Huntington, Samuel P., and Clement H. Moore. *Authoritarian Politics in Modern Society: The Dynamics of Established One-Party Systems.* New York: Basic Books, 1970.

Ilchman, Warren F., and Normal T. Uphoff. *The Political Economy of Change.* Berkeley: University of California Press, 1969.

Joseph, Richard, ed. *State, Conflict, and Democracy in Africa.* Boulder: Lynne Rienner Publishers, 1998.

Jung, Kim Dae. "Is Culture Destiny? The Myth of Asia's Anti-Democratic Values." *Foreign Affairs,* 73/5 (November/December 1994): 189–194.

Kautsky, John H. *Political Change in Underdeveloped Countries: Nationalism and Communism.* New York : John Wiley & Sons, 1962.

Kebschull, Harvey G., ed. *Politics in Transitional Societies: The Challenge of Change in Asia, Africa, and Latin America.* New York: Appleton-Century-Crofts, 1968.

Kryzanek, Michael J. *Latin American: Change and Challenge.* New York: HarperCollins, 1995.

LaPalombara, Joseph, ed. *Bureaucracy and Political Development.* Princeton: Princeton University Press, 1963.

Lewis, Peter, ed. *Africa: Dilemmas of Development and Change.* Boulder: Westview Press, 1998.

Leys, Colin, ed. *Politics and Change in Developing Countries: Studies in the Theory and Practice of Development.* Charlotte, N.C.: UNI Publications, 1969.

Linz, Juan, et al., eds. *Politics in Developing Countries: Experiences With Democracy.* Boulder: Lynne Rienner Publishers, 1990.

Lipset, Seymour Martin. *Political Man: The Social Bases of Politics.* New York: Doubleday - Anchor, 1959.

_____. "Some Social Requisites of Democracy." *American Political Science Review* (March 1959) : 69–105.

_____. The First New Nation: *The United States in Historical and Comparative Perspective.* New York: W.W. Norton & Company, 1979.

Little, Daniel. *The Paradox of Wealth and Poverty: Mapping the Ethical Dilemmas of Global Development.* Boulder: Westview Press, 2003.

Long, David E., and Bernard Reich. *The Government and Politics of the Middle East and North Africa.* 4th ed. Boulder: Westview Press.

Lovatt, Debbie. "Islam, Secularism, and Civil Society." *The World Today* (August/September 1997) : 226–228.

Lowy, Michael. *The Politics of Combined and Uneven Development: The Theory of Permanent Revolution.* London: New Left Books, 1981.

Mahmood, N., ed. *Rethinking Political Development in Southeast Asia.* Kuala Lumpur: University of Malaya Press, 1994.

Malloy, James, ed. *Authoritarianism and Corporatism in Latin America.* Pittsburgh: University of Pittsburgh Press, 1977.

Maniruzzaman, Talukder. *Military Withdrawal From Politics: A Comparative Study.* Cambridge, Mass.: Ballinger, 1987.

Marcussen, Henrik, and Jens Erik Torp. *Internationalization of Capital: Prospects for the Third World, a Reexamination of Dependency Theory.* London: Zed Press, 1982.

Martin, Guy. *Africa in World Politics: A Pan-African Perspective.* Lawrenceville: Africa World Press, 2003.

Martz, John D., and David J. Myers. "Understanding Latin American Politics: Analytical Models and Intellectual Traditions." *Policy,* 16 (Winter 1983): 214–241.

Midgal, Joel. *Strong Societies and Weak States.* Princeton: Princeton University Press, 1986.

Miller, John D. *Politics of the Third World.* New York: Oxford University Press, 1967.

Millikan, Max F., and Donald L. Blackmer, eds. *Emerging Nations: Their Growth and United States Policy.* Boston: Little, Brown, 1967.

Monga, Celestin. *The Anthropology of Anger: Civil Society and Democracy in Africa.* Boulder: Lynne Rienner Publishers, 1996.

Norton, A. R. "The Future of Civil Society in the Middle East." *Middle East Journal,* 47, 2 (Spring 1993): 205–216 .

O'Brien, Donal B. Cruise, John Dunn, and Richard Rathbone, eds. *Contemporary West African States.* New York: Cambridge University Press, 1989.

O'Donnell, Guillermo, Philippe C. Schmitter, and Laurence Whitehead, eds. *Transitions from Authoritarian Rule.* Baltimore: Johns Hopkins University Press, 1986.

Organski, Kenneth. *The Stages of Political Development.* New York: Alfred A. Knopf, 1965.

Oxhorn, Philip D., and Graciela Ducatenzeiler, eds. *What Kind of Democracy? What Kind of Market? : Latin America in the Age of Neoliberalism.* University Park, PA: Penn State University Press, 1998.

Palmer, Monte, ed. *Dilemmas of Political Development.* Itasca, Ill.: Peacock Publishers, 1989.

Payne, Richard J., and Jamal N. Nassar. *Politics and Culture in the Developing World: The Impact of Globalization.* New York: Longman Press, 2003.

Pinkney, Robert. *Democracy in the Third World.* Boulder: Lynne Rienner Publishers, 1994.

Pipes, Daniel. *In the Path of God: Islam and Political Power.* New York: Basic Books, 1983.

Poulantzas, Nicos. *Political Power and Social Classes.* London: New Left Books and Sheed and Ward, 1973.

Pye, Lucian W. *Asian Power and Politics: The Cultural Dimensions of Authority.* Cambridge, Mass.: Harvard University Press, 1985.

Pye, Lucian W., and Sidney Verba, eds. *Political Culture and Political Development.* Princeton: Princeton University Press, 1965.

Richards, Alan, and John Waterbury. *A Political Economy of the Middle East.* Boulder: Westview Press, 1996.

Riggs, Fred W. *Administration in Developing Countries.* New York: Holmes and Meier, 1964.

Robinson, Thomas, ed. *Democracy and Development in East Asia.* Washington, D.C.: The American Enterprise Institute for Public Policy Research, 1991.

Rodney, Walter. *How Europe Underdeveloped Africa.* London and Dar es Salaam: Bogle - L'Ouverture and Tansania Publishing House, 1972.

Rostow, W. W. *The Stages of Economic Growth.* New York: Cambridge University Press, 1960.

Rothchild, D., and Naomi Chazan, eds. *The Precarious Balance: State and Society in Africa.* Boulder: Westview Press, 1988.

Rothchild, D., and V. A. Olorunsola, eds. *State versus Ethnic Claims: African Policy Dilemmas.* Boulder: Westview Press, 1983.

Rudolph, Lloyd I., and Suzanne Rudolph. *The Modernity of Tradition.* Chicago: University of Chicago Press, 1967.

Rustow, Dankwart. *A World of Nations: Problems with Political Modernization.* Washington, D.C.: Brookings Institution, 1967.

———. "Transitions to Democracy: Towards a Dynamic Model." *Comparative Politics,* 2 (1970): 337–363.

Said, Edward. *Orientalism*. New York: Pantheon, 1978.

Schmitt, David E., ed. *Dynamics of the Third World*. Cambridge, Mass.: Winthrop, 1974.

Schmitter, Philippe. "Paths to Political Development in Latin America." In D. Chalmers, ed., *Changing Latin America*. New York: Academy of Political Science, 1974.

Seligson, Mitchell A., and John T. Passe-Smith, eds. *Development and Underdevelopment: The Political Economy of Global Inequality*. Boulder: Lynne Rienner Publishers, 2003.

Shils, Edward. *Center and Periphery*. Chicago: University of Chicago Press, 1975.

_____. *Political Development in New States*. Paris: Moulton, 1966.

Sigmund, Paul E., ed. *The Ideologies of Developing Nations*. New York: Praeger, 1972.

Smith, Peter, ed. *Latin America in Comparative Perspective*. Boulder: Westview Press, 1995.

Somjee, A.H. *Parallels and Actuals of Political Development*. London: MacMillan, 1986.

_____. *Political Capacity in Developing Societies*. New York: St. Martin's Press, 1982.

Tachau, Frank, ed. *The Developing Nations: What Path to Modernization?* New York: Dodd, Mead, 1972.

Tangri, R. *Politics in Sub-Saharan Africa*. London: James Currey, 1985.

Vatikiotis, Michael R. J. *Political Change in Southeast Asia: Trimming the Banyan Tree*. London: Routledge, 1996.

Veliz, Claudio. *The Centralist Tradition in Latin America*. Princeton: Princeton University Press, 1980.

Viberto Selochan, ed. *The Military, State and Development in Asia and the Pacific*. Boulder: Westview Press, 1991.

Villalón, Leonardo, and Phillip Huxtable, eds. *The African State at a Critical Juncture: Between Disintegration and Reconfiguration*. Boulder: Lynne Rienner Publishers, 1997.

Vogel, Ezra. *The Four Little Dragons*. Cambridge, Mass.: Harvard University Press, 1991.

Wallerstein, I. *Africa: The Politics of Unity*. New York: Random House, 1967.

Weatherby, Joseph N., et al. *The Other World: Issues and Politics of the Developing World*. New York: Longman Press, 2003.

Weiner, Myron, ed. *Modernization: The Dynamics of Growth*. New York: Basic Books, 1966.

Weiner, Myron, and Samuel P. Huntington, eds. *Understanding Political Development*. Boston: Little, Brown, 1987.

Welsh, Bridget. "Lessons from Southeast Asia: Growth, Equity, and Vulnerability." In *Models of Capitalism*. B. Stallings and E. Huber Stephens, eds.: Penn University Press, 2000.

Wiarda, Howard J. *Civil Society: The American Model and Third World Development*. Boulder: Westview Press, 2002.

_____. *Corporatism and National Development in Latin America*. Boulder: Westview Press, 1981.

_____. *Latin American Politics: A New World of Possibilities*. Belmont: Wadsworth Publishers, 1994.

_____. *The Soul of Latin America: The Cultural and Political Transition*. New Haven: Yale University Press, 2001.

Wiarda, Howard J., ed. *Authoritarianism and Corporatism in Latin America, Revisited*. Gainesville: University of Florida Press, 2003.

_____. *Comparative Democracy and Democratization*. Fort Worth, Texas: Harcourt Brace, 2001.

_____. *Non-Western Theories of Development*. Fort Worth, Texas: Harcourt Brace, 2001.

_____, and Harvey F. Kline, eds. *Latin American Politics and Development*. 5th ed. Boulder: Westview Press, 2000.

World Bank. *World Development Report*. Yearly.

Subject Index